GLORY DAYS

GLORY DAYS

LIFE WITH THE DALLAS COWBOYS, 1973-1998

WILLIAM T. "BUCK" BUCHANAN
and
STEPHEN D. STAINKAMP

Taylor Trade Publishing
Lanham • New York • Boulder • Toronto • Plymouth, UK

First Taylor Trade Publishing edition 2006

This Taylor Trade Publishing hardback edition of *Glory Days* is an original publication. It is published by arrangement with the author.

Published by Taylor Trade Publishing
An imprint of The Rowman & Littlefield Publishing Group, Inc.
4501 Forbes Boulevard, Suite 200, Lanham, Maryland 20706

Estover Road
Plymouth PL6 7PY
United Kingdom

Distributed by NATIONAL BOOK NETWORK

Library of Congress Cataloging-in-Publication Data

Buchanan, William T., 1933–
Glory days : life with the Dallas Cowboys, 1973–1998 / William T. "Buck" Buchanan and Stephen D. Stainkamp.
p. cm.
Includes index.
ISBN-13: 978-1-58979-364-4 (cloth : alk. paper)
ISBN-10: 1-58979-364-1 (cloth : alk. paper)
1. Buchanan, William T., 1933– 2. Dallas Cowboys (Football team)—Officials and employees–Biography. I. Stainkamp, Stephen D., 1949– II. Title.

GV939.B795 2006
796.332092—dc22

2006006544

∞™ The paper used in this publication meets the minimum requirements of American National Standard for Information Sciences—Permanence of Paper for Printed Library Materials, ANSI/NISO Z39.48-1992.

Manufactured in the United States of America.

CONTENTS

CONTENTS

FOREWORD

Roger Staubach

As a player with the Dallas Cowboys from 1969 to 1979, I was privileged to work for the most ethical, decent man in the NFL. Head Coach Tom Landry was a great man, a resourceful and brilliant coach, a shrewd tactician, and a tremendous judge of character. More often than not, the personnel Coach Landry acquired reflected his good judgment in people. I met a lot of good men during my career in Dallas and Buck Buchanan was one of those.

In the forty-five-plus years of the franchise, the Cowboys have had three equipment managers—Jack Eskridge, Buck Buchanan, and Mike McCord. When Eskridge left in 1973, a key element of the Cowboys' infrastructure was lacking. Coach Landry searched long and hard for a suitable replacement—sifting through more than two hundred job applicants.

During the interview process, Lt. Col. Floyd G. Davis, U.S. Air Force Academy Prep School director of athletics and military training, contacted Tex Schramm.

I'm told that conversation went something like this: "Tex, I suggest you give Senior Master Sergeant Buchanan a shot at the equipment manager job. If you aren't thrilled with Sgt. Buchanan at the end of the season, I'll reimburse the Dallas Cowboys his annual salary." Days later, Coach Landry invited Buck to Dallas for an interview, and the rest is history.

I met Buck prior to our 1973 training camp. At 6 feet, 3 inches tall, and 180 pounds, Buck was a tall drink of water. Our last equipment manager had been a large man, too. But the job of equipment manager for the Cowboys required more than size; it required *stature*. More than a uniform conveyor belt, more than a repairer of football equipment and playing fields, a really *good* equipment manager must be plugged into his team's needs. He must be willing to listen. He must be good with people—outside and inside the organization. He must be observant, and he must care about his players' well-being. To be really good at the job, a man must be willing to go the extra mile.

Buck always did.

As I got to know him, I learned Buck was an affable guy with a can-do attitude. I came to like and admire him. As we worked together and traveled to distant cities, I found Buck to be resourceful, gracious, and hard working. He was always eager to accommodate everyone—from rookies and vets to coaches and trainers.

There was never any job too big or too small for him.

Buck poured himself into his job—and it was noticed and appreciated.

In 1973, Conditioning Coach Alvin Roy asked the rookie equipment manager to jog with me as part of my conditioning regimen during training camp. Buck leapt at the opportunity. At forty years old, despite damaged knees from catching baseballs and more than thirty-eight parachute jumps, the former 82nd Airborne trooper and U.S. Air Force bronze star recipient, never hesitated to test his endurance against a man ten years his junior.

Before the 1975 Divisional Playoff Game in Minnesota against the Vikings, Buck came through for me big-time. He engineered a bodysuit—a combined rib and shoulder pad system—which protected my bruised ribs and afforded me greater freedom to pass.

We won that contest with Minnesota, 17 to 14, and went on to beat the Los Angeles Rams in the NFC Championship Game in Los Angeles, 37 to 7. Without Buck's help, we might never have made it to Super Bowl X that season.

Buck is a decent man, a family man with an unbridled sense of integrity and work ethic. Offensive Line Coach and former U.S. Marine Jim Myers characterized Buck as the most regimented person he'd ever had the pleasure of knowing and working with—no small tribute from a tough old work horse like Coach Myers. Coach Roy spoke of Buck's attention to detail, a trait that inspired Alvin to fondly nickname Buck the "General."

With time, Coach Landry and the Cowboys conferred increasingly more responsibilities on Buck, entrusting him with their absolute faith and confidence. Buck never hesitated or buckled beneath the burden.

Coach Landry trusted him with the care of the fields and the equipment and the transportation of the equipment, to and from each game. And in the performance of his myriad duties, Buck was always resourceful and flexible, always ready to change plans and divert the contents of several truckloads of equipment from one coast to the other—at a moment's notice—if Coach Landry asked him to.

Coach Landry knew he could depend on Buck for all that and much more. He relied on Buck to clean up, dress up, police up, and secure our facilities—whether at home, at training camp, or on the road. He knew Buck would have every uniform cleaned, repaired, and inventoried, every helmet repaired and spit-shined before game day.

Coach Landry trusted Buck to get it done—and it was, generally with a smile or a joke, without as much as a whimper or a harsh word.

Buck's expertise and reputation were universally admired, so much so that Tex Schramm gave him free rein over the design of the equipment room at Valley Ranch.

Buck was lured from a secure career in the Air Force to an NFL job with long hours, difficult family separation, and an uncertain future. He was sought for his athletic prowess, his expertise with equipment and field maintenance, his organizational skills, his team camaraderie, and his devotion to service. But Buck is perhaps best remembered for his attitude, his kindness, his people skills, and his humor in the face of adversity.

Buck never said much about himself. In that way, he was a lot like Coach Landry.

What follows is an enlightening glimpse of the man—from his colorful west Texas childhood, through his military career, to his adventures with the Cowboys.

For those of us who know and love Buck, the book is entertaining and revealing.

For those who never met Buck Buchanan, you're in for a real treat—a glimpse of the behind-the-scenes, locker room life of the Dallas Cowboys' Glory Years.

So sit back and enjoy Buck's story.

You'll be glad you did.

PREFACE

I waited eight years to write a book I never intended to write in the first place. I spent twenty-five glorious years with the Dallas Cowboys—the first twenty-one (1973–1993) as the full-time equipment manager for the team—the last four (1994–1998) as a part-timer working with my protégé Mike McCord and my son, Bucky Buchanan.

Toward the end of my career, I was asked frequently by sportswriters if I planned to write my Cowboys memoirs. "No, sir," came my immediate and stock response.

But I was never really able to answer their next question, "Why not?"

After finishing *Glory Days* I am not certain I know the answer to that question. My half-hearted retort, in keeping with Coach Landry's "loose lips sink ships" philosophy, might have been, "I consider the Cowboys family, and I don't want to air family laundry in public." But that would not have been completely accurate or truthful.

Jerry and I are proud parents. We have been blessed with two wonderful children and three terrific grandchildren: Thomas (19), Andrew (17), and Brett (16). It is an extreme joy to have them around us and, in that way, stay hip with the younger generation. We are quick to share how wonderful those kids are, especially when they do something we deem worthy, which is practically every day.

Then why not toot the horn of my extended Cowboys family?

More accurately, what kept me from writing this book was the Herculean effort required. Even more so, I felt compelled to record a story that paid proper tribute to my Cowboys family. To do so, I required a worthy writer who could get inside my head and accomplish the job to my complete satisfaction.

I found that writer in Stephen Stainkamp.

But write it I have, and I'm proud to have done so.

Glory Days is one man's perspective. It is my personal account as I remember it. The book is not a football play-by-play primer, so coaches and players, don't rush out to buy it if you are looking for a how-to-guide to football.

Although the reader won't glean the building blocks or the stratagem for a winning football program, hopefully he or she will discern the character traits, work ethic, and attitudes of winning. Indeed, I can't think of a better template for success, in any human endeavor, than an introspective and comprehensive look at America's Team.

In the final analysis, *Glory Days* is not a tutorial. It is, however, a lighthearted look down memory lane, a peek into the inner sanctum, an insider's look at the world-famous Dallas Cowboys in their heyday.

My desire is that the reader enjoys this adventure half as much as I loved living it.

I am a very lucky man.

I had a one-in-a-million opportunity most men only dream of—to associate with, to work with on a daily basis, and, over a period of years, to get to know a remarkable cast of sports personalities most mortals only read about in the newspaper or see on TV.

I don't consider myself an especially talented or gifted man. I am a blessed man, however, one who spent a quarter-century in the company of giants, the most special and gifted sports personalities to have ever trod this earth, often in the cramped, sweat-stained, odorous locker rooms and stadium team meeting rooms throughout America.

Yes, *Glory Days* is one man's perspective. As of its writing, I am seventy-two years old. As men my age know all too well, our bodies and our minds aren't what they once were. Neither are our memories. I have faithfully recounted my story with the Dallas Cowboys as honestly as I could. I never took notes, and I never used a tape recorder during my Cowboys career. Perhaps I should have.

I worked with literally thousands of players, coaches, trainers, officials, stadium managers, NFL equipment managers, security personnel, and sportscasters, many of whom I have not credited in this book only because I lacked the time and space.

If I have failed to include friends or associates, or not given them the credit they are due, it is not because I don't remember them fondly—I do. There were just so many wonderful men and women with whom I worked those many years that it is impossible to include them all.

Looking back at my NFL career, I consider myself a very fortunate man.

To everyone in the Cowboys organization, thanks for the memories!

It is not, nor has it ever been, my desire to discredit anyone.

Every story in this book is told with fond recollection.

It has been my goal from the beginning to tell it like I lived it, and remember it—with all its joys and blemishes—much like I have tried to live my life. What follows are my memories as best I can remember them. I trust you enjoy them.

I have many friends who are former Cowboys and some who are still with the organization. In many instances I have availed myself of their memories in the compilation of this story. Many of the accounts are paraphrased memories, some imprecise quotes.

PREFACE

Glory Days is what it is, a compilation of twenty-five years with the Dallas Cowboys.

Like my heroes—my Dad, Andrew T. Buchanan, and Dallas Head Coach Tom Landry—I rarely discussed personal matters on the job. Like my heroes, I have tried to treat everyone with respect.

This is my legacy: that I have walked in the footsteps of Great Men.

ACKNOWLEDGMENTS

I owe a special debt of gratitude to my wife, Jerry, my daughter, Julie, and my son, Bucky, for hanging tough with me through all those difficult years of separation.

To my dad, Andrew T. Buchanan, and Mom, Ina Ruth Buchanan, thanks for your loving example and tutelage. I wish you could have been there, Dad, to enjoy the Cowboys experience with me.

To my half-brother, Hoyt Smith, and to my sister, Marianne Buchanan, thanks for your love and support.

Thanks to all the wonderful coaches, athletes, and staff who helped make those years of long, hard hours and separation from family tolerable.

Special thanks to Jerry Jones, Roger Staubach, Gene Stallings, Bob Ward, Jim Myers, Rich Dalrymple, Brett Daniels, Marylyn Love, Barbara Goodman, the *Dallas Cowboys Official Weekly* (old pals Russ Russell, Cheryl Harris, and Sharon Carnahan), and all the players and coaches who contributed to the development of *Glory Days.*

And thanks to all the equipment managers throughout the NFL, and to the Cowboys' staff who helped make my career possible. My time at Dallas couldn't have been more enjoyable. For that, I have been truly blessed.

1

HAIL MARY

BLOOMINGTON, MINNESOTA
DECEMBER 28, 1975

The sidelines were iced over and slicker than snot.

Rival teams, seated on the same sideline—muddied, bloodied, grass-stained, bodies venting steam—sat mannequin-like facing the field.

An angry sky, overcast and gun-barrel gray, covered the baseball field turned gridiron. Metropolitan Stadium was a seething hornet's nest of 48,341 screaming sports fans. The mercury hovered at 30 degrees Fahrenheit, but I was oblivious to the cold.

Three layers of Dallas Cowboys winter wear covered my 6-foot 3-inch lanky frame. Beneath a pair of black, unlined, waterproofed, four-buckle overshoes, I wore my favorite sideline footgear—coaches' shoes with patented ripple soles—a Gene Stallings favorite. Tucked within my boots, I wore a pair of athletic socks, calf-high.

No, sir, I wasn't cold. I had too much to do and too much to consider.

My only sensation was the nagging ache in my posterior, a result of the inglorious spill I'd taken on the sideline prepping for the game—dad gum ice—and my palpitating heart, the result of another Divisional Playoff Game too close to call in the final seconds.

Piles of snow lay stacked in grimy mounds against the shaking bleachers.

I glanced at the scoreboard, and my heart sank—HOME-14—VISITORS-10.

I began picking up for the return trip home.

Head Coach Tom Landry stood fifteen yards from where I labored.

Huddled with him were the offensive coaches, Myers, Ditka, and Reeves.

To my left, ten yards removed, stood a stunned Cowboys defensive staff.

I surveyed the field and quickly scanned the Cowboys' huddle.

I snuck a peek at the clock, packed a parka, and noted the time remaining—forty-four seconds. The Vikings mascot, a burly fellow in shaggy costume, danced behind his team's bench. Bundled Vikings cheerleaders vied for space and a chance to be heard over the din.

We had the ball in our end of the field—at about the 35-yard line.

The Cowboys broke the huddle.

It was fourth and long—a *very* long sixteen yards.

Working out of the shotgun, No. 12, quarterback Roger Staubach, stood poised. On the count, Cowboy center Kyle Davis, No. 57, snapped the ball.

The pigskin sailed the distance to Roger's outstretched fingertips.

The Minnesota line, veteran defensive linemen all, surged the Cowboys' offense.

The clash of titans could be heard over the deafening roar of the crowd.

Roger faded to his own 30-yard line and looked downfield.

He saw Drew Pearson, No. 88—open—and lofted the ball to his wide receiver. Roger connected to Drew, making the first down and stopping the clock.

I dropped a parka and shook my head in disbelief.

The comeback kid was back to his old tricks—way to go, Roger.

Once more, out of the shotgun, Kyle snapped the ball.

No. 12 dropped back and looked downfield.

Roger saw Drew and heaved the ball as hard as he could.

The spiraled pass floated high overhead and threatened to leave the stadium.

Time froze.

Drew leapt.

There was contact, between Drew and Vikings defender Nate Wright.

But was it offensive or defensive interference, or neither?

We may never know. The NFL had no instant replay in 1975.

Drew came down with the ball—inbounds.

Nate lost his footing and went down.

Drew scampered untouched into the end zone for the touchdown and the win.

He spiked the ball and was immediately met by his celebrating teammates.

The loudspeaker roared, "Touchdown Dallas!"

The roaring crowd instantly turned deathly still.

The scoreboard registered the score—HOME-14—VISITORS-16.

The crowd directed its wrath at the back judge official.

A beer bottle hurled from the stands struck the official on the head. Bleeding, his hat lying on the turf, the official was quickly escorted off the field.

Drew Pearson scores the winning touchdown against Minnesota in 1975

Cowboys players, both on and off the field, continued to celebrate.

The Cowboys' coaching staff joined in the celebration.

Standing there in stony silence, Coach Landry checked his game plan.

I stood over a pile of parkas, my hands extended at both sides, my mouth agape.

Coach Landry hurried Toni Fritsch, No. 15, onto the field.

Kyle snapped the ball to the holder, defensive back Charlie Waters, No. 41.

Toni, our Vienna, Austria–born kicker, booted the extra point.

The scoreboard changed—HOME-14—VISITORS-17.

The Vikings regained possession, but Minnesota never came close to another first down. We won that Divisional Playoff Game and advanced to the NFC Championship.

After the legion of supporters, family members, and the press had left the dressing room, Head Trainer Don Cochren pulled me aside and asked, "Buck, Don't you ever get emotional about a close game like this? How the hell can you remain so composed?"

My answer was truthful, candid: "Guess I don't have the luxury of getting excited. I'm a lot like Coach Landry—and my Dad—I've never seen either man show emotion."

2

TEXAS TOUGH

Born William T. Buchanan on May 24, 1933, I was raised in the sleepy west Texas town of Ballinger, Texas, county seat of Runnels County, a tiny dot on the Texas road map located forty miles northeast of San Angelo and fifty-five miles south of Abilene.

Ranching, farming, and bootlegging were the area's economic mainstays until the oil and gas boom of the 1950s, and that industry's gradual decline there a decade later.

Dad was Andrew T. "Buck" Buchanan, former special Texas Ranger, and Deputy Sheriff/Jailer for Ballinger. Mom was Ina Ruth Buchanan, known for her Christian charity and the delicious meals she prepared for her family and the jail's incarcerated.

As a Texas Ranger, Dad rode border patrol during the Mexican Insurrection, and he had an old, scarred leather belt in his souvenir collection that had saved his life from a bandit's knife while on patrol. Dad served on a Texas Rangers detail at the King Ranch, and he was on special Ranger duty in Eastland, Texas, during the oil boom there.

In 1926, Dad moved to Fort Stockton, Texas, and became a barber. He never went to barber school, but he learned to cut hair and shave cowboys on numerous cattle drives.

Dad met and married Mom in Fort Stockton in 1930.

Andrew T. Buchanan, my Dad and former Texas Ranger

That year, the newlyweds moved to Ballinger where Dad became the town barber. Mom and Dad started a family there, and we grew up in two houses—the first at 402 Eleventh Street and the second at 501 Tenth Street. I was born at our Eleventh Street home.

In 1939, Dad was appointed chief deputy sheriff under Sheriff Calvin Robinson. And in October of that year, in his official capacity as town jailer, Dad moved his small family into the living quarters on the first floor of the Runnels County Jail.

The jail was a three-story brown-brick structure. There was a boiler in the basement for the building's heat. The office and booking area were located on the first floor, as were our family's living quarters. In short order, I learned how to work every handle and lever in that jail to gain access to, or exit, any room or cell on all three floors. That knowledge proved invaluable when Mom wanted food delivered to the prisoners.

The second floor was called the bullpen, and it housed the white criminals. There was a big cell on the third floor for the general population of blacks and Hispanics. Three smaller cells, one padded, were reserved for the women and the mentally incapacitated. Those accused of or suspected of being insane were kept in one of the three smaller third-floor cells pending a determination of their competence by the court.

My earliest recollection of life in Ballinger was when I was three and a half years old.

All kids do stupid things, and I was no exception. In a freak accident, I severely cut my right palm ferrying glass milk bottles. At the time, I was suffering with tonsillitis. Dad was a practical man. That day, he marched me across the street to the doctor's office.

My Ballinger birthplace

My third home—the Ballinger Jail

"Doc," Dad began, "young Tom cut his hand putting the empties out by the curb. Think you could take a look at it for me?"

Doc Lassiter accommodated Dad and stitched my damaged hand with catgut.

"While I got him here," Dad continued, "could you take a look at his throat? Tom's been suffering with tonsillitis, doc. It has been going around you know."

Doc Lassiter nodded. After a cursory exam, he concurred with Dad's prognosis, peered over his wire-rimmed spectacles, and looked about his tiny office. We were alone.

"Shoot, might just as well take 'em out while you've got him here," he said.

And my tonsils were just as quickly removed.

Suffering blood loss and trauma, I was feeling puny.

"Might see to his privates, too, doc," Dad said, motioning to my lap.

"Meaning?"

"Meaning the boy's not been circumcised," Dad whispered.

"Oh," the doctor replied.

"Well, then, young Buck," the doctor said, patting the elevated table. "Best climb up here, and let's take a look."

I don't remember what that doctor's visit cost.

Back then, medical bills were often paid with a chicken or a bag of produce. I was too much under the weather at the time to care about our family's medical payment plan.

Dad carried me home from Doc Lassiter's—stitched hand, *sans* tonsils, and circumcised. It had been a banner day for that country doctor. Years later, reflecting on that episode, I figured that if I had survived three surgeries in one day, at the age of three, I could survive anything life had to throw at me.

But survive I did, and in 1939, I started the first grade in Ballinger.

As a three-year-old, with friends in Ballinger. Photo courtesy of Eva Jo Flynt Scott.

Dad was widely known and respected throughout Runnels County. He had enjoyed a colorful and distinguished career as a Texas peace officer, and he was quite an accomplished rodeo performer, having ridden the rodeo circuit from Mexico to Canada.

As a law enforcement officer during a particularly rough and stormy era of Texas toughs and notorious outlaws, Dad owned a sizeable cache of weapons. Often, on a cold winter's day, he and I would take those guns apart and clean them with Hoppe's Gun Oil.

Dad's service pistols were nickel-plated, his mainstay a single-action, pearl-handled .38/.40 Bisley that fired a rifle cartridge. He had a bone-handled .41 Colt, built on a .45 Peacemaker frame; a Super .38, on a .45 automatic frame; and a .30/.40 Krag. And just in case, Dad kept a shiny .25 automatic tucked inconspicuously inside his belt.

On special occasions, Dad carried a double-barreled, sawed-off shotgun, or a .45 caliber Thompson's submachine gun, a Runnels County loaner, for official business. The bad guys steered clear of Dad and that scattergun, and the Thompson's, with its round drum, the kind you see in those Elliott Ness movies, that held fifty lead-nosed bullets.

Dad knew his way around criminals—and weapons—and I don't remember a day growing up in Ballinger when he wasn't packing several concealed weapons. He also owned several shotguns and deer rifles the two of us used for hunting.

Dad cast a long shadow, and he definitely stood out in a crowd. He wore a large white cowboy hat, a white shirt and tie, a black suit, and black kangaroo boots made by Mercer Boots in San Angelo. Dad seldom wore anything but boots, and he only took them off before going to bed. He anchored his tie with a diamond stickpin I still have.

In his early years with *Los Diablos Tejanos*, the not-so-complimentary Mexican version of the famed Texas Rangers, Dad had numerous scrapes with nasty *bandidos* and near-death brushes with border outlaws and criminals. As Ballinger's deputy sheriff and jailer, he had his fair share of encounters with troublemakers, drunks, and bootleggers.

Runnels County is a dry county. When I got older, Dad let me ride with him, several members of the State Liquor Board, and the Ballinger City Police on a raid to nab a suspected bootlegger. They left me in the car when they went inside to apprehend the suspect.

"I'll leave a gun in the glove box for you, Tommy," he'd said, "just in case."

I was ten years old.

"If he comes out, make him stop," Dad warned.

When Dad left, I looked in the glove compartment, and sure enough, there was a pistol. An expert gun-handler by that time, I retrieved and inspected my service revolver, but found it was unloaded. Dad and the others had little trouble apprehending the suspect, and I remember them escorting the handcuffed prisoner to a patrol car outside. Good thing for me there was no gunplay.

Illicit drinking, generally on the weekends, was common in those days, and often I was forced to listen to the all-night bellowing of intoxicated prisoners upstairs.

This one night, Dad brought in the town undertaker, drunk as a skunk. As I tried to sleep, that undertaker would not stop his tirade against my father, the arresting officer.

"Mr. Buck," the inebriated, foul-mouthed undertaker hollered, "you're nothing but a gall-durned son of a gun." The tirade continued nonstop. Finally, unable to sleep, I crawled out of bed and asked my father, "How can you stand that?"

Surely, Dad had written the book on patience.

"I know old George," he replied. "Old boy's drunk, and he doesn't mean what he's saying. Best we let him sleep it off tonight, Tom. He'll be alright in the morning."

Another drinking incident involved a black man who got intoxicated every weekend. Elijah had a bad eye that twirled uncontrollably in its socket. I guess the eye lacked muscularity and must not have been anchored right.

Dad had been working on the oil furnace in the basement, and it blew up on him, burning his face and hands. Doc Lassiter applied salve and wrapped Dad's arms and much of his face in gauze.

Chief of Police J. L. Moreland had arrested Elijah on the charge of public intoxication and brought him to the jail that night. Chief Moreland rang the bell outside and Dad answered the door. When Elijah saw Dad wrapped up in that gauze like a mummy, he screamed, and that eye straightened up in its socket.

Elijah turned and ran screaming from the jail.

"Aren't you going after him, J. L.?" Dad asked the Chief.

"No, sir," Chief Moreland said, "I imagine he's sobered up by now."

Years later, I witnessed Dad, the night watchman, and another officer, all older gentlemen at the time, attempt to book members of the dread *pachucos.*

Pachucos were gang members who sported tattoos on the fleshy area between their thumb and index finger. Reportedly, they were involved in dope and other nefarious activities.

That night, when my half-brother Hoyt Smith and I heard a ruckus in the jail's booking area, we entered to see four gang members fighting with Dad and the two officers. One of the officers had to use his three-cell flashlight on an unruly gang member in an effort to subdue the man, rapping the offender soundly about the skull.

We watched briefly from the shadows, then stepped into full sight clad in our red pajamas. The gang members must have thought we were police reinforcements, because after we showed up they calmed down some.

There were other local gangs Dad had to be concerned with at the time. Rowena, Texas, six miles down the road from Ballinger,

With siblings, Hoyt and Marianne, at home in the Ballinger jail, 1958

is the home of Bonnie Parker of Bonnie and Clyde fame. Members of the infamous Barrow Gang were jailed in Ballinger, but to my knowledge, neither Clyde nor Bonnie ever spent a night beneath our humble roof.

Many a night as a young boy I lay in bed listening to the howling, the ranting, and the raving that came from the occupants of the jail's second and third floors.

One day a drunk prisoner stripped naked and climbed to the top rung of his jail cell, hanging there, his contorted face squeezed through the bars, barking like a dog.

But growing up in Ballinger, living in its jail, wasn't that bad. My friends would drop by, and not one thought my family's living conditions odd. In fact they thought visiting was pretty neat, preferable to hanging out at any of the other kids' houses.

The courthouse lawn took up two city blocks of Ballinger and was a favorite place for the kids to play baseball and football. After Dad got permission from the county commissioners, we created a makeshift baseball field with a chicken-wire backstop. It must have been quite a sight—two five-man teams of youngsters playing baseball on the court lawn while cheering inmates hung from the jail's barred windows rooting us on.

Like most kids, Hoyt and I owned bicycles—second-hand contraptions Dad had picked up for us in San Angelo. I thrilled at riding my bike around the jail, screeching around hairpin curves like a race car driver. I noticed the family's laundry too late one morning, put out to dry on my mother's clothesline, and like to hung myself. After that, I restricted my bike riding to the areas where Mom did not have her clothesline strung.

Hoyt was my older sibling by four years; Marianne Buchanan, my sister, was four years my junior. Now and then, Hoyt let me run with his friends. It was neat hanging out with the older guys. Being a girl, however, Marianne had a different set of friends.

In one way or another, the Buchanans were familiar to the area's criminals. Dad locked them up. Mom prepared their meals, and we kids entertained those jailbirds and listened to their daily chatter. Most were respectful, and I enjoyed talking with them.

There was one prisoner, Jim Price, whom I really liked. Jim was an excellent carpenter. He just had a drinking problem. Every weekend Jim got liquored up on whatever it was he drank, and he'd peacefully admit himself into the jail.

Jim would stagger up to the door, ring the bell, and announce, "Mr. Buck, you're gonna have to lock old Jim up." Between bouts with the bottle, however, whenever I saw Jim in town, he was always respectful and had a kind word for me. And he usually gave

Runnels County Courthouse

me the change in his pockets. When I left Ballinger in 1953, Jim was still going strong.

The penalty in Ballinger for drunk and disorderly conduct could be as severe as ten days in jail—especially if gunplay was involved. I suppose Jim's only crime was public drunkenness. After all, he was a contributing member to society, and he did admit himself into our jail. Jim must have been interested in Mom's home-cooked meals—they were that good—and a clean bed to sleep in. Come Monday, his boss got him out and Jim was good to go for the week—till Friday night.

There was no air conditioning, and the boiler—a continuous source of mechanical aggravation for Dad—provided the only heat for the jail's tenants. The steam produced by that boiler noisily wound its way through the building's pipes and into each room's radiators.

With all its imperfections, the jail was home sweet home to the Buchanan clan as well as a host of disparate, unwilling guests collected from throughout Runnels County.

In general, life in Ballinger was peaceful and great for kids. My friends and Hoyt and I played all the games kids played—hide and seek, kick the bucket, and annie over. We built a play set in the backyard of our home on Tenth street, and we named our Western-style saloon, the Buck Horn Saloon, after the deer antlers Dad provided us.

We played cowboys and indians, and we drank our own pretend sarsaparilla—a frothy mix of soda and vinegar that was short on taste and long on imagination. My all-time favorite *real* soda pop was RC Cola, and nothing beat the taste of an ice-cold RC with a handful of salted peanuts thrown into the frosty bottle for taste.

Occasionally, on weekends we'd spend ten cents and take in a double feature at one of Ballinger's two theaters—the Texas Theater or the Palace. In the 1950s, however, when drive-in theaters became popular, the Palace closed its doors for good.

We had no grass or manicured lawns—just a whole lot of weeds, as water was scarce and no one in Ballinger owned a water sprinkler, if they even existed at the time.

People spent a lot more time together.

Families were close.

When I walked around town with Dad, townsfolk tipped their hats and waved.

Dad had a fourth-grade education, but he could read and write with the best of them. His favorite book was *Judge Roy Bean: Justice West of the Pecos.*

On Sundays, Dad loved to come home, prop his feet up on the table, one boot on either side of the radio on account of his varicose veins, listen to his favorite gospel quartet, and sing along. Dad had an excellent voice. His favorite Sunday evening radio shows were *Mr. District Attorney* and *Doctor IQ.*

Being the son of the deputy sheriff had its advantages. Sometimes the county judge allowed me to sit in the jury box, when there was no jury seated, and observe the proceedings. When I got older, Dad gave me a single-shot 12-gauge shotgun—a gift to him from one of the jail's drunks, who had unwisely used the gun to celebrate one night. When he sobered up, the man wanted nothing more to do with that scattergun, so Dad let me use it on our dove-hunting trips outside Ballinger's city limits.

This one hunting trip, my first with that new gun, we set up in a field of towering sunflowers, beside a cattle tank, waiting for the doves to fly over. When they did I stood up and fired. That old gun knocked me back, butt-first, into a patch of prickly pear cactus.

Dad laughed and laughed, as I tried to remove those stickers from my rear end.

On the way home, he stopped the car and stepped into the brush by the side of the road. Dad located one of his hidden watering holes—a spring-fed trickle that bubbled up out of the ground. We cleaned those birds, and wet our whistles at that watering hole before heading home with that night's supper.

My life in Ballinger was filled with kids' games, wanted posters, interesting inmates, sports, hunting with Dad, and dime movies. It could not have been better.

We didn't own a television, and we had few of today's so-called amenities. The family owned a 1938 Ford—a used car Dad bought from the county when the sheriff got his new squad car. That Runnels County Sheriff's car sure scared the socks off those older kids who had parked at Ballinger's secluded Lover's Lane, the night best friend Jimmy Parish and I pulled up in a cloud of dust.

Our lives were full, happy, and content.

Dad was a gardener, which was a great complement to Mom's cooking.

He was a real handyman, too. Dad built a shoeshine bench from scrap two-by-fours, and each Sunday, after he had given us our weekly haircuts, he'd shine our shoes. Hoyt and I became pretty good at shining each other's shoes, too.

Being a lawman, Dad always followed the law to the letter. To avoid breaking it, he made certain his barber's license was current so he could legally cut our hair. And years later, after I reached manhood at the advanced age of sixteen, Dad gave me my first shave, on account of my severe acne, with that old, sharp, straight razor of his.

In 1946, at the age of thirteen, I started playing baseball on the American Legion team in Ballinger. The coach was ER Earnshaw, a former professional baseball catcher. Because of Coach Earnshaw's influence I decided I had to be a professional baseball catcher, too.

The Legion supplied most of our equipment, but I ordered my catcher's mask, shin pads, chest protector, and mitt from Sears. And that year I fell in love with baseball.

I lettered in baseball four years, and I started each year as the team's catcher. I lettered in football my junior and senior year as right tackle for the Ballinger Bearcats. I graduated from Ballinger High School on May 20, 1950, one of sixty-two graduating seniors.

Much as I enjoy football my first love has always been baseball. My favorite teams were the New York Yankees, the St. Louis Cardinals, and the Brooklyn Dodgers.

My favorite player was Enos "Country" Slaughter, outfielder for the St. Louis Cardinals. Country was one heck of a talented right fielder. And he was a good hitter and a brawler, when it was necessary to win. I admired Enos because he was one of those take-no-prisoners, whatever-it-takes-to-win players common to that era of baseball.

I played semipro ball with the Plymouth Oilers in Big Lake, Texas, in 1950. And I signed a contract with the Brooklyn Dodgers in February 1951. Later, when I checked the Dodgers' roster and saw that Roy Campanella was the starting catcher and Johnny Roseboro was Campanella's backup, I knew I had my work cut out for me.

Cliff Gustafson, our Oilers' shortstop, went on to coach baseball for the University of Texas in Austin. Cliff was a gifted player, a great guy, and a terrific coach who had a successful career at UT.

But a career with the Brooklyn Dodgers was not in the cards for me and after six weeks in training camp I was released. Upon returning home I worked for Lone Star Gas from 1951 to 1953, where I played semipro baseball for the Ballinger Cats.

3

UNCLE SAM WANTS YOU!

Rather than wait to be drafted, a certainty for a healthy kid just out of high school in 1953, I decided to enlist in the Army. The United States was winding down a costly war on the Korean peninsula, one that had cost the lives of some five million Koreans and Chinese, and more than fifty-four thousand U.S. soldiers. Later dubbed the Forgotten War by some, a cease-fire was in the works, but an agreement would not be signed until July 27, 1953.

I'd spoken with a buddy of mine from Ballinger, Troyce O'Neal, who had heeded Uncle Sam's call and was stationed at Ft. Sill, Oklahoma. Troyce suggested I consider the Army Airborne—with its fifty-five-dollar-a-month-bonus for jumping out of perfectly good airplanes, and the treat of wearing those fancy, spit-shined Corcoran jump boots.

In March of 1953, I signed the papers and Uncle Sam shipped me off to Basic Combat Training at Ft. Campbell, Kentucky. Four months later, I attended the Army's grueling Parachute Jump School at Ft. Benning, Georgia, and upon graduating proudly with my jump wings, I was attached to the 82nd Airborne at Ft. Bragg, North Carolina.

I was stationed at Ft. Bragg three years. The crowning glory of that assignment was not my thirty-eight parachute jumps, but what took place on February 4, 1956, the happiest day of my life,

Pvt. E-1 Buck Buchanan at Ft. Bragg, North Carolina

when I married Geraldine "Jerry" Quick of Rockingham, North Carolina.

After completing my military hitch, I got out of the Army and Jerry and I moved back to Rockingham. Restless, in the spring of 1956, after a short visit to Ballinger, I signed the enlistment papers with the United States Air Force. After a brief basic training refresher course, I received orders for Donaldson Air Force Base, South Carolina.

That tour in South Carolina, from 1956 to 1959, was wonderful. We were close to family, and Jerry and I loved our neighbors and the community. Unlike the Army, the Air Force gave me something to do that was immensely more to my liking—a job involved with base athletics. And on March 5, 1957, the Buchanan family was blessed with the arrival of our first child—Julie Renee Buchanan.

My next job, Non-Commissioned Officer in Charge (NCOIC) of Base Athletics and Recreation at Washington National Airport, with the Special Missions Group, ran from 1959 to 1961.

William Andrew "Bucky" Buchanan, our second child, was born at Ft. Belvoir, Virginia, on June 9, 1961. The Buchanans enjoyed that assignment, and life in our nation's Capitol, on an enlisted man's salary with two children, was both austere and short-lived.

At the conclusion of our assignment in Washington, DC, I received orders for Elmendorf AFB, in Anchorage, Alaska. We lived in Anchorage from 1961 to 1964. For the first three years, we enjoyed Alaska immensely. But on March 27, 1964, the Good Friday Earthquake, and subsequent tsunami generated by that temblor, officially scored by the United States Geological Survey at 9.2 on the Richter scale, shook our tiny household to the core.

The Buchanan home was a tiny trailer outside town, at the base of the Chugach Mountains. Fortunately, we avoided most of the destruction caused by that terrible quake. Our electricity was knocked out, and Jerry and I weren't happy with the broken glass and the baby diapers that had to be washed by hand. But we avoided any significant structural damage, and family and friends suffered no injuries or loss of life.

THE UNITED STATES AIR FORCE ACADEMY

Shortly after the earth shook our humble Alaskan home, I received orders for the U.S. Air Force Academy in Colorado Springs, Colorado. Jerry could not have been happier to leave Anchorage. She had no desire to fly either, so we drove the entire way, 3,378 scenic miles, in caravan with another Air Force family.

I was assigned to the Department of Athletics at the academy from 1964 to 1968. But for the first ten weeks, my commanding officer, Lt. Col. William Quinlan, had me clean horse stables on base.

The job of stablehand wasn't all that bad, and although it required some degree of physical dexterity, handling a pitchfork

Master Sergeant Buck Buchanan in Thailand

and wheelbarrow, it wasn't exactly what I'd signed up for. Perhaps the Air Force was short on stablehands; perhaps the colonel thought I needed a humbling experience to prepare me for my job as NCOIC of the academy's athletic program. I don't know, but I have my suspicions.

Nonetheless, after graduating from equestrian duty, I assumed responsibility for the cadet gymnasiums and the maintenance of the athletic fields—133 acres in all.

Academy cadets have an impressive athletic program from which to choose, with the full complement of sports—baseball, track and field, cross country, football, lacrosse, soccer, rugby, swimming and diving, gymnastics, cadet rifle team, wrestling, and boxing.

I managed five military and four civilian subordinates who worked inside, plus a crew of fifteen whose responsibility was the care and maintenance of the athletic fields.

Julie and Bucky were growing like weeds, and we loved our Colorado Springs assignment. But it was not to last. In June of 1968, I received a hardship-duty assignment—family could not accompany me—to Thailand's Takhli Royal Thai Air Force Base.

During my Thai assignment, I had the opportunity to tour much of Southeast Asia as NCOIC of Personnel Services. I was stationed at Takhli from June 1968 to June 1969, and I earned the Bronze Star for Meritorious Service during that tour. Much as I am proud of that distinguished military award, it paled by comparison to the joy I felt when I received orders for home, and a second tour at the U.S. Air Force Academy.

DÉJÀ VU

Jerry and the kids were thrilled to have me home. During my tour in Thailand, they had lived in a small apartment close to Jerry's family in Rockingham. But nobody was happier to be back in the good old U.S. of A., with his family and friends, than I was.

My second academy assignment ran from 1969 to 1973, and I served as the NCOIC for the Preparatory School's athletic program. It was great revisiting old Air Force colleagues and friends, and mom and the kids quickly readjusted to Colorado's altitude, thin air, and lack of humidity.

Little did I know what career changes lay ahead.

My cumulative military experience, especially at the academy, a total of eight years by the end of my second tour there, would soon open exciting new civilian doors. That military experience, in athletics, facilities, and grounds care, would prove instrumental in my being hired by the Dallas Cowboys in 1973.

It would be my equipment-handling experience at the academy that most impressed Cowboys Head Coach Tom Landry during our 1973 interview. Due to the scope of my work with the cadets, I often wore four or five hats. My experience putting two thousand kids on the field every day, my expertise with game set-up, transportation, meals, and lodging for away games, and my instructional and classroom work proved invaluable at the Cowboys' interview.

My hands-on experience at the academy helped determine the outcome of my interview with Coach Landry, but my references sealed the deal. Mr. Brandt, director of player personnel for the Cowboys, expedited background checks after the interviews with Coach Landry. Brandt contacted every one of my references and spoke with my Air Force boss in Colorado Springs, Colonel Floyd G. Davis.

But then, I'm getting ahead of myself.

BACK IN THE U.S.S.R.

During my tenure as NCOIC at the Prep School, I met Colonel Floyd Davis, a tremendous athlete and former basketball star from the University of Utah.

Nicknamed Shot Davis by his teammates, Colonel Davis was the best basketball coach I have ever known. Certainly, his record at the academy speaks highly of his coaching credentials. I doubled as a trainer for Colonel Davis during my four-year hitch at the Academy Prep School, my last assignment before retiring from the Air Force.

The colonel received a new batch of preppies each year. Working from scratch with the most promising new students, he forged winning basketball teams every season.

Colonel Davis shaped those kids into tremendous players with winning records and winning attitudes. And we won the majority of the contests we played against freshmen teams throughout Colorado and Kansas.

In 1972, Colonel Davis was asked to coach the All–Air Force Basketball Team in interservice competition. In head-to-head contests with the Navy, the Marines, and the favored Army basketball team, we won that tournament for the first time in six years.

As a result of those victories, Colonel Davis was selected to coach an All-Military Team to compete in the Amateur Athletic Union (AAU) against amateur and semipro teams in London, Kentucky. No military team had won that contest before, but in 1972, Colonel Davis' boys did.

In April, the AAU asked the colonel to coach the AAU All-Star Team for a goodwill basketball tour of the Soviet Union. The United States and the U.S.S.R. were embroiled in a bitter Cold War. Tensions were high, and like the earlier American Ping-Pong tours in China, the AAU must have thought the contests between American and Soviet athletes would go a long way toward easing international tensions.

Upon being notified of his selection by the AAU, Colonel Davis asked me if I would like to accompany him on the team's six-week tour behind the Iron Curtain.

He did not have to twist my arm. I immediately volunteered, pending my wife, Jerry's, blessings. She agreed, and after the request had been approved through channels, I became the official trainer for the United States All-Star Basketball Team.

We practiced at Georgetown College in Georgetown, Kentucky, for a week before boarding a flight from Louisville to New York, bound for Prague, Czechoslovakia. Since I had just returned from Thailand, I still had my red U.S. passport.

In Prague, I was the last person in our contingent to clear customs, as I had to ensure that all our athletes were successfully processed.

When I got to the immigration counter, the officials were stymied by my red passport and refused to allow me entry. The pair of Czech officials called another official over for consultation. After lengthy discussions, they explained that, in the Soviet Bloc, the red passport denoted official U.S. government business.

Concerned that my trip might be cancelled, I called an old friend from the academy, whom I knew was stationed in Prague. Sgt. Paul Turner and another embassy staffer had to leave the American Embassy and come to the airport to help with my dilemma. Fortunately, I was successful in gaining entry.

Paul and I chatted about the incident at the embassy reception that night. He told me that, despite being outranked by an Air Force colonel, a pair of Air Force captains, and a Marine major, in Soviet protocol, the holder of the red passport was considered head honcho.

Paul advised me that if anything went wrong on the trip, it would fall on my shoulders. Needless to say, I was concerned to hear my friend's report, and I took special care throughout our visit to ensure that our athletes were on their best behavior.

Our trip was carefully orchestrated and strictly monitored by our Soviet hosts. Mr. Ivanhof, our official tour guide, turned out to be a member of the KGB. We called him 007. We had another caretaker—a man simply introduced to us as Leon. Both Russians spoke flawless English and were our constant translators and travel companions.

Our social calendar was predictable. We flew into the designated city in the afternoon, attended a reception at the embassy that night, or at a party held elsewhere, and spent the night at a hotel of our hosts' choosing.

We practiced the next day, spent the night in the hotel, and played the scheduled team the second night. We spent that night in our hotel, and left on the next leg of our Soviet journey the following morning.

Of all the cities we visited throughout the Soviet Union, Prague—with its delightful old churches, magnificent architecture, and the Moldau River—was the most beautiful. We lost our first game, a cliffhanger, to a determined Czech Olympic Team. In Czechoslovakia, fans show their approval by whistling. And boy, could they whistle.

By agreement, we played international rules, a decidedly more physical game than we were accustomed to. In the days that followed, the American team won the majority of our contests, when oddsmakers at home gave us a shot at one or two wins, at best.

After losing our first game to the Czechs, we boarded an older Aeroflot jet in Prague and flew to Moscow for a scheduled four-day visit. Moscow's no-frills airport lacked the modern conveniences common in the West. It had no escalators, no baggage carousels, and no cafeteria snack bars. After enduring customs, our bags were placed in the middle of a large room for our retrieval, and we were loaded onto buses.

A towering, dense forest was snugly nestled between the airport and the city of Moscow. It was mid-April and still very cold. The stark, black-and-white Russian landscape was blanketed in snow. But despite its centuries-old architecture, Moscow proper was nowhere near as lovely as Prague. In fact, its tenements were depressing.

It took about ninety minutes to get to the Hotel Metropol, a half block from Red Square, opposite the Bolshoi Theater. We were a few minutes' walk from the Kremlin, but we never received a formal invitation.

The most elegant of Moscow's historic hotels, the Metropol was built between 1899 and 1903, in a rich, luxurious décor. Eight years before we stayed there, the Metropol was used as a historic setting during the filming of the Russian classic, *Doctor Zhivago*, the David Lean film based on Boris Pasternak's novel.

At that night's reception Colonel Davis and I wondered, in hushed voices, how many hidden bugs—Cold War listening devices—must have been buried within the walls of the American Embassy. I have often wondered if our Soviet hosts enjoyed our whispered discussion of their eavesdropping techniques that night as much as we did.

Colonel Davis dressed casually for that evening meal; I wore a coat and tie. The American ambassador, an older gentleman, must have thought I was in charge of the delegation. Perhaps he'd been told I held the red passport. Perhaps he assumed I, the oldest-*looking* man in our contingent, *was* the senior guy. Either way, he talked my leg off.

The meal—pork roast—was tasty, and we were waited on like royalty.

During our stay in Moscow, we ate at several restaurants on the economy. When we did, we were served standard Russian table fare. Their food is nothing like American food. The Russians have great bread and toast. Their jelly is good, too. Their steaks were hard to come by, or small. The Russians ate a ton of potatoes, and their borscht was certainly nothing to write home about.

Our AAU representative was a gentleman by the name of Jim Fox. Jim lacked, shall I say, certain people skills. Most of the time, he was uptight, and to say the man was humorless and unfriendly would be to give Mr. Fox more credit than he is due.

Our seventeen-man-contingent included a pair of Air Force captains and academy graduates, Cliff Parsons and Gregg Popovich, Colonel Davis, a Marine major, myself, and a dozen superb young American athletes. Gregg Popovich continued in basketball after his Air Force tour, and today, after a string of exemplary athletic accomplishments, is the general manager and head coach of the world champion San Antonio Spurs.

Hank Egan, former assistant coach to Coach Popovich and the Spurs, was the former head coach of the Air Force Academy Falcons Basketball Team, a delightful officer and gentleman whom I had the pleasure of working with my first tour there.

AMERICAN-BORN, AMERICAN-PROUD

Every time I have stood at attention before the American flag, I've gotten choked up, whether my right hand was held over my left breast, or if I was saluting, in uniform.

Gregg Popovich

During that Soviet goodwill tour, I enjoyed the pomp and pageantry before and after every game. Each team lined its players up before its bench, and the American national anthem, then the host team's national anthem, was played. Players exchanged small country flags, and after the contest, no matter how hard fought or who won, the players met on center court to shake hands and exchange pleasantries.

Three decades later, I wear my Bavarian hat with pride, adorned with the pins of our host countries.

Before playing our first basketball game in Moscow, we were given a tour that included the world-famous Soviet weightlifting program. The Russians were very proud of that program, and they had every right to be, as it was the most impressive conditioning regimen I have seen—before or since.

That night we attended a performance of *Swan Lake* at the Bolshoi Theater. The presentation was impressive, but despite being forewarned not to take photographs, several American players' flash cubes illumined our seats midway through the performance, giving new meaning to the term Ugly American. Our hosts were not pleased.

Leon squeezed a special thirty-minute tour of the countryside outside Moscow into the schedule. To a man, we were unimpressed by the small, plain houses in the neighborhood. When Leon beamed, "And this was the house of Peter the Great!" not a word was said by the American contingent. When we got back to the Metropol, I tried to smooth Leon's obviously ruffled pride: "You don't say, Peter the Great."

Leon's countenance lit up. And in the moments that followed, I learned that Peter the Great is to the Russian people what George Washington is to Americans—the father of their country.

Our second day in Moscow, we played and beat the famous Red Army Team. I don't know who was more surprised—the Soviets or us. Two days later, we lost to the Russian Olympic Team, a squad comprised of athletes drawn from the republic states.

From Moscow we flew to Kiev, Ukraine, where we beat the Ukraine National Team. The colonel liked to walk after dinner, so he and I took a stroll that night on the darkened streets of Kiev. During that walk, we encountered a pair of Ukrainians who must have consumed their monthly quota of vodka that night. The men greeted us amicably at street side and asked for a light. But when I announced that we were *Americanski*, they clammed up and crossed over the cobblestone road to the other side.

Upon leaving Ukraine, we flew to Lithuania where we beat their Republic Team in Vilnius. After the game, Mr. Ivanhof demonstrated his clout in an incident that took place in a Lithuanian cafe.

With Leon's help we had placed our orders and the waiter was especially slow in delivering our dinner requests to the cook. After a lengthy wait, seeing our obvious impatience, 007 jumped into action. In no time, he had the waiter pinned against the wall between our table and the kitchen. And in Russian that required no translation, 007 told our waiter how the Soviet cow ate the Lithuanian cabbage. A short time later, grinning, sweating profusely, our waiter delivered our meal.

Next, we flew to Tallinn, Estonia, across the Gulf of Finland from Helsinki, and beat the Estonian Republic Team. Before the game, our Estonian hosts treated us to a brilliant performance of *Man of La Mancha*.

During the fifteen-minute intermission, the audience left the theater and moved to a large rotunda inside the front door. Hand in hand, the men walked their ladies around that rotunda until the performance resumed. We stood and stared. During that break, I saw no one speak or smile. After intermission, everyone returned in stony silence to their seats.

The flight to the Republic of Georgia was our longest in duration. Leon emphatically warned us of Georgians, insisting we not get drunk and not make any moves on their women—otherwise, we might be killed. He reminded us that Stalin was a Georgian, and that the Georgian men were easily provoked and prone to violence.

I don't know if that's true, but we didn't test the waters.

We beat the Republic of Georgia team in Tbilisi, but after that night's dinner and festivities, I got sick. Throughout our tour of the U.S.S.R., I was carried on our roster as the team's trainer. In the Soviet Union, trainers have medical training. Consequently, I was seated beside the Georgian team's doctor, one of the preeminent cardiovascular surgeons in Russia. During the meal, the surgeon offered me vodka, and I graciously declined.

"I don't drink the stuff," I told him.

"But you are a doctor," he insisted, "and you don't drink vodka?"

Later, Colonel Davis escorted the Soviet doctor to my room to treat me for severe dysentery, the result we assumed of poor dishwashing practices.

On the last leg of our journey, back in Moscow, we played the Russian Olympic Team a second time, and they soundly beat us once more. After that loss, we flew to Helsinki, Finland, a modern city by Soviet standards, and concluded our trip, and salvaged our reputations, with a win over the National Team of Finland.

The American team won six of our nine games.

Since that goodwill tour, I have come to wonder if the Soviets might not have had a particularly insidious motive for agreeing to host the American basketball team in 1972.

In Olympic competition in the intervening years, the Soviet basketball program fared very well against American teams. I have considered the possibility that the Soviets studied our play during that trip and adapted their play accordingly. Brilliant strategy!

4

COME ON DOWN!

Several NFL coaches attended a football camp. To save money, they decided to share accommodations, but no one wanted to room with Coach Daryl because he snored.

They decided it wasn't fair to make one of them stay with Daryl the whole time, so they voted to take turns. Coach Rick slept with Daryl the first night and came to breakfast the following morning with his hair a mess and his eyes bloodshot.

"What happened to you?" the other coaches asked.

Coach Rick lamented, "Daryl snored so loud, I just sat up and watched him all night."

The next evening, it was Coach Dave's turn. In the morning, the same scene was repeated, with Dave joining the group with his hair tussled and his eyes bloodshot.

"What happened?" the coaches intoned. "You look awful!"

"Man," Dave groaned, "Daryl shakes the roof. I watched him all night."

The third night was Coach Frank's turn. Frank was a burly, no-nonsense tackle.

Next morning at breakfast, Frank showed up bright-eyed and bushy-tailed.

"Man, what happened?" the coaches asked.

"Well, we got ready for bed," Frank explained, "I went and tucked Daryl into bed and kissed him good night. He watched me all night long."

—Author Unknown

Those who have spent any time in the military know that noncommissioned officers, sergeants, are the backbone of the United States armed forces. NCOs know their way around the system, and they represent the bulwark of this country's finest.

My nephew, Ralph Rhye (USAF Lt. Col., Retired), tells of a classroom problem posed to him when he was a student cadet at the United States Air Force Academy (1971–1975).

The instructor asked Ralph and his fellow classmates how best to erect a fifty-foot pole. The cadets pondered the problem all week, and by week's end, only one had solved the problem to the instructor's satisfaction: "Find the NCO in charge and have *him* do it."

When I was at the Air Force Academy I accompanied four hockey players/cadets to a game with Notre Dame in Colorado Springs. Wally Grinewich, a fellow sergeant I worked with, had told me about an NFL job as equipment manager with the Cowboys. Wally was the ticket manager at the academy, and he was at that hockey game that night.

Wally told me that Sid Brooks, who also worked with us at the academy as the cadet athletic supply sergeant, had recently accepted a job with the San Diego Chargers as their equipment manager. Wally had heard about the Cowboys job from another sergeant, Artis Smith, the Air Force Academy's equipment manager.

Wally secured the address for me, and in March 1973, I typed my resume and sent it to the Dallas Cowboys, attention Head Coach Tom Landry.

Ten days later I received a call from Cowboys Business Manager Joe Bailey saying the team wanted to interview me in Dallas.

Before hanging up Mr. Bailey told me that a round-trip ticket was awaiting me at the American Airlines ticket counter at Stapleton Airport in Denver, Colorado.

On March 30, 1973, I flew to Dallas and met my sister, Marianne, at Love Field. Marianne agreed to take me to the Dallas Cowboys' Expressway Towers, located at 6116 North Central Expressway, to interview with Coach Landry.

When we got to the hotel I changed out of my military uniform into a pressed sports shirt and a pair of dress slacks. And in the most forceful of terms I suggested to Marianne that we get there early, no later than eight for my eight-thirty meeting with Coach Landry.

The interview was to take place in Coach Landry's office, located on the eleventh floor of Expressway Towers. But as I walked into that empty elevator, Coach Landry stepped inside and joined me. During the brief time it took to go from the ground floor to the eleventh, I suffered a bad case of the jitters, and I engaged Coach Landry in idle chitchat.

BUT FOR A PAIR OF SOCKS

The interview lasted less than an hour. During that time I learned Coach Landry and I had something in common besides being Air Force veterans—we were both men of few words.

We discussed the position of equipment manager—how at that time it was a one-man operation, responsible for keeping the Cowboys' athletic equipment and uniforms neat and clean, refurbished, clearly marked, and ready for the team's use.

We discussed the equipment brands used by the Cowboys, and Coach Landry mentioned he was a former Army Air Corps pilot. During World War II, with the Eighth Air Force, Coach flew thirty missions over Germany in a B-17 bomber. He asked me about my work at the Air Force Academy, and I discussed

Head Coach Tom Landry

its extensive athletic program and my involvement working with cadets.

Toward the end of the interview he asked, "If one of my players comes up to you, Buck, and asks you, say, for a pair of socks, what would you do?"

The question seemed innocent, and I responded, "I would sure let the player have the socks, Coach." I remember thinking, "Is this some sort of trick question?"

In retrospect, Coach Landry's question was actually packed with a lot more meaning than it would have seemed. Over time as I got to know him, I learned he had a habit of stating or asking the obvious in simple terms. And he always expected a simple, direct answer.

"I don't want my players upset on the field because some guy won't give them what they need," he said. "I want my guys concentrating on what they're doing."

Given my military background, I couldn't imagine doing anything less.

I remember rendering the stock response, "If that's the important thing, Coach, then that's what we'll do. In college athletics you need to maintain control of your stock. I'm pretty sure it's the same in the NFL. Still, I would let the player have those socks."

After the interview Coach Landry's secretary, Marge Kelley, took me down the hall to meet Joe Bailey. Marge introduced us and left.

Mr. Bailey provided me with an overview of the job and the organization, and he suggested we tour the practice facility at Forest Lane.

The Forest Lane facility was modest with a small, nondescript Butler building and a single field. My resume reflected my experience caring for the 133 acres of athletic fields at the USAF Academy. During my interview with Coach Landry, I explained how I had supervised the maintenance of the playing fields for the cadets.

Mr. Bailey gave me a quick tour and asked me what my recommendations were for caring for the Cowboys' practice field. I told Mr. Bailey that to keep a grass field in good shape, it must be fertilized, aerated, and watered, with care to top-dress with sand.

I also recommended rotating team practices to prolong the life of the turf.

At Forest Lane I met Head Trainer Don Cochren. Don and I quickly became good friends, and we spent the next twenty-one years working together for the Dallas Cowboys.

After touring the practice facility, Joe drove me across town to Texas Stadium. Joe introduced me to the stadium operations manager, retired Air Force Lt. Colonel Jim Berling, and Jim provided me with a nickel tour of the facility.

During my career at the Dallas Cowboys, I saw Jim Berling each Sunday morning before every home game when he performed a systems check of the electricity, plumbing, and water. Jim retired in 1977.

Although I had viewed shots of the stadium on television, you really must stand in the middle of that sprawling playing surface, in the midst of nearly ninety-one thousand square feet of Tartan Turf, staring 208 feet overhead—at the open ceiling—to appreciate its grandeur.

Jim explained that groundbreaking for Texas Stadium had been in 1969, that the stadium comprised ten acres of prime Dallas real estate, and that the sprawling facility seated more than sixty-five thousand fans. I told Jim—and Joe—that I had seen enough; I was sold.

Joe took me back to the hotel where I changed back into my military uniform. He then took me back to his office with time remaining to catch my three o'clock flight from Love Field to Denver.

"We'll get back to you, Buck, after Coach Landry makes his decision. Just hang tight, and I'll be sure to keep you informed. Coach Landry has other interviews."

The part about "other interviews" made me a little nervous. I'd had a golden opportunity to meet with the principals, the movers and shakers with whom I hoped I would work, and I felt pretty good about my chances for the job of equipment manager.

Joe dropped me at the airport, and I boarded my flight bound for Colorado. After landing at Stapleton, I caught a shuttle from Denver to Colorado Springs.

When I got home, Jerry conducted a lengthy interrogation of the trip.

"How did the interview go?" she began.

"I really don't know, mom," I said. "The money's right, but the competition's got to be stiff." Little did I know at the time how tough the competition really was!

We had not planned on retiring from the Air Force until Julie had gotten out of her full-body brace. Julie had scoliosis, and the military doctors had agreed that it might be another two to three years before she could go it alone without the brace.

Mom and I were excited about the Cowboys job, yet apprehensive about leaving the security of military life. There was the unknown—would we like the NFL?

Three weeks later, on April 20, 1973, one of my NCO friends fielded a call for me in the academy gymnasium. He wrote down the phone number and hung up. When we spoke later that day, he was beaming. He handed me the slip of paper with the number transcribed on it and said, "I think you might want to call them ASAP, Sgt. Buchanan."

I raced to the nearest phone and placed the call.

Marge Kelley answered. "Just one moment, Sgt. Buchanan."

I heard Ms. Kelley whisper, "It's him."

Seconds later, Cowboys Head Coach Tom Landry was on the phone.

"Buck," Coach Landry said, "we've made our decision."

My heart was pounding in my chest. Not since my tour in Southeast Asia, or the birth of our two children, had I been so nervous.

"We'd like to have you come down and work for us," Coach Landry said.

I nearly dropped the phone.

"Yes, sir," I said.

Coach Landry paused, waiting for me to say something.

"Then you accept our offer?" he asked.

I heard a strange voice—not my own—respond in the affirmative.

"Yes, sir. I do. How soon do you need me there?"

I held my breath and waited for his long-distance reply.

"Right away," Coach Landry said.

"Yes, sir," I said. "I'll submit my retirement papers."

"You do that," Coach Landry said, "and keep us posted."

"Thank you, sir," I said, and we hung up.

I called Jerry and shared the news.

"I want to hear every word," she insisted.

That afternoon at work, I thought the day would never end.

That night mom and I discussed the ramifications of taking the job. Since the interview, Julie's spinal curvature had improved markedly, almost miraculously—from 33 to 12 degrees. More than anyone, Julie was anxious to shed her confinement, the brace she had worn twenty-three hours of every day for two years.

But processing my retirement papers could take eight weeks, and Coach Landry had said he wanted me there as soon as possible.

I submitted my request for retirement on April 25, 1973, and I had my retirement orders in hand on May 25. Jerry and I were stunned that the paperwork had gone through so quickly, and we both agreed someone up above had been looking out for us.

My last day of duty at the academy was the 29th of May, although my Air Force retirement would not be official until July 1. I declined a retirement parade, but my work group gave me a nice going-away party.

I was still uncertain about leaving the security of the military, and mom was even slightly more apprehensive. The kids felt about the same, apprehensive but excited.

In days the moving company had everything packed into its truck and our small caravan, the family Pontiac Catalina and Opel, were headed south to Dallas, Texas.

Marianne had found us a three-bedroom home in Lake Highlands, east of Dallas, and our modest rented house was waiting for us when we pulled into town the evening of May 31, 1973, awaiting the arrival of our worldly goods.

My first official day on the Cowboys' payroll was June 1, 1973. But before I ever received my military retirement papers, I had taken leave and squeezed in a trip in mid-May to reconnoiter the training facilities at Thousand Oaks, California, for the Cowboys.

While I was in California, Jerry packed her bags and got the kids ready to spend time with her family in Rockingham, North Carolina. As I was preparing for my first training camp, Julie, aged sixteen, and Bucky, aged twelve, and their mother left for North Carolina.

CIVILIAN LIFE

I was totally unaccustomed to the nuances of civilian life. Before leaving for Thousand Oaks, in all the confusion of unpacking, packing, and getting prepared for the new job with the Cowboys, I completely forgot to cut off service to our new home. Consumed by the changes in our lives, I never thought to stop the newspaper or the mail.

I'd been gone a few weeks, anxiously preparing for my rookie year and the Cowboys' first preseason opener August 3, 1973, against the Los Angeles Rams, when I received a long-distance telephone call from the Lake Highlands Police Department.

The detective I spoke with had called to inform me that our house had been broken into and extensively vandalized. The culprits stole Julie's ten-speed bicycle, and they lavishly painted our furniture with catsup, mayonnaise, and mustard, ransacked from the refrigerator. The house was a mess.

The burglars stole Jerry's jewelry, and they had even taken my Dad's prized gun collection—irreplaceable family heirlooms my father had carried during the commission of his duties as Texas Ranger and jailer in Ballinger, Texas.

I was tied up with the job, so I called Jerry in North Carolina and asked her to fly back to Texas. The Cowboys graciously offered their support, and with Joe Bailey and the team's help, Jerry salvaged what she could.

She had never been happy there to begin with. And after the break-in, Jerry wanted nothing more to do with that house. We ended up buying a new home in Plano, Texas, in September, and we've lived there for thirty-two glorious years. We spent just three months in the rented house my sister secured for us in Lake Highlands, and we've never been back.

LIFE AS A COWBOY

It was exciting and a little nerve-rattling going from the military and my job at the Air Force Academy to the NFL, working with the caliber of players/celebrities on the Cowboys' roster and coaching staff there in 1973. My first team meeting at Forest Lane in mid-June proved pivotal toward launching my career and cementing my position on the team.

The coaches were waiting when I entered the meeting room at Forest Lane. The veterans came in, and everyone who was anyone in the Cowboys organization was there. The experience was darned near overwhelming for this old country boy from west Texas.

Coach Landry announced the changes to the coaching and training staff. Then he introduced the only change in the equipment room.

"Our new equipment manager comes to us by way of the United States Air Force," Coach Landry said. "Let's welcome Buck Buchanan to the Cowboys."

The room broke out in applause.

Within that cramped space, no larger than twice the size of an average American living room, resided a wealth of athletic talent. There were fifty-five professional football players, eight coaches, and two trainers—and yours truly. There were celebrity sports figures crammed into that room most fans only read about in the paper, or see on TV.

Truly, I was surrounded by legend, an arm's length from such noted athletes as linebacker Lee Roy Jordan; tight end Billy Truax, defensive backs Charlie Waters and Mel Renfro, tackle Ralph Neely, guard Blaine Nye, running backs Walt Garrison and Calvin Hill, and the Cowboys' great starting quarterback Roger Staubach.

The coaching talent was equally distinguished and included Head Coach Tom Landry, Special Assistant Ermal Allen, Defensive Back Coach Gene Stallings, Offensive Line Coach Jim Myers, Defensive Coordinator Ernie Stautner, Linebacker Coach Jerry Tubbs, Running Back Coach Ed Hughes, and rookie Tight End Coach Mike Ditka.

Coach Ditka had played for the Cowboys the year before. Coincidentally, that year "Iron Mike" was in the same boat I was in. Ditka was a rookie. When Coach Landry introduced Buck Buchanan, and that room broke out in applause, it was surreal.

I was in awe.

Then the reality of it all began to sink in.

The experience was humbling, intimidating.

But, as it turned out in the months to come, every one of those guys proved to be genuinely nice, and they could not have made me feel more welcomed.

I didn't panic. But after the meeting, when I was able to check out what we had in the way of inventory and the time frame I had to get everything itemized, packed, and shipped to training camp in California, just three weeks later, I got really nervous.

I prayed that I would have everything I needed—that the team needed—for training camp in southern California, that I would be able to get it all loaded on the trucks and delivered on schedule to our training camp at California Lutheran College.

I had no idea what the state of the equipment was like at the Cowboys, what we had and what we lacked. I worked seven days a week, often more than twelve hours per day, whatever it took to get ready. And that schedule remained the same for the next twenty-one years.

Essentially, I was thrown into the job without any supervision or direction. But there was an individual who helped me immensely in the early days, uniform representative Jack Davis from Terrell, Texas.

From 1960 to 1980 Southland Athletic Company made the Cowboys' uniforms and practice pants, and Jack wrote the orders and supplied the uniforms. But he did a lot more than his job at Southland required.

Before my first day at work, Jack had inventoried every Cowboys locker and developed a comprehensive list of equipment and uniform requirements. When I arrived, Jack presented me with that list and a Southland uniform order form.

Jack had been with the Cowboys since the beginning. He knew the ropes, and he helped me every step of the way. Ultimately, Jack worked beside me at every home game until I retired in 1994. His help and his friendship those twenty-one years are deeply appreciated.

THE PRINCIPALS

During my career at the Cowboys, I was fortunate to have known and worked with a cadre of extraordinary personalities. I had the great fortune to meet media announcers, team owners, celebrated athletes, the crème de la crème of the coaching world, talented trainers, extraordinary medical personnel, movie stars, and a whole cast of common folks—like me—who just happened to be caught up in the moment.

The three Dallas icons who follow—Tex Schramm, Gil Brandt, and Tom Landry—may have had the greatest impact on my 1970s world. With a certainty, the trio's influence on the National Football League, the Dallas Cowboys, and the state of Texas is the stuff legends are made of. I am proud to have known and served with such great men.

Tex Schramm

A lot has been said of Tex Schramm, president and general manager for the Dallas Cowboys from 1960 to 1989. In my estimation, there are few individuals who have had such a profound and long-lasting effect on the league and the Cowboy franchise.

For his many accomplishments, Tex was inducted into the Pro Football Hall of Fame in Canton, Ohio, in 1991. Schramm joins six Dallas teammates who were similarly selected based on their accomplishments with the Cowboys—Bob Lilly (1980), Roger Staubach (1985), Tom Landry (1990), Tony Dorsett and Randy White (1994), and Mel Renfro (1996).

Schramm was selected to the Cowboys' Ring of Honor in 2003, joining Cowboy greats Tony Dorsett, Cliff Harris, Bob Hayes, Chuck Howley, Lee Roy Jordan, Tom Landry, Bob Lilly, Don Meredith, Don Perkins, Mel Renfro, Roger Staubach, Randy White, and Rayfield Wright. (Before *Glory Days* went to press, Dallas greats Emmitt Smith, Troy Aikman, and Michael Irvin were selected for the Ring of Honor.)

I reported for duty with the Cowboys the 1st of June 1973.

Those early days were the most exhilarating and toughest of my long and far-ranging athletic career. I worked my tail off. We all did. It was expected.

Two or three days after reporting, I was at Expressway Towers, when Mr. Schramm stopped me in the hall and asked me to step into his office.

Schramm (far left) with Bum Phillips and Gil Brandt

He pointed to a chair, "Sit down. I have a few things I'd like to cover with you."

During that first meeting, we discussed everything Coach Landry and I had spoken about during my job interview—and more—how I would manage the equipment room, maintain the equipment, the costs involved, and what I would do and how I should respond when players needed help.

Then we got into his favorite subject: *uniforms*.

Tex Schramm was a visual kind of guy. He chose the color for the Cowboys' game pants after seeing the metallic, bluish-green paint job on an early '60s Pontiac in Dallas. Tex was *really* impressed with that color, and he insisted the team's game pants match that automobile's paint job.

I still think those pants looked better on TV than in person. I remember thinking, "That's the ugliest pair of pants I've seen."

Tex liked them, and they *were* prettier on TV.

That's how the man's mind worked.

We discussed socks and how they complemented, or failed to complement, the uniform. Tex was emphatic that socks be worn with the two stripes showing. This, he explained, was to make them more distinctive for television. Tex Schramm's overriding concern was with the Cowboys' uniform and that it show up well on TV.

The sock issue began with receiver Bob Hayes. Bob and several Cowboys players liked to pull their white athletic socks over the blue game socks, believing that made their legs look larger. Hayes and the others put their game socks on, much like a baseball sock with a stirrup, with white socks on top.

Tex told me that he didn't like it, and he wanted it fixed. I told him I'd see what I could do. "Buck," Tex said, "I know some of the players are set in their ways, but there's a company I've heard about that makes a one-piece game sock that goes all the way up to the player's knee with the two white stripes woven in."

I assured Tex that I'd look into it and left his office.

Like the rest of the league, the Cowboys had players with size 8½ and 9 shoes and offensive and defensive linemen with gargantuan size 14s—and every size in between.

I knew the sock issue was going to be a problem. And it was. At any rate, I called a man I knew and ordered new socks and had them delivered by the end of training camp. We planned to wear those socks the first game of the season against the Chicago Bears.

As it turned out, the socks looked really bad. Given the customary heavy tape jobs many of the players preferred from the trainers, the stripes were displayed way down around the guys' ankles. We ended up scrubbing the new sock idea that year and going back to the blue baseball stirrups with the white athletic socks—what most players wanted to begin with.

In 1974, we tried solid blue stirrup socks beneath the white athletic socks.

That first preseason game, after warm-up, Tex came into the locker room, beaming. "I sure do like those socks, Buck. They look great." By the end of the game, after several guys had been tackled, the white socks had been pulled down, and there were no stripes showing.

So, it was back to the drawing board.

I contacted Russell National, the company that made the one-piece sock, and their sales rep told me they had solved our problem. According to the rep, Russell made socks for receivers, running backs, linebackers, and offensive and defensive linemen. They simply put a different-colored thread on the toe of each sock to identify its size.

We started using the new socks, but it took some time for the players to get used to them. The socks were extremely thick and bulky. Still, some of the players insisted that they wear athletic socks over the new socks to make their calves appear larger. And each game, as was his custom, Tex appeared on the field to inspect the players' uniforms.

During that preseason warm-up, Tex sidled up to me.

"Buck," he said, "That player doesn't have his stripes showing." And then he said, pointing, "That player's jersey isn't tucked in. Take care of it."

If Tex Schramm was big on uniforms, he was even bigger on neatness. Before a NFL dress code was ever established, Tex had one drawn up for the Dallas Cowboys.

He insisted on jerseys being tucked in. Tex wanted the players' socks the way *he* wanted them to look, with the stripes showing. And he wanted every helmet strapped down. In retrospect, everything Tex Schramm liked eventually became NFL code.

After my second year, Tex wanted to change jerseys once more. He wanted the player's number back where it had been before, on each shoulder where it would show up better on TV.

Everything Tex thought of, and every uniform adaptation he came up with, was for the media's sake. Tex was insistent that the player's identity be clearly visible in the photographs whether the player was running, being tackled or flat on the ground.

At the end of the 1979 season, Tex summoned me to his office.

"I don't like the blue jerseys. I want a different color. Call your jersey people, and see if they can send us more swatches of blue material so I can decide which one I like."

I called our jersey supplier and told them what Mr. Schramm wanted. I learned early in my career that name-dropping paid off. Tex always got exceptional service from our vendors, and the mere mention of his name accelerated the process.

After my call the supplier sent several dozen swatches of blue material, which I promptly delivered to Mr. Schramm's office. Tex carefully laid out the pieces of material on his couch and studied each one.

He continued to study that material until I called him back several weeks later.

"Mr. Schramm," I said, "we really ought to make a decision so the vendor can get started. We're leaving for training camp in another month."

"Okay, Buck," he said, "I'm just about there."

At the time, Tex was driving a Buick Riviera with a blue interior. He later chose the blue swatch that most closely matched that car's upholstery. I sent the chosen swatch to the vendor and told them to get started on the jerseys. We also had them change out the numbers in gray, with a white, feathered edge to show up better on camera.

We got two sets of the jerseys while we were in training camp. I had our laundry guy pick them up, and they were ready for our opening game in DC with the Redskins.

I thought they looked great. After the game, Tex called, "We're going to have to do something with those numbers, Buck."

"What's the problem, Mr. Schramm?"

"In the press box and on the film, with that white feathered edge touching the gray number, when you're up high, you have a hard time distinguishing the numerals."

Every year teams shot game film and exchanged it with the other NFL teams for review. In the film, it was difficult to identify the players who were involved in the action. Their numbers didn't show up clearly.

"We're going to have to change those, Buck," Tex said.

"Yes, sir, Mr. Schramm," I said, "I'll get right on it."

And it was back to the drawing board.

As luck would have it, we didn't use the blue jerseys for several weeks. I called the vendor and they were shocked. "We've never had that problem before," they insisted.

Weeks later, during a Chargers Monday Night Football game, Tex called.

"Buck," he said, "are you watching the Chargers game?"

"Yes, sir," I replied.

"That's the kind of numbers I want," he said.

"Yes, sir."

I called my buddy Sid Brooks, the Chargers' equipment manager, and got his specs for the numbers and called the vendor with the correction. They cut all new patterns, and they did a great job on the jerseys. We got them back two weeks before our next game, and Tex could not have been happier.

Tex was the chairman of the NFL Competition Committee for twenty-three years. In that capacity, he was instrumental in many of the leagues' rule changes.

In 1973, we played the Minnesota Vikings in the NFC Championship Game in Dallas, the winner destined to go to the Super Bowl. Minnesota won that contest 27–10. The outcome of the game was never really in question, but there was a field goal that was.

#73 Ralph Neely on the Cowboys' sideline

Because of that questionable call, Tex instigated a rule that extended the goalpost uprights an extra ten feet—that way, the officials were sure to get it right.

Whenever possible, it was Tex Schramm's purpose in life to improve the game of football, and without hesitation he'd jump on it. I was usually the purveyor of his whims.

During our 1976 Bicentennial, he changed one of the blue stripes on our helmets to red, rendering the Cowboys' headgear a patriotic red, white, and blue.

During a preseason game with the Pittsburgh Steelers, Cowboy tackle Ralph Neely was asked by the opposing Pittsburgh lineman, "How long have you been wearing that red stripe on your helmets?"

The ball was snapped, and Ralph knocked his man on his butt.

Ralph turned to walk back to the huddle and fired over his shoulder, "First year, but we may keep wearing 'em."

Tex was instrumental in getting the instant replay instituted in the NFL.

He was on the rules committee with Miami Dolphins Head Coach Don Shula, with whom Tex was close friends. The pair effected significant rules changes to the NFL.

In the old days, we only had first down chains on one side of the field. Tex believed a running back had to know the precise location of the first down marker, especially if he happened to be on the opposite side of the field. In part because of Mr. Schramm's insistence, the NFL pushed for the orange arrow marker indicating first down location on the side of the field absent the chains.

When the Cowboys played in cold weather, our sideline jackets had no numerals showing. Tex insisted on having the players' numbers discernible for media and fan identification, so we ordered numbered sideline jackets for the receivers, running backs, and quarterbacks. The rationale—linemen were never recognized unless they got a penalty. The plan was a bucket of worms.

When the players came off the field, they grabbed the first jacket available, and we didn't have the staff to ensure that the correct jacket went to the right player.

Before Super Bowl X, the league issued written instructions dictating where to sew the Bicentennial Patch on our jerseys.

"What do you think, Buck?" Mr. Schramm asked.

"Could be distracting to the quarterback," I replied.

"Damned right," he said. "Put the patch on the jersey sleeve."

"The NFL letter says to put the patch on the upper left breast," I said.

"No, sir," he said. "Put it on the sleeve."

"But the letter was signed by Pete Rozelle," I insisted.

"Buck, listen to me," Tex insisted, "put the patch where I told you to put it."

Roger Staubach hands the ball to Duane Thomas

Unlike our opponents, the Pittsburgh Steelers, the Dallas Cowboys wore their Bicentennial Patch during Super Bowl X precisely where Tex had insisted, on the jersey's left sleeve. And we didn't catch any flack from the league.

Tex and NFL Commissioner Pete Rozelle were friends.

Tex Schramm got along well with most Cowboy players. He did not get along with No. 33, running back Duane Thomas

(1970–1971) from West Texas State. After his first year with the Cowboys, Duane reportedly became difficult to get along with.

You could call guys like Duane high-maintenance players.

Duane and Tex weren't getting along, and the press was quick to catch on. A local newspaper reporter queried Duane about the tiff, and Duane responded candidly, saying in effect that Tex Schramm was sick, demented, and dishonest. When that article hit the newsstands, its content quickly made its way back to Mr. Schramm.

"That's not bad," he said, "at least Duane got two out of three correct."

Tex Schramm was a special person to work for, and he took great care of his employees. He loved the people who worked for him, and he hated firing anyone.

Was he outspoken? Sure. Like most powerful men, Tex Schramm wanted things done his way. But at the end of the day, at the end of the season, when those checks were in the mail, we were more than adequately compensated.

During the 1986 season, Tex got this notion that he wanted a complete, one-piece uniform that stretched the length of the athlete's frame, from his feet to his shoulders—a bodysuit. The lady at Russell Athletics freaked when I conveyed his intent to her.

"Meaning you want this next week, or the week after?" she sarcastically replied.

Later, the San Diego Chargers tried the bodysuit concept on a receiver who agreed to test it. He wore it one game.

The bodysuit never worked, but Tex tried.

He gave everything a shot until it was proven that it wouldn't work.

Tex Schramm was a gentleman, and I'm proud to say, a good friend.

I could not have worked for a better man.

Gil Brandt

Gil Brandt

Without a doubt, Vice President and Director of Player Personnel Gil Brandt (1960–1989) wrote the book on schmoozing and college recruiting. Mr. Brandt was a terrific organizer, and he was great with those he wanted to be great with.

He worked harder at developing relationships with college coaches, trainers, and equipment managers than anyone I have ever known. And he thought, I believe correctly so, there was more player data to be gleaned from college trainers, in particular, than anyone else in college athletics.

Brandt was one of the premier directors of player personnel—and it definitely showed in the Cowboys draft selections made throughout his career at Dallas. He was one of the pioneers in computer draft data compilation, and his database paid off handsomely for the team.

Each draft, Brandt sent as many as twenty Cowboys reps out to scour the countryside. And when a player wound up not being drafted, one of us was there to sign him. As a result of Brandt's efforts during the 1970s, the Cowboys made many lucrative draft deals.

Brandt developed relationships with all the right college coaches, and he often did so by extending favors. He sponsored golf tournaments in Dallas, and he had coaches flown in from all over the country. The coaches were shuttled to and from the airport, and they were wined and dined like royalty.

During playoffs and bowl games, Brandt set up hospitality suites and invited his favorite coaches. He was a personal friend of Coach Bobby Knight of Indiana, and he came to know and be known by virtually every sports personality in athletics. And as a result of his extensive network, Brandt worked the NFL draft like a true master.

He maintained a close working relationship with track, basketball, and baseball coaches, believing it was possible to convert their athletes into football stars.

And Brandt's efforts were, more often than not, successful.

Brandt may not have been the most popular guy in the Cowboys organization, but in many ways he was light years ahead of his time as director of player personnel.

In my capacity as Cowboys equipment manager, I knew firsthand of Brandt's horse-trading activities. Cowboys jerseys, tee shirts, and baseball caps were prized gifts coveted by college coaches, and their friends and families. And Brandt spent considerable time in my office, shopping for gratuitous uniforms for his horse-trading schemes.

I made the mistake of mentioning the outflow of stock to Tex Schramm.

"If it helps him gather player information, or helps us with the draft," Tex said, "then it's damn worth the expense to the club. Don't worry about it." Tex winked, "So in the future, Mr. Buck, if Mr. Brandt needs *anything* you have in stock, see to it he gets it."

Brandt's efforts proved to be a tremendous advantage for the Cowboys vis-à-vis the draft. We weren't constrained by today's rules. If the club wanted to pay for the extra players in training camp, and foot the bill to ferry them to and from their homes, so be it.

Today, it's altogether different, with NFL teams cut back to a maximum of eighty players. Then, however, it was not unusual to field one hundred rookies and fifty to fifty-five veterans.

Brandt was as successful in securing players from the big schools as he was from the smaller ones. Undrafted college players weren't considered draft choices, rather free agents. We secured a number of really good players via the free agency route.

Jethro Pugh was drafted from Elizabeth City, a small college. Cliff Harris, one of the best players I've had the good fortune to work with, came from a small school, Ouachita. Brandt picked up world-class sprinter Bob Hayes from Florida A&M and basketball great Cornell Green from Utah State. In college, Cornell was strictly a basketball player, but he went on to become an outstanding cornerback.

At the end of his reign, when Jerry Jones bought the team in 1989, a number of Cowboys assistant coaches were released, their posts going to men Jones and Coach Jimmy Johnson brought with them. But Brandt remained a short time while Jerry Jones developed his NFL sea legs. When he did leave the Cowboys later in 1989, that milestone marked the end of an era.

Coach Tom Landry

Head Coach Tom Landry served with the Cowboys from 1960 to 1989. The first head coach of the Cowboys, Coach led Dallas to two Super Bowl wins and five NFC titles in his twenty-nine-year career. He compiled a career record of 270–178–6, the third most wins in NFL history, and was elected to the Pro Football Hall of Fame in 1990. Coach was inducted into the Ring of Honor in 1993.

Coach Landry

Other than the job interview in March of 1973, when I rode up in the elevator with him, I saw Coach Landry only once more before leaving for my first training camp.

Coach Landry walked off the practice field, strode directly to the equipment room, and asked, "Is everything going okay, Buck?" I learned that unless he said something, or worse yet, gave me the old squint-eye glare, all was well between Coach Landry and me.

Schedules were everything to him. And *his* schedule was the only one that mattered. Other than having such short notice to get prepared—just three weeks from the time I accepted the job, to the time we left for training camp—everything was going well.

"Yes, sir, coach," I said. "Couldn't be better."

Coach Landry was calm and regimented. He always had his training camp schedules completed for each and every day before we left Dallas—and he never varied that schedule, no matter what. The Cowboys had two-a-day practice, six days a week with one on Sunday and *everything* was scripted beforehand. We followed that script religiously.

Coach was always punctual for meetings, and he expected everyone else to be. He held an after-breakfast staff meeting during training camp and a players' meeting after lunch. At the appointed time, he closed the doors to the meeting room, and if anyone was a minute late, he was fined fifty to three hundred dollars. At the end of each season, we spent the money generated from Coach Landry's fines for a team party.

My rookie season I ordered a dozen whistles for the coaching staff. I had not seen any worn about the necks of the assistant coaches, and it seemed the heads-up thing to do. After all, I was always looking for ways to improve the "system" and help the team.

Puzzled by the lack of enthusiasm for the whistles, I asked Assistant Head Coach Jim Myers (1962–1986), a long-time offensive line coach from UCLA, and former head coach for Texas A&M, why the assistant coaches didn't sport whistles about their necks.

"Buck," Coach Myers said, in his typical stern fashion, "we only need one whistle on the Cowboys' practice field, and that whistle will be around Coach Landry's neck."

Coach Landry controlled every practice. He controlled everyone and everything on the field. And he controlled everything within his organization. But he did so with respect and discipline—never out of fear or intimidation.

We had one regular football field at training camp, and it remained that way my first three years with the team. The Cowboys used Cal Lutheran's baseball outfield in the morning and the full-sized field each afternoon for practice. Some years later, the college built a second regulation football field for our use and theirs.

Our film crew used a thirty-foot, three-tiered tower to film practices. Coach Landry stood, megaphone in hand, directing the action from the tower's second tier. He knew every detail of every practice, and he controlled the action, concurrently directing offensive and defensive plays, with the skill and finesse of a symphony conductor.

Coach Landry worked his players hard. But occasionally, when they were worn out, he let them work out on the game field nearest the dressing room.

Every practice excluding Sunday's was in full gear. His rationale was simple: If players practiced in full gear, they would be accustomed to the added weight come Game Day. Consequently, there would be fewer injuries. He had another standing rule relating to the prevention of injuries: Whenever possible, never practice on a wet surface.

I never heard a harsh word directed at Coach Landry by any Cowboy player. The man was tough. He insisted on having things done his way, but I can't recall anyone complaining about him. The Cowboys loved and respected him. Coach Landry respected his players, and in turn, they did whatever he asked, without fail.

In 1996, I attended a team reunion. I was retired then, employed part-time, helping my successor, Mike McCord, and my son, Bucky Buchanan, assistant equipment manager. The get-together was at a Country-Western joint downtown and many of the veterans and coaches were there. We had eaten and linebacker/emcee Lee Roy Jordan attempted to quiet the crowd.

Lee Roy was the inspirational leader of the Cowboys' first championship teams. He was the first-round draft choice in 1963 following an All-American career at Alabama. Lee Roy anchored the "Doomsday Defense" from his middle linebacker position for fourteen years, and he was named to the Pro Bowl five times and All-Pro twice. He was inducted into the Ring of Honor in 1989.

"Okay, guys," Lee Roy said, "Let's hold it down. We have business to discuss."

The roar continued unabated.

Lee Roy repeated his request, "Hey, guys. I said, hold it down."

Nothing changed.

Lee Roy got irritated. "Coach Landry says to be quiet!" The room became still.

Lee Roy Jordan attributed much of his success to defensive tackle Larry Cole (1968–1980) from the University of Hawaii. Cole was a big, lumbering guy who didn't go forward that much, but he didn't take many steps back, either, which allowed Jordan to read the play and make the tackle.

In 1980, in a game played in San Francisco against the 49ers, we weren't having a good game, and we ended up losing. I was in the equipment room preparing for our return trip home, when three plainclothes San Francisco police officers strode in and flashed their shields. They insisted on inspecting everything—each bag, trunk, locker, and hamper. Everything was packed, locked up, and ready to be taken to the airport.

"You've got to be kidding," I moaned.

"No, sir. We've had a bomb threat."

I couldn't believe it. We had a flight to catch, and there would be heck to pay if the chartered jet was delayed. Coach Landry hated to get home late, especially after a losing effort. I complied with the authorities and everything was searched. They found nothing, but the search set me back forty-five minutes.

In the mid-1980s, against the Los Angeles Rams, it was our first playoff game and we weren't doing well against the Rams' talented Eric Dickerson. Early in the third quarter, two suits approached Coach Landry on the sideline and consulted with him in hushed voices.

Expressionless, Coach Landry pirouetted and walked off the field with a Los Angeles Police Detective at either elbow. Coach was gone about thirty minutes, during which time Coach Myers took over head coaching responsibilities for the Cowboys.

When Coach Landry returned, word spread quickly that there had been a threat made on his life. The police had taken him into the locker room and provided him with a bulletproof vest that they insisted he wear. They also suggested he remain inside. Coach Landry insisted on returning to the game, and the officers escorted him to the sideline.

Dickerson had a record-setting 200-yard day and we lost that game.

That incident had an ironic and humorous twist. My assistant, Jerry Fowler (1979–1992), was accustomed to the limelight, preferring to stick close to Coach Landry's side when the cameras were rolling.

When the police put Coach Landry in a vest and returned him to the sideline, Jerry was nowhere to be seen. After some searching, I finally located Jerry at the far end of the bench—far from his usual proximity to Coach Landry and the bright lights.

Training camp was open to spectators. At Thousand Oaks, Coach Landry was in his elevated perch, megaphone in hand, directing the action when he spotted a ten-year-old culprit making off with a football. The boy was seated on his bicycle holding the pigskin ready to flee the scene when Coach raised that megaphone. Squinting, he hollered at the kid, "Young man, you don't need that football. Bring it back."

The kid dutifully got off his bike, ran back, and tossed that ball to a player.

Like a battlefield general, Coach Landry was able to focus on everything, on and off the field, both in games and during practice—despite bomb and death threats.

In a game with the Pittsburgh Steelers, Coach Ditka said something unflattering to an official, resulting in a 15-yard

Jerry Fowler using the kick-off gun

penalty, putting the Steelers in position to boot a 15-yard field goal. Those three points cost Dallas the game.

The following Monday during postgame review, mention of the sideline infraction came up, and squinting, Coach Landry vowed, "That 15-yard penalty won't happen again."

And it never did.

Coach Landry never hollered. He never screamed or got upset, he squinted, and without looking directly at you, he would narrow those eyelids and speak slowly and deliberately. And there was never any doubt as to his intent. In that sense and many others, Coach Landry reminded me a lot of my father—Andrew T. Buchanan.

Cliff Harris shared a story with me during the compilation of this book. During a team meeting, Coach Landry was going over defensive coverage for an upcoming game.

"Cliff," he said, "I want you to line up on the left side. They're going to line up two receivers on your side. Like they have in the past, they're probably going to come down ten to twelve yards.

Cliff Harris tackles O. J. Simpson as Charlie Waters closes in

One is going to run a post, and the other should run a flag pattern. You have to be ready to handle that receiver."

Cliff raised his hand. "Which one do you want me to cover, Coach?"

Coach Landry replied, "The one he throws the ball to!"

Coach was emphatic about punctuality. He was usually early to meetings, allowing himself ample time to change out of his suit and tie and into his blue shorts and Cowboys T-shirt.

One morning he came running into my office minutes before the meeting, still wearing his suit and tie. "Buck," he said, "I locked my keys in the car. While I'm in the meeting, call a locksmith and have him drop by."

I said, "Sure thing, Coach."

"Do it quick," Coach Landry said, "my keys are in it, and it's running."

I ate breakfast in the cafeteria every morning at half-past five. I generally shared a table with Coach Landry and Dallas defensive back coach Gene Stallings (1972–1985).

Coach Stallings had been the head coach at Texas A&M, and he is a native son of Paris, Texas. As a Cowboys coach, he was known for his ability to take free agents and low-round draft choices and develop them into top-notch defensive backfield players.

Coach Stallings was head coach for his alma mater, Texas A&M, from 1965 to 1972, and he was instrumental in developing four Cowboys All-Pro players: Cliff Harris, Charlie Waters, Everson Walls, and Michael Downs.

He was an All-Southwest Conference receiver at A&M under Coach Paul "Bear" Bryant and a tri-captain on Bryant's undefeated 1956 team—the famous "Junction Boys."

When Stallings' A&M team defeated Bear Bryant's Alabama squad in the Cotton Bowl in 1968, Bryant walked across the field, picked up Stallings, and carried him off the field.

Stallings was a successful college recruiter and is an outstanding family man.

Those early-morning breakfasts were relaxed, and they provided me great insight into both men's character. And it didn't hurt to learn the latest scuttlebutt from the top.

Coach Landry was predictable—he never drank coffee or soft drinks. He drank water, iced tea, or hot tea. At breakfast he ate one egg, fried medium, with two pieces of bacon and a slice of toast.

He kept in great shape. Most of the Cowboys coaches did. And especially in my early days at Dallas, I would have wagered that Coach Landry could still don the pads and play football with the best of them.

Everything good that has been said about Coach Landry is no doubt true. I worked with him sixteen years, and I never once saw him upset, and I never heard him utter anything derogatory about anyone. And I never heard him curse or use bad language.

If I had a question, he would stop and listen. And Coach Landry was honest, as honest as any man I've known—including my Dad. For years, I have said: "If Coach Landry or my Dad were

Adjusting Charlie Waters' shoulder pad straps

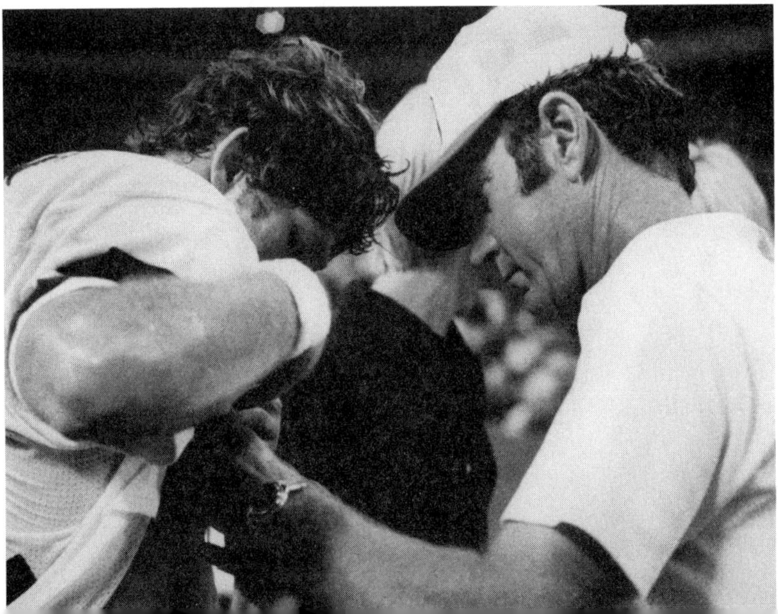

elected president of these United States, the day they left office, they would both be as honest and trustworthy as the day they entered the office."

Such character traits made Coach Landry a pleasure to work for. If I ever forgot something, I knew he would not explode at me and come unglued. Casually and deliberately, he would correct me and let me know what he expected—in a civil manner.

Cowboy linebacker Jeff Rohrer (1982–1987) from Yale used a special inflatable belt for back support. Jeff cut his jersey short, a Coach Landry and an NFL infraction, to let air in and out of that bladder. Toward the end of the first quarter, I saw the official's ribbon fly onto the field, and I thought, "Oh, no. Jeff's in trouble, now."

Squinting, Coach Landry asked, "Buck, did you know Jeff cut his jersey?"

"No, sir," I replied. "You know, he has to get another jersey," Coach said.

"Jeff's got a bad back," I stuttered.

"Get him another jersey, Buck."

Jerry and I with former "Junction Boys" Coach Gene Stallings

Jeff Rohrer in action

Fortunately, I had already sent Bucky to the equipment room to get one.

Coach Landry utilized a successful conditioning regimen for his players. After morning practice he would have all the defensive players line up across the field and one of the coaches simulated the snap motion, trying to draw a player offside.

If a guy jumped, Coach had them repeat the drill five times. If another man jumped, they would repeat the process until they got it right. Coach conducted the same drill with the offense, and if there were any illegal procedures, or someone jumped offside, they'd run it again and again until they had five consecutive infraction-free plays.

After the afternoon practice, when the team was tired, Coach Landry had grass drills. He'd get on the second rung of the training tower, and with his megaphone blaring, he lined everyone up facing him.

From that position, he made the team run in place before yelling, "Front!"

The guys fell on their chests.

Coach yelled, "Back!" and the guys flopped over on their backs.

Coach yelled, "Up!" and they ran in place.

Coach ran the team for several more minutes.

He hollered, "Left," and the players fell on their left sides.

When he yelled, "Up!" the process began anew.

Coach Landry's workouts were so grueling they even elicited dissent from the most experienced, battle-hardened veteran—Mr. Cowboy, Bob Lilly—according to offensive lineman Ralph Neely.

"Bob tended to be a habitual complainer," Ralph recalled. "During Coach Landry's grass drills, he continually yelled, for all to hear, 'You're killing us, coach!'

"The next morning," Ralph continued, "At the team meeting, Coach Landry said, 'I know Lilly complains a lot, but when you play as good as he does, that's okay by me.' "

In late October of 1973, Coach Landry had team practice in Dallas before our November 11, 1973, game against the New York Giants. The Giants' Meadowlands Stadium was under construction, so the game was played at Yale University's stadium.

The Wednesday before Game Day, during an offensive practice, Roger Staubach was working a pass play with the offense. Dallas running back/wide receiver Mike Montgomery (1972–1973) caught the ball, and Cliff Harris attempted to hit his man full force. The goalposts were not on the end line, but were set back in the end zone. The post had a yoke on it, but it had been wrapped with a cheap pad.

When Roger ran the play, pursuing his man, "Crash" Harris ran into the goalpost and knocked himself out. Cliff had his helmet on, but it still rang his bell. The force of the impact had the coaching staff worried Cliff might not play on Sunday. But he did.

A couple of the guys helped Cliff off the field to have him checked out by the team doctors. When he returned, Cliff said, "Buck, Roger called that play just to run me into that goalpost."

I ordered new goalpost covers and we had them up by Friday.

MY PREDECESSOR

It would have been nice had the former equipment manager been there to pass the baton to the new guy, to show me the ropes. But unlike the military, civilian life isn't always so accommodating.

I didn't meet my predecessor, the former Cowboys' equipment manager, for another five years. Jack Eskridge served in that capacity from 1960 to 1973. Jack sealed his fate and opened the door to my NFL career the year the team won Super Bowl VI.

At that time, by league mandate, coaches were guaranteed a share of the team's playoff revenues. Divisional playoffs, championship games, and Super Bowl contests translated into sizeable paydays. Trainers and equipment managers were not guaranteed any portion of the team's revenues, however. Players voted each season for the trainers and equipment managers they deemed worthy of receiving a share of the playoff money.

I was told there was conflict between Jack and the Cowboys players. Apparently, team captains Roger Staubach, quarterback and offensive captain; Lee Roy Jordan, linebacker and defensive captain; and Mel Renfro, defensive back and special teams captain, had complained about Mr. Eskridge well before he was terminated early in 1973.

Enter west Texas son Buck Buchanan, new Cowboys' equipment manager.

Unlike the military there was no instruction manual that came with the job, no job description or manual titled "*Equipment Manager, Standard Operating Procedures.*"

I relied on my eight years' experience at the Air Force Academy, my lifelong knowledge of athletics, and the inside help of several seasoned veterans—fellow employees Otis Jackson and Don Cochren, and uniform representative Jack Davis.

New to the NFL, I winged it my rookie season.

And, oh what a year that was!

THOUSAND OAKS, CALIFORNIA

Before my Air Force retirement was a done deal, the Cowboys sent me to Thousand Oaks to reconnoiter the West Coast facilities and ensure that everything was up and running for training camp. Don Cochren flew out with me.

Most NFL trainers are too busy taping players and tending to their myriad of team duties to care, much less pay attention to, what goes on in the equipment cage next door. Not so Don. Busy as he was, Don always found time to take this fledgling rookie equipment manager under his wing and show him the ropes.

I worked every day, from my first day onboard to the time we went to training camp and beyond, from o'dark thirty to late at night. As far as the equipment area was concerned, I was the only help the Cowboys had.

Otis Jackson helped me with field maintenance, and I couldn't have done it without his help. A carpenter by trade, Otis pitched in and helped me fold and put away tons of laundry, every item of clothing worn by the coaches and players. And from the beginning, when the team was at home, I relied on my young son, Bucky, to help out.

Otherwise, the equipment side of the operation was my baby.

On my first trip to Thousand Oaks, I met Mr. Fred Ford, a retired seamster. Mr. Ford and his lovely wife laundered and repaired the Cowboys' uniforms. He picked up our dirty laundry after the morning practice, about 1:00 p.m., and he was back at seven that night for our afternoon laundry.

Ken Locker and Don Cochren talk shop

Otis Jackson

The following morning at five, Mr. Ford was there to deliver the team's clean uniforms for the morning practice. The Fords were a real godsend.

Rookies reported to training camp between June 26 and June 29.

Coach Landry had ten days, twenty practice sessions, to fully evaluate rookies and, if necessary, weed them out before the veterans arrived.

Three weeks into training camp, I had as many as 110 players—rookies and veterans—to suit up. And that many players required a whole lot of socks and jocks.

I was responsible for the uniform and equipment needs of more than one hundred Dallas Cowboys—players, coaches, and trainers. With two-a-day workouts, I was up and at 'em by five every morning, and I was at it hard, long after every team member had retired to his dorm room late at night.

THAT OLD LEATHER BELT

My military background shaped me into a disciplined individual. Certainly, my childhood in Ballinger at my father's side had much to do with my regimentation.

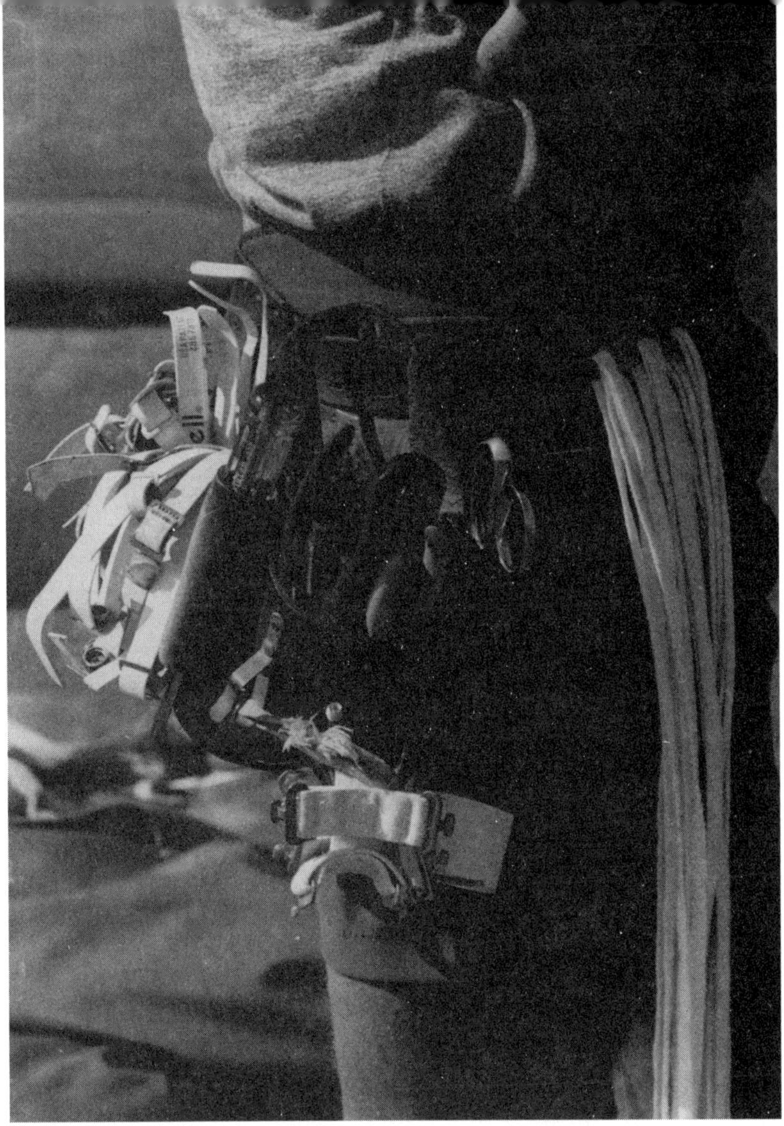

That Old Leather Belt

Everything had a place and there was a place for everything within my purview. Because of that discipline, I started a tradition in Dallas that has endured to this day.

There was never enough room in my pockets to accommodate all the tools and accessories I needed to keep the team running. As a result I fashioned a leather pouch that was attached to a leather belt to tote the tools and extra items I needed to perform my sideline duties—the screwdrivers, pliers, and wrenches to work on the team's equipment.

The belt had holes all the way around, and extra shoelaces dangled from each hole. And my pants pockets were always filled with more stuff. I was a walking hardware store.

To my knowledge, I am the only equipment manager in the NFL to have used such a system. After retirement I passed the belt to my successor, Mike McCord (1989–2005), whom I had the pleasure of training. Mike still wears that old leather pouch and belt proudly on game day.

EQUIPMENT UPKEEP

Several tons of equipment—from the shoes, *software* (shorts, jocks, socks, and uniforms), footballs, and helmets—to the sleds, the team's conditioning equipment, and weights, had to precede the Cowboys to their training camp in the desert region of Thousand Oaks, California.

Getting it all cleaned, repaired, sorted, inventoried, and shipped was my primary responsibility. That included liaising with vendors, the trucking companies, and the laundry staff.

Every helmet had to be reconditioned, painted, and tested. Shoulder pads had to be safety tested, repaired, and refurbished. Sleds, used by the linemen to simulate contact, had to be dismantled and the pads removed, cleaned, and refurbished.

I had no idea how many tee shirts, shorts, socks, and jocks we had, but with two-a-day workouts I knew I would need at least three of everything for each player and coach.

In 1973, NFL teams were not given free shoes like they are today. We had to buy our own. Puma and Adidas had only recently begun operations, so I consulted with their representatives. And I barely got the shoes ordered and stocked before we left for camp.

Taping Lincoln Coleman

After inventorying the equipment, I had to make sure it got there. That required packing, boxing, and shipping everything to Thousand Oaks. For the latter, I relied on the team's moving company, Billy Cox Trucking. That first year we left with one truck. By the time I retired in 1994, our equipment inventory had burgeoned to four truckloads.

I would need two sets of practice uniforms, two sets of game uniforms, and nameplates for every signed rookie—all of which had to be ordered from the supplier.

Within ten to twelve days after the outset of training camp, the coaches were discussing rookie cuts to make room for the veterans. And with every rookie cut, I had to inventory and account for those discarded uniforms and set them aside as backups.

The gear we took to California had to suffice for the team's nine-week stay there, up to and including the first preseason games played on the West Coast. It proved to be a long way from Southland Athletics in Texas to Thousand Oaks and the team relied on me, and me alone, to supply all their equipment needs during their absence from home.

FORTY-YEAR-OLD ROOKIE

From the beginning I was aware that my relationship with my fellow Cowboys was critical. There's more to a job than the performance of its basic responsibilities. There is the knack of working well alongside others, especially in the NFL, given the stresses of winning (and losing), the tight deadlines, the travel, and the long hours.

Since retiring I have had ample time to reflect on my career at Dallas. Cowboys great, and former defensive back and friend, Charlie Waters, shared these kind thoughts:

"The true unsung hero for the Dallas Cowboys, America's Team, was Buck Buchanan. He won the award every year (twelve) I played professional football."

"Buck was a consummate professional. He performed his job with efficiency and exactness, with no recognition, except for those who appreciated his work habit. Our entire team knew how great a job Buck did for the team and each player."

"He was always pleasant in his demeanor despite the most bizarre requests. He was a friend, a psychiatrist, a confidant, a workmate, and an untiring laborer for our Cowboy team, an unsung hero."

Over the course of my athletic career I had come to recognize the need for getting along, maintaining a positive attitude, and keeping things light under pressure. And the sum of what I learned before coming to work for the Cowboys was applied, out of sheer necessity and often, during my career at Dallas.

I had a young guy ask me once, "Buck, what does an equipment manager do?"

I replied, "Whatever is necessary."

During my career there was no task too great or too small. I did it all—trainer, weatherman, conditioner, groundskeeper, launderer, soda jerk, referee, counselor, security guard, handyman, and scout. But ask anyone who has worked in professional football and they will agree—NFL employees wear many hats. It just comes with the territory.

When an athlete needed his ankles taped, I taped. Although defensive back Benny Barnes (1972–1982) from Stanford might have preferred I had not. After I taped Benny's ankles for practice, he said, "I thought I was going to lose all my blood out there today, Buck."

When Coach Landry needed a weather forecast, I called the weather center.

When an athlete needed someone to run with him, I jogged.

When the practice field was in bad shape, I pitched in.

When dirty laundry piled up, I filled the washing machines.

When players needed Gatorade, I got it.

When a fight broke out, I waded in.

When a player was down, I was there.

When security was in question, I slept on a cot in the locker room.

When a helmet broke, I repaired it.

And when Mr. Brandt was short-handed, I signed free agents.

During the off-season, Mr. Brandt used as many as twenty staff members to travel the highways and byways in search of hot new prospects. League competition was fierce.

We set out two days before Draft Day, and when a player remained undrafted, we'd try to woo him as a free agent with a bonus, a three-year contract offer, and an irresistible offer to play NFL football in a Dallas Cowboys uniform.

Mr. Brandt sent me to North Dakota my rookie year.

In 1974, he sent me to Rochester, New York.

My third year with the team, he sent me to Utah.

Thereafter, to my wife's delight, he sent me to the Raleigh/Durham, North Carolina, area, Jerry's family home.

In twenty-one years I signed only one player who was not later cut, Duke University offensive lineman Brian "Baldy" Baldinger (1982–1984, 1986–1987). Brian played with the Cowboys for five years before leaving to play for the Philadelphia Eagles.

After retiring from football, Brian served as the play-by-play announcer in the NFL Europe League. Today, Baldinger is an announcer at FOX. And to think, when I first met him, Brian couldn't even *spell* announcer.

During seven years working together, I think I only really irritated Baldy once. It was after the Thanksgiving Day Game of 1984, when I sent a number of the vets' helmets to Ft. Worth to be reconditioned and painted. The helmets had not been refurbished since before training camp, and they really needed it.

After getting the helmets back, I put them in each player's locker. Baldy came by the cage with a horrified look and asked, "What did you do to my helmet, Buck?"

"I had it repainted," I said.

Baldinger asked, "Why?"

"Because it was all scratched up and looked terrible," I said.

"Don't do me like that again, Buck. I like those battle scars," Baldy replied.

At training camp we'd enlist the help of our college aides to record video plays.

One of my kids carried a slate board, and he would transcribe each offensive play on the board in chalk. He'd turn around and hold up the printed message so the film crew could record the play. When we returned to Dallas from Thousand Oaks, we didn't have any extra help to perform the video sideline duties, and Coach Landry asked me to help.

The Cowboys ran a play dubbed *FAN RIGHT-34*. I couldn't get all those words to fit on that tiny chalkboard, so I got inventive. For FAN, I wrote FA. For RIGHT, I abbreviated the word, RT. And the play became immortalized on film as FART-34.

The next day, Coach Landry stopped by, grinning. "Buck," he said, "I like your work on the board, but think about changing some of your abbreviations. We were watching the film last night, and we didn't know we had a play called FART."

Coach Dan Reeves later used a script format and the chalkboard went away. Running back Dan Reeves from South Carolina University played for the Cowboys from 1965–1972. During the overlapping period, 1970–1972, Reeves served as a player/coach for the Dallas Cowboys.

Reeves served as offensive backfield coach from 1970 to 1972 and 1975. He was the Cowboys' special teams coach in 1974 and our quarterbacks/receivers coach in 1976. From 1977 to 1979, Coach Reeves served as our offensive coordinator and offensive backs coach. In 1980, he served as the Dallas quarterbacks/receivers coach.

Reeves scored four touchdowns in the November 5, 1967, game with Atlanta—two running and two passing. As a result, he is tied for most touchdowns scored in one game—four—with Cowboys players Bob Hayes, Calvin Hill, Duane Thomas, and Emmitt Smith.

Coach Reeves was a talented quarterback coach who mentored Staubach.

Coach Dan Reeves

He was also skillful with his hands. Coach Reeves was accustomed to betting others that he could perform certain tricks. He had large, bulbous hands, and he often bet he could bounce a racquetball on the floor and catch it on the back of his hand.

"Bet you a dollar I can do it," he would say.

And he did.

I never saw him collect the money.

He was also quite remarkable when it came to blowing dimes into an 8-ounce Styrofoam coffee cup. After betting an unsuspecting Cowboy he could do so, he would place a dime and a cup on a flat surface two inches apart. He then put his lips to the edge of the table, and with a huff and a puff, eight times out of ten, blew the dime into the cup.

Quite remarkable what NFL players and coaches do in their spare time.

I've always liked working with athletes and coaches. I played high school and semipro sports, and I've worked with players and coaches since I was a kid.

I enjoy people and I like helping them.

I joked and laughed with Cowboys players, trainers, and coaches, and a few, over time, became devoted and long-time friends.

But like my mentors, my Dad and Coach Landry, I never talked about myself.

My predecessor had grown unpopular over time, leading to his dismissal. I've never been fired from a job, and that was never an option for me. I hit it off with the team from day one. I didn't holler, rant and rave, or threaten—as if I could have. That just isn't my style. And as it turned out, my way of coping with stress—and people—was compatible with, if not identical to, Coach Landry's.

I gave the players what they needed, when they asked for it. The team quickly realized that I was determined to take care of them. Dad used to say, "If a job's worth doing, Tom, do it to the best of your ability, or don't do it at all."

I was there to serve the players and coaches. That's why I checked every shoe, every shoestring, every cleat, and every snap on every helmet before every game.

I took my duties seriously, and I poured myself into the job—110 percent.

I was a forty-year-old equipment manager, a rookie, so it's not like I was a kid thrown into a tough and demanding job. In point of fact, I was a middle-aged family man, an old codger on his second career, thrown into an extremely tough and demanding job.

A DIFFERENT BREED

Most Cowboys players were young, twenty-something men. Many were mature; others were not. Some, like my all-time favorite, Roger Staubach, surely have been mature since birth. There was an altogether different breed of player in 1973. Generally, they were older, responsible, and mature. Certainly the vast majority were fiercely independent.

In nearly every way, Roger was mature and level headed. But that contention might be argued in light of his unorthodox contract negotiations with Tex Schramm. Some might say the Dallas franchise quarterback had had his bell rung once too often.

Shortly after my rookie season at Dallas, Roger was anxious to renegotiate his contract with the Cowboys. Tex was on the phone in his office, and Roger had been told that he was not to be disturbed. Impatient, the Cowboys' star quarterback made his way to an outside exit and climbed out onto the ledge of the Cowboys' eleventh-floor Expressway Towers Office.

Roger inched his way around the building to Schramm's office window and peered inside, making a face at and putting the fear of God into the Cowboys' otherwise fearless president and general manager. Staubach got his audience with Tex, and he successfully negotiated his own contract.

Players didn't move from team to team then, as players do today. There was no such thing as free agency, and players were dedicated to one organization. And some, like Roger, fulfilled their military obligations prior to coming onboard the NFL. It was a different time, and football was played—and coached—by a different breed of men.

SUPERB LEADERSHIP

Much of what took place on and off the Cowboys' field of play was a direct result of superlative leadership and planning. Coach Landry was a man of character, a combat veteran, a man of unquestioned principle. He worked the Cowboys hard and the results of his efforts paid off. And Coach Landry usually hired like-minded assistant coaches.

He expected 110 percent from his players and staff, and Coach Landry always gave 150 percent of himself. He had no fire-up speech before games. He told his team what the other team might do, come Game Day, and he made sure they were prepared.

Football was their job; he *expected* them to do it to the very best of their ability.

Coach Landry never gave windy speeches, but then every coach in the NFL has his own style of coaching. Coach Johnson, for example, came from a college background, and Jimmy, as he asked his players to call him, believed in the value of rallying speeches.

Coach Landry was all business, no nonsense, preparation, and all hard work.

And as Coach Bob Ward noted, "It's tough chopping wood and carrying water for that long a time." Coach Landry's illustrious reign at the Cowboys lasted twenty-nine seasons.

TITLES

Since that first meeting my rookie year, Coach Landry called me Buck. So did the team. My wife, Jerry, calls me Tom—and a few other choice words, now and then. In turn, I never called Coach Landry anything but Coach or Coach Landry—to this day.

The only Cowboy I ever heard call him Tom was Cowboys President and General Manager Tex Schramm. Quarterback great Joe Theismann shocked Cowboys veterans Pat Donovan (1975–1983), Tony Dorsett (1977–1987), and myself on the sidelines at the 1983 Hawaii Pro Bowl, when he casually addressed Coach Landry as Tom.

Theismann even shocked Coach Landry. None of us were accustomed to hearing our vaunted leader spoken to in such common terms. I'm sure Theismann meant nothing by it.

Alicia Landry called her husband Tommy, but wives have that luxury.

Barbara Goodman, Landry's secretary (1981–1989), called her boss Mr. Landry.

These many years since, when I'm around former Cowboy players, coaches and staff, we speak of Coach Landry in respectful, almost reverential terms.

But he is *never* called Tom.

In addition to our given names, some of us were blessed with nicknames during our athletic careers. If you were lucky to be so honored, it *usually* spoke well of you.

Roger Staubach was nicknamed "Captain America"; Bob Lilly, "Mr. Cowboy"; Mel Renfro, "Fro"; Thomas Henderson, "Hollywood"; Mike Ditka, "Chipmunk"; Cliff Harris, "Crash"; Bob Hayes, "Bullet" and "Speedo"; Jethro Pugh, "Buzzy"; Tony Dorsett, "TD"; Emmitt Smith, "EM"; Cowboys charter pilot Wally Nicholson, "Sky King"; and yours truly, the "Hanging Judge."

Most everyone had a nickname.

No doubt we have other handles that are unprintable.

TRAINING CAMP

On June 28, 1973, the Cowboys left Dallas for training camp in Thousand Oaks, California, three short weeks into my rookie year. Three staff members flew with me to southern California—trainers Don Cochren and Ken Locker—and Joe Bailey.

I stood watching in the parking lot when the truck pulled away from Forest Lane early that Saturday morning, and I was there when it pulled up to the empty practice field at Thousand Oaks early the next Monday.

I helped the movers unpack, and I bid them farewell. Standing alone in the university locker room, staring at all those stacked, padlocked trunks and boxes, I wondered if I'd ever get everything set up in time for camp. Somehow I did. After another late night I called it a day and crawled into bed shortly after midnight.

The next day, June 29, 1973, was the beginning of my first Cowboys training camp, and I had ten days to get set up for the rookies. Many of those kids would end up being released and sent home, their NFL experiences cut short, their hopes dashed.

Players were given physicals their first day in camp. That afternoon, they were suited up in full gear and pads. From that point on, Coach Landry had the team practice twice a day, six days a week. On Sunday, players and staff were allowed an opportunity to attend church, as did Coach Landry, and by that afternoon the players were on the field in full gear.

Two weeks later after the surviving rookies had endured their first NFL trial, the real fun would begin and the veterans would arrive to make the rookies' lives hell.

At Thousand Oaks

Coach Landry had an orientation at the outset of training camp. During that informal meeting he introduced the rookie hopefuls and identified the positions they were vying for. He introduced each member of his staff and asked that we provide the team with a brief description of ourselves and our responsibilities.

Team rules, by-laws, and player fines were discussed. The players were told how to report to be taped, and there were instructions on player weigh-in and weigh-out.

Each player was expected to weigh out before going on the practice field, and after practice he was expected to weigh in upon reentering the dressing room. Players who failed to do so were fined fifty dollars. It may not seem like much now, but in training camp every player was paid the same, nominal salary and several fifty dollar fines could add up quickly.

Unlike the team meetings that followed, the orientation was cordial and relaxed. But for us rookies it was nerve-wracking. For all its spirited jockeying it was still a Coach Landry meeting with all the elements of business and no nonsense typical of his style of coaching. I'll admit to having suffered a bad case of butterflies that morning.

Thousand Oaks was akin to military boot camp. Training camp represented rigorous physical and mental training, tempered with intense discipline and a Spartan lifestyle. Like it or not, we were there till the third week of August—nine long, hard weeks.

There was no time to consider the enormity of the job, no time for distractions, and family life was nonexistent. Much like my Air Force tour of Southeast Asia, I did not have the luxury or the comfort of loved ones. I was a professional soldier, in or out of uniform, on TDY—temporary duty assignment. That part of the job was familiar to me whether I found myself in the NFL or in the military—it was my chosen way of life.

During training camp I had no paid assistants. I did have four teenagers, loaners from the university who helped me with my duties. There were Chris Kindem, Mike Hagen, Steve Hagen, and Jeff Garrison, without whose help I might never have survived my rookie year. Those guys were tremendous, helping me get the fields set up and the dressing rooms and equipment readied for the players.

I kept track of three of my "kids" from Cal Lutheran. Chris is currently a university professor in Minnesota. Mike is the director of college personnel with the Atlanta Falcons. Steve is the football coach at the University of Nevada in Reno.

I lost track of Jeff, so if you read this, buddy, give me a call.

My kids ranged in age from fourteen to eighteen, and their parents worked at the college. Those guys really helped during camp, and I was tickled to death to have them.

Coach Landry liked having the guys as extra hands. In large part because of them, he could run four concurrent drills—two offensive and two defensive. Among their other duties, my kids helped control the footballs, snagging them when they went out of play.

Prior to each new day, Coach Jim Myers, offensive line and assistant head coach, provided me with a copy of the schedule and the field assignment for that day's practice. We used three areas to work out on at Cal Lutheran: the stadium field, the baseball outfield, and a regulation practice field.

During my first ten days, the rookies, the only players in camp at the time, used the school's baseball outfield for morning practice. In the afternoon, we used Cal Lutheran's practice field.

Part of my responsibility was to check field conditions before practice.

One morning I discovered that the water sprinklers had run all night, flooding the practice field from one 25-yard line to the other. I sat with Coach Landry and Coach Stallings at breakfast, and that morning I told them about the poor field conditions.

"Don't worry about it, Buck," Coach Landry said. "Let me know when it's dry. In the meantime, we'll use the stadium field."

That was Coach Landry's typical response. Nothing ever rattled him.

Despite the pressures of that first camp I enjoyed the experience immensely. But the happy-go-lucky man my wife knew in the Air Force had already begun to change.

Jerry was fond of telling friends and family that her husband, the Cowboys' equipment manager, had three distinct football personalities. There was my preseason/training camp personality, which Jerry characterized as easygoing; my regular season personality, which she said, was uptight; and there was my playoff personality, which she described as being "a grumpy old man."

Sometimes I think my personality best fit the grumpy old man description throughout all twenty-one of those long seasons. Given the pressures of the game we all tended to be that way at times—players, coaches, and staff. The exception was Coach Landry, who remained placid and serene throughout every trial—but his last.

Training camp was open to the public and security was strictly enforced at Thousand Oaks. During regular season our training facilities were off-limits to the public.

Our twenty-four-hour security service nabbed several teens one night that had been attending a football camp down the road. The kids had broken into the rooks' locker room and were making off with some jerseys when they were nabbed by the night watchman.

Cal Lutheran's president called the next morning and asked what I intended to do with the offenders. Was it not an open-and-shut case of breaking and entering?

"Prosecute the hoodlums," I told the president.

An hour later, the kids' camp manager and the president of Cal Lutheran dropped by to see me, the former clearly agitated.

"Come on, man," he pleaded, "tell me you're not gonna charge those kids."

"Yes, sir," I said. "They have to face up to what they've done."

The red-faced camp manager tried another tack, a somewhat more personal approach. "Buck, you apparently haven't got a lot of experience working with kids."

"Well, sir," I said, "I just completed eight years with a super bunch of young men at the Air Force Academy in Colorado Springs, and I never had this kind of problem there."

The camp manager spun about angrily and left without saying another word.

Cal Lutheran's president quietly departed the scene.

At lunch that day, Tex Schramm joined me in the cafeteria.

"I understand you intend to press charges."

My mouth was full so I dutifully nodded.

Tex leaned closer, his palms leaving sweaty impressions on the table.

"Those kids are leaving camp. Their parents have agreed to pay for the damages."

"Yes, sir," I said.

Tex grinned and turned to leave.

"I understand," I said.

Tex patted me on the shoulder and left.

We never pressed charges against those youthful offenders. But shortly afterwards, Public Relations Director Doug Todd assigned me a new nickname, and sounded it with his best west Texas drawl.

"Yes, sir, Buck. We're gonna start calling you the Hanging Judge."

Coach Landry never said a word to me about the jersey incident, but my new handle stuck with me throughout my rookie training camp.

CONJUGAL VISITS

In general, wives and family members were discouraged from visiting Thousand Oaks. There were few exceptions. On occasion, Alicia Landry visited her husband. Mrs. Landry brought her knitting and a book and watched her husband's practices, but she was the exception to the rule.

One weekend, under extenuating circumstances, my wife, Jerry, was granted permission by Coach Landry to visit me at training camp. After seeing how hard I worked and how little time I had to spend with her, she never asked to return.

All-Pro defensive lineman Bob Lilly wanted to have his sixteen-year-old son, Bob Jr., stay with him at training camp, so he talked to Mr. Schramm. Bob Jr. had some problems at home and Bob Sr. wanted his son nearby. Mr. Schramm agreed to the arrangement, but that was one of the rare exceptions to the rule. Bob Jr. stayed with us about two weeks.

Bob Lilly retired the following year, ending a Cowboys tradition. Bob Jr. was a good kid, and once he joined us in camp, he was never any problem. There just wasn't much a teenager could do at Thousand Oaks with his dad tied up all day on the job.

MEETINGS

Life in football, not unlike life in the corporate sector, can be punctuated with endless meetings. At our Forest Lane and Valley Ranch facilities, the Cowboys held all-inclusive team meetings, followed by daily offensive and defensive minimeetings. I was spared from attending. Instead, I used the lull in the action to catch up on my work.

At both training facilities, after the team meeting was concluded, players separated into offensive and defensive groups to discuss their various assignments. The offense split into quarterback and running back, receiver and offensive lineman groups, and the defense met in lineman, linebacker, and defensive back meetings.

Forest Lane didn't have adequate space, and meetings tended to be raucous, with players vying to be heard over the noise of their teammates. In 1985, the new Valley Ranch facility made up for Forest Lane's space deficiencies and lack of privacy.

At training camp, players met before practice every day but Sunday. In the afternoon, they had meetings before and after each practice.

Practice was filmed, to include end zone and sideline shots, and the film was reviewed in both team and specialty-team meetings. Coach Landry kept our video department busy, documenting every drill, practice, and game.

TRAINERS AND MEDICAL STAFF

I put in long hours, but the coaches and trainers outhustled me. We had two full-time trainers for taping, tending to the players' dietary needs, monitoring their health and weight, and rehabilitating their injuries. With upwards of 110 players at any given time, trainers had 220 ankles to tape—shoulders, elbows, and knees not included—twice a day.

Because of the workload, Head Trainer Don Cochren brought in an extra trainer that year from Southern University in Baton Rouge, Louisiana. Carl Williams was as tall as he was wide. Carl loved to eat, and he was always threatening to go on a diet.

Carl was a personable fellow with great jokes that went a long way toward boosting morale. Weeks into the season, after getting their heads bashed in twice a day, Cowboys players enjoyed having the stress relieved with Carl's good-natured humor.

Our trainers worked in concert with four dedicated team doctors to tend to player injuries. My rookie season, Dallas had a cadre of distinguished surgeons and general practitioners—Dr. Marvin P. Knight, chief orthopedic surgeon; Dr. Pat Evans, orthopedic surgeon; Dr. Pepe Zamorano, general practitioner; and Dr. Mitch Aboussie, radiologist. We also had an orthopedic surgeon who lived in Thousand Oaks.

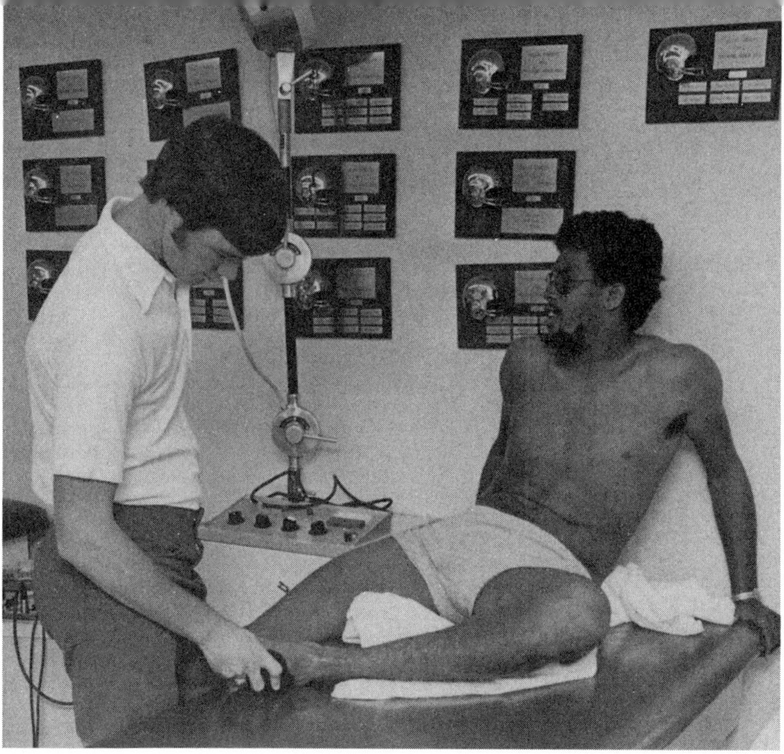

Ken Locker and Jean Fugett

Each was licensed in California, certified to write player prescriptions.

A legend in his own right, a surgeon of renown, Dr. Knight was one of the first sports medicine doctors in the United States. He joined the franchise in 1960, and he retired to his ranch in 1987 after a long and distinguished career.

Dr. Knight was a native of Muenster, Texas, and he often admitted players to Muenster Memorial Hospital for surgeries, where they were treated like royalty.

Dr. Knight was a surgeon during World War II, where he served his internship in a MASH (mobile army surgical hospital) unit. Although he was direct and often blunt, Dr. Knight was much loved by the players and staff.

In many ways he reminded me of my Dad—especially the way he dressed. That old country doctor made quite a first impression

Ken Locker and Dr. Zamorano

in his white cowboy hat, dark suit, white shirt, dark tie, and black cowboy boots.

Dr. Knight had little patience for complaining players distressed with the bumps and bruises of life in the National Football League. It was not uncommon for him to scold players for seeking medical attention when, in Dr. Knight's opinion, their requests were frivolous. One occasion comes to mind in the case of wide receiver Golden Richards.

Golden was many things, but durable he was not. In one game, the wide receiver was hurt twice and Dr. Knight had to rush to the far side of the field to attend to Golden's injuries. Golden was injured a third time, across the field on the opponents' sideline, and when Dr. Knight arrived, panting, he knelt down beside the injured Dallas player.

Knight was reported to have said, and I paraphrase, "Next time you get hurt, Golden, do it on your own sideline. And don't expect me to be running across the field to take care of you."

Another Cowboy complained to Dr. Knight about an injured shoulder. The doctor asked, and again I paraphrase, "How high can you lift your arm?" The player lifted his arm shoulder high. "How high," Dr. Knight continued, "could you lift your arm before the injury?" The player lifted his arm only slightly higher

Dr. Knight helps Don Meredith from the field

than before. "Don't lift your arm like that again," Knight said, "and get your ass back on the field. You're not hurt."

Walt Garrison spoke at Dr. Knight's funeral in 2000, where he recounted a personal experience with the good doctor. Dr. Knight had operated on Walt's knee and later asked Garrison to visit his ranch in Muenster for a follow-up visit.

When Walt got to the Knight's home, he found Dr. Knight working in his cow pasture. "What do you want?" Knight demanded.

Walt reminded Dr. Knight that he was only complying with doctor's instructions.

"Well, get up in the back of the truck," Dr. Knight said, "and drop your pants." After examining Walt's knee in the bed of that pickup truck, Dr. Knight made his medical pronouncement. "You're ready to play on Sunday. Now put your pants back on."

Dr. Knight and Tex Schramm were good friends. Leaving our Texas Stadium locker room, as Dr. Knight and I made our way through the tunnel toward the field one Game Day, I pointed to the "No Smoking" sign prominently displayed above our heads.

It was common knowledge that the stadium's artificial turf was flammable, and Mr. Schramm had a hard-and-fast no-smoking rule for the team. At the time, Dr. Knight held a lit cigarette in his hand. He took a drag and wafted smoke in the direction of the sign as we exited the tunnel. "Tex can fire me, if he wants to," he growled.

The NFL requires a minimum of forty-eight hours after a game for players to recuperate. But in 1973 we were doing good to get one day off after Thanksgiving. Monday night games were the hardest on us. Our doctors were the best and they went to great lengths to keep the team healthy, but they were about as unconventional as they could have been.

Dr. Knight dressed in cowboy boots and jeans and drove a truck. Dr. Zamorano was a neat, classy dresser who loved large, expensive cars. Dr. Evans dressed in casual Western garb and was a connoisseur of fine wines and upscale restaurants. Team radiologist Dr. Aboussie was a sharp dresser and a sports car nut.

Every Dallas doctor was unique, yet each lent his flavor to the team mix. Without a doubt the atmosphere in the Cowboys locker room, when the doctors were there, was more akin to an episode from *M* A* S* H* than one from *General Hospital*—another reason why working for America's Team in 1973 was so much fun.

HOLIDAYS

Independence Day, July 4, coincided with training camp. Scratch that holiday.

The Cowboys played every Thanksgiving, and we worked out on Christmas Day. For NFL players and staff, there are no traditional holidays until the season is over, you're cut from the team, or you expire.

For those of us who had family, holidays were squeezed in whenever time could be found. The Buchanans celebrated

Christmas after practice, late the evening of December 25. And we celebrated Thanksgiving the following Saturday or Sunday.

DORM LIFE

The dorms at Cal Lutheran were comfortable, although anything but luxurious. Having served in the U.S. Armed Forces I had considerable experience with dorm life and cafeteria-style cuisine.

Cal Lutheran's dormitory and cafeteria were a cut above most. The cafeteria provided a full breakfast, lunch, and dinner, and the food was exceptionally good. It had to be. NFL players, by necessity, must eat well and often.

The cafeteria offered a variety of fresh fruits and nutritionally balanced meals.

Strength and Conditioning Coach Alvin Roy (1973–1975) made certain of it.

It was Coach Roy's responsibility to advise players of their ideal playing weights.

And if a player exceeded his limitations, he was given two weeks by Coach Roy to trim down. If he did not, the player was forced to go on a diet, which meant his meals were carefully scrutinized, and he wasn't allowed seconds.

Every year there were players who couldn't meet weight, and it was usually one of the offensive or defensive linemen. In 1973, there were only a handful of players pushing three hundred pounds. In the 1990s there may have been four dozen. In today's NFL training camps, there are more than five hundred players in excess of three hundred pounds. Insofar as linemen are concerned, today's game of football is more about mass than finesse.

Mr. Schramm made certain that the trainers and I had everything we needed in training camp. We had a dayroom with a TV, and ample snacks and beverages were always available. Tex encouraged us, before the players' arrival, to take in a movie or go into town to enjoy a good meal. We even had sodas and beer. But after the players got there, it was all business and off-campus excursions were the exception and not the rule.

In Roger Staubach, Bob Breunig, Charlie Waters, and Cliff Harris' room, when you walked in, there was always a bowl of cereal snacks on a table by the door. Each room had its own snack bowl, but some players weren't satisfied with their supply and resorted to borrowing from their teammates.

Bob Breunig and the guys befriended a homeless pooch that training camp in Thousand Oaks, and to feed the hapless stray, they bought him a bag of dried dog food.

About that time, the snacks in Roger, Bob, Charlie, and Cliff's room had been mysteriously disappearing, so Breunig got the bright idea to switch out dried dog food for the human snack offering. An offensive lineman ate the dog food "snacks" for three days before his teammates finally told "Ruff" what he'd been eating.

For the remainder of training camp, former Penn State center Tom Rafferty came to be known as "Ruff," not "Raff" as he had formerly been nicknamed by his teammates.

During practice the veterans dressed in the college varsity room. The rookies had a less auspicious dressing area, the K Building. Neither was especially spacious or luxurious, but the rookies always seemed to have it worse.

In the NFL, rookies have no rights. New players were forced to endure hardships, usually one form or another of training-camp hazing. Singing to the veterans, fetching their coffee, or performing demeaning, menial tasks was the norm.

Rookies were at the veterans' beck and call, and the vets delighted in pushing the rooks' buttons. And if the rookies graduated to become veterans, they were more than happy to return the favor to the next year's batch of unseasoned players.

Upon leaving the cafeteria one night, veteran running back Walt Garrison stopped me outside. "Hey, Buck," Walt chortled, a pinch of Copenhagen tucked between his cheek and gum, "Unless I'm mistaken, you're a rookie."

Unable to sidestep the charge, I replied, "That's right, Walt."

"Then you sing tomorrow," Walt said.

I didn't eat supper in the cafeteria for days. I'm no public speaker, and I am most definitely no entertainer. Almost a week later, at practice, Walt joined me on the sideline grinning like the Cheshire cat. "I was just kidding, Buck. You don't have to sing for us."

I missed a week's chow to avoid singing to the veterans because of that turkey. But just in case, I had practiced my Air Force song in the privacy of my dorm room during my forced absence. That week I subsisted on snacks, ice cream, and sodas.

CURFEW

Lights out was shortly after the day's last meeting, and players could be fined for being absent without leave (AWOL). A designated coach checked each player's bed every night to ensure compliance. Penalties depended on the severity of the infraction and Coach Landry's mood. Upon returning from his AWOL status, it was necessary for the player to report directly to Coach Landry to determine the degree of his punishment. A stern taskmaster, Coach Jim Myers, was the dorm monitor that first year. Coach Myers was a hard-nosed, no-nonsense offensive line coach. By his own admission, he'd had that trademark beak of his broken several times. His face more closely resembled a piece of rawhide, weathered by the elements. That, and his status of World War II–era United States Marine, made Coach Myers a formidable hall monitor.

Coach Myers

I've seen Coach Myers instruct body blocking by hurling his own, unpadded frame at padded players twice his size—and half his age—knocking them aside.

Throughout the course of his collegiate and NFL career, Coach Myers was said to have engaged in fisticuffs, now and then knocking out players with a helmet, those who would not subordinate their will to his.

Coach Myers has changed little in all these years. A cursory glimpse of the man's rugged demeanor, then and now, tells the same tough story. As a young man growing up in West Virginia, Jim Myers hauled nitroglycerine over rugged mountain roads to miners in a rickety oxen-drawn wagon.

Famed *Los Angeles Times* sports reporter Jim Murray said of Coach Myers in his January 18, 1979, newspaper column: "His face looks as if he just went 10 hard rounds with Dempsey or as if he were the last guy out of a plane wreck. It would have to improve to be called "craggy"—a relief map of Colorado with eyes. . . . Life never dealt Jim Myers many aces. Every card he ever turned over broke the flush. It made him hard and his face got the message."

Myers served as head coach at Texas A&M before Bear Bryant.

He was a classic head football coach and an awesome offensive line coach.

At Dallas, Coach Myers was organized, dedicated, and smart. In my long career, I have not met a better line coach. Unlike others, he could change during the course of a game—a mark of true genius.

Never shy, Coach Myers was unabashed about standing up in meetings to question the prevailing wisdom, if he thought it was warranted. Coach Ditka was that bold, but most assistant coaches never dreamed of doing so in a Coach Landry meeting.

In large measure, Coach Myers was pivotal to the Cowboys' success. And to his and his team's credit, Coach Landry listened to such dissenting voices.

Today, the Dallas resident, and my personal friend, has a full head of white, flaxen hair, bright blue eyes, and a brilliant mind, capable of reciting prose on demand. As of this writing, he is a spry eighty-five-year-old who walks four miles a day.

But don't let age fool you; Coach Myers is as tough as ever.

Players in 1973 were not unlike those of today, young, testosterone-driven males averse to any restrictions being placed on their extracurricular activities, anxious to spend their hard-earned cash. Given the dynamics of the Cowboys' curfew, the mix made for an interesting game of cat and mouse.

All-Pro defensive back Charlie Waters reminds me of a story that involved our European kicker, Toni Fritsch. Coach Myers was on bed check when he discovered the little Austrian missing, whereupon he reported Toni's absence to Coach Landry.

Charlie reminisced, "We snuck Toni out to buy us a pizza. On the way to the pizza joint, he was pulled over by the Thousand

Oaks Police. Problem was, Toni couldn't speak much English. All he could say was, 'Me, Dallas Cowboy. Me, Dallas Cowboy!' "

The officer, no doubt having heard one story too many that night, replied, " 'Yeah, right. And I'm Superman.' "

Toni spent the night in jail, and he received a Coach Landry reprimand and a fine the next morning—after he was bailed out.

Toni Fritsch signed with the Cowboys in 1971, and he was there when the team won its first Super Bowl game, Super Bowl VI, in New Orleans.

In 1972 the world celebrated the Twentieth Olympiad in Munich, Germany. It was the year the world witnessed the horror on September 5, when eight terrorists slipped into the Olympic Village and killed two Israeli team members and seized nine others.

That year, twenty-two-year-old American swimmer Mark Spitz set an Olympic record by winning four individual and three relay events in record-breaking time.

Those Olympics set the tone for our conversations—and jokes—before I retired from the Air Force and during my rookie year with the Cowboys. It seemed every time we listened to the news, there was a mention of some European athlete, an Eric Von something or other. So I nicknamed Toni, Eric Von Wolfgang Fritsch. And the perky little kicker returned the favor, dubbing his tall west Texas friend "Bucky Boy."

"Bucky Boy," Toni would say in his broken English, "No polish shoes."

What Toni meant was he didn't want me to unwittingly ruin his kicking win-streak with a little unsolicited shoe polish. Toni was a soccer-style kicker, and like so many NFL players, domestically grown or otherwise, he was extremely superstitious.

Toni wasn't the only Cowboy who expressed his superstitions in unconventional ways. Harvey Martin and Golden Richards had their own, shall we say, peculiarities, when it came to football and magic potions.

All-Pro Harvey Martin, the 6′-5″, 262-pound defensive end from East Texas State, went ballistic if he had not eaten at least two hot dogs before a game. If we weren't able to supply Harvey with a couple of wieners, he insisted on visiting a concession stand or a stadium vendor to get his fix before game time.

Golden was compelled to wear his right sock lower than the left. Seems the sock thing was a tradition in high school that carried over into his college and NFL career.

Not changing one's uniform or equipment is commonplace within the NFL and certainly within sports in general. 6′-3″, 250-pound center Tom Rafferty (1976–1989) kept the same shoulder, thigh, and knee pads his entire fourteen-year career. And Raff's last three years with the Cowboys, he wore the same tailored game-day jersey—No. 64.

Life in the NFL can be tough on kickers like Toni Fritsch, especially when they're born outside the United States. We had three or four kickers in training camp at any given time, and the competition was intense. Kickers just don't stick around long.

After my NFL debut, Toni left the team in 1974 due to an injury—lucky soccer shoes and all. Toni returned after rehabilitation and contributed to the Cowboys' Super Bowl X effort in 1976.

Before leaving the Dallas Cowboys, Toni racked up an impressive team record. He booted a 54-yard field goal against the Giants in 1972, and he attempted six field goals during a single game against the Los Angeles Rams in 1975.

During his four-year career at Dallas, Toni tied Danny Villanueva's (1965–1967) record for most field goals made in one game with four against the St. Louis Cardinals and an equal number against the Los Angeles Rams. Toni had an impressive points-after-touchdown record of 119 of 121 attempts and 66 of 107 field goal attempts, for a total of 317 career points.

In the final minutes of a pair of regular season games, Toni made a field goal, winning the first contest, and missed the second field goal, losing the second game.

On the plane ride home, Toni lamented the plight of NFL kickers. "Bucky Boy," he said, "when you kick and you win the game, you're a big hero. When you kick and you lose the game, you're a piece of shit."

Coach Myers is fond of telling the story of 6′-2″, 198-pound wide receiver Tony Hill's (1977–1986) missing his eleven o'clock bed check at training camp in Thousand Oaks.

"I notified Coach Landry," Coach Myers reminisced, "and fined Tony $17,000 for being AWOL. Against my protests, Coach Landry reduced Tony's fine to a mere $5,000."

Roger Staubach failed to show for a pregame breakfast, a major infraction of a Coach Landry directive. "The fine continued until the player met with Coach Landry in person," Coach Myers explained. "Never mind that the Cowboys' starting quarterback preferred to eat breakfast with his wife. Roger still got fined."

Celebrity or team status did not prevent players from being punished. In fact it may have contributed. "I fined Staubach $50 for throwing his helmet during a short-yardage practice," Coach Myers recalled. "Roger came unglued."

"'That's a $25 fine, coach!' he protested."

"I explained to our starting QB, 'It's $50 because your helmet *bounced*!' "

Chief of the Cowboys' bed check, Coach Myers, spied on the empty room of 5′-11″, 190-pound running back Tony Dorsett; 5′-10″, 202-pound fullback Robert Newhouse; 6′-1″, 225-pound linebacker Mike Hegman; and 5′-11″, 180-pound defensive back Dennis Thurman one night through the players' closed venetian blinds.

When confronted with the charge, the players became incensed.

Coach Myers tells of the AWOL status of Ed Jones, who he could not help but see sneaking away from the defensive end's dorm room crouched behind a thicket of shrubs. Keep in mind,

Coach Stautner

Ed was a 6′-9″, 270-pound player who often wore elevator shoes in public.

Offensive lineman Brian Baldinger authenticated that cat-and-mouse episode the night Ed's dormitory escape was thwarted, as one of his all-time funniest moments at the Cowboys. "The summer at Thousand Oaks when Too Tall was busted for missing curfew and pretended to be a tree, as Coach Myers searched around in the bushes."

"Another player was able to conceal himself," Myers later explained, "and his identity, in the tall bushes outside Ed's room. But 'Too Tall' was just too damned tall."

Ultimately, Ed was unable to duck below Coach Myers' radar to avoid detection, and he was hauled before Coach Landry for curfew infraction.

Players got up when they wanted to every morning—as long as they weren't late for a Coach Landry meeting. The rookies began showing up in the cafeteria around 7:00 a.m., and the vets arrived around 7:30 or 8:00, with the nine o'clock practice looming.

After workouts, they were off again at 11:30, whereupon they showered and ate lunch. There were more meetings, and they were back on the field no later than 3:00 p.m. and off again at 5:30. Players ate dinner, attended meetings, and went to bed—or pretended to do so. Such was the glamorous NFL lifestyle of Dallas players in 1973.

Occasionally the vets rented TVs; some rented cars. Veteran 6′-1″, 193-pound defensive back Charlie Waters drove his motorcycle to California from Dallas my first year. Coach Landry put a stop to such road trips and made sure the motorcycle rode safely in the back of the equipment truck on the trip home.

Charlie took the chartered team jet.

At Thousand Oaks, exposure to the outside world was minimal, the dorm phones being the players' only means of communicating with family, friends, and agents.

There were no cell phones in 1973 for personal communications, only the dorm phones and a pair of telephones in the locker room—one for the trainers, the other for myself. The phone situation was a training camp reality I relished, because I wasn't dashing about madly all day, fielding player, coach, and trainer phone communiqués.

Phone communications were another story at Forest Lane. We had three telephone lines in the dressing room—two for the players and one for the trainers and me.

Players were free to answer their phones, but when they could not, or simply chose not to, that task fell to me. And just in case I didn't have enough to keep me busy, those phones rang nonstop on my desk in the equipment cage.

Life at training camp was isolated, insofar as the phones were concerned, and I was relieved of the extra burden of answering dozens of phone calls every day.

Unlike today, we had no-frill training camp bathrooms in 1973. At best, our facilities were Spartan compared to today's NFL locker-room conditions. But the college set-up at Thousand Oaks was vastly superior to Forest Lane's, although it didn't come close to the luxurious conditions I was accustomed to at the Air Force Academy.

After eight years working with Air Force cadets, living in the lap of government luxury, I was stunned at the austere conditions within the NFL—at training camp, at home, and on the road. It puzzled me how the Super Bowl VI Champs could live like that.

My rookie training camp went by fast.

The trainers worked their butts off, the players did too, and the coaches seldom got any sleep. As experience has demonstrated, this is the reality, not the glamour depicted in the movies.

HOLLYWOOD FILMMAKING

Twice during my NFL career I was involved in Hollywood moviemaking efforts. Two weeks after our 17–21 Super Bowl X loss to the Pittsburgh Steelers on January 18, 1976, in Miami, I returned to the Orange Bowl to help with the making of the John Frankenheimer film *Black Sunday*.

I had just gotten unpacked when Joe Bailey called me in Dallas and insisted I catch a flight to Miami. Joe had "volunteered" Don Cochren and me for a movie project.

Given our new marching orders, Don and I flew to Miami where we hooked up with Steelers Equipment Manager Tony Parisi. The three of us had been chosen to serve as consultants on the adventure flick, adapted from the Thomas Harris book.

The movie was shot in Miami during and after Super Bowl X; Frankenheimer's people filmed the crowds at the Orange Bowl for realism. At one juncture, during the Super Bowl game with the Steelers, actor Robert Shaw raced along the sideline behind me, as a film crew captured the action. I had no idea the production crew was filming.

Mine was the tiniest of roles in the production of that film classic, where terrorists planned an aerial attack on a Super Bowl crowd of more than eighty thousand football fans. Yet despite having no filmmaking experience, other than being a diehard film fan since my early years in Ballinger, I managed to be seen in the film.

In a scene at the end of the picture, as Israeli antiterrorist Major David Kabakov (Robert Shaw) tracks the terrorists, the explosives-laden Goodyear blimp descends on the horrified crowd and my backside appears in the scene—so much for fleeting fame.

Our primary responsibility as NFL film consultants was to ensure that the lockers were authentically displayed and the uniforms and equipment were properly worn.

We worked ten ten-hour days, not all that hard, for which we were more than adequately compensated. The food was quite good, and plentiful, and I ate often. My first Hollywood experience was a lot of fun, and just being there, exposed to that great cast—Robert Shaw, Bruce Dern, and Marthe Keller—made the experience worthwhile.

Twenty-two years later, Oliver Stone directed *Any Given Sunday*. The film had a stellar cast that included Al Pacino, Cameron Diaz, Dennis Quaid, Charlton Heston, James Woods, Ann-Margret, Jamie Foxx, LL Cool J, Matthew Modine, and

NFL greats Jim Brown (Montezuma Monroe) and Lawrence Taylor (Luther "Shark" Lavay).

Texas Stadium manager and long-time friend Bruce Hardy called during the off-season and asked if I might be interested in working on a movie set. I jumped at the chance.

I met Oliver Stone my first day on the set, and that was the last time we spoke.

"Nice to meet you, Buck," Stone said. "I don't run my operation like the NFL."

And as we all learned, Oliver most definitely did not.

Life in the NFL means long hours that begin early every morning. Life on a Hollywood movie set, with Oliver Stone directing, is defined by long hours that begin in the afternoon and extend into the wee hours of the morning.

Oliver Stone is a night owl with a penchant for perfectionism.

Texas Stadium underwent a radical facelift. The Cowboys blue was painted over with red. The dressing rooms were repainted. The white Cowboys stars—mounted on Cowboys blue—were taken down. And the lights in the tunnel leading from the locker room to the field were switched from a perpendicular to a horizontal format—a change that has lasted at Texas Stadium to this day.

For realism, Mr. Stone insisted his "players" play full bore for the cameras.

His costume manager took Polaroid photographs of each player every time he left the locker room, to ensure a consistent look throughout the production process.

High school coaches and student athletes doubled as extras and stand-ins, and the stadium parking lot was filled for the duration with actors' trailers, tents, and caterers' trucks. Security was tight, and the general public was restricted from the area.

The filming of *Any Given Sunday* reminded me a lot of my hurry-up-and-wait Army days—long hours of tedium punctuated with frantic bursts of activity.

The highlight of my Oliver Stone/Hollywood moviemaking experience, other than seeing and getting to meet several of the actors, was the food. I believe I ate all day.

Every actor had his or her double, and I never was able to distinguish one from the other. Just when I thought I could, I failed miserably. I remember saying to one of the film crew, "That guy is a spitting image of Al Pacino." To which the person replied, "That *is* Al Pacino, Buck."

Mr. Pacino would film two scenes and leave Dallas. Hours or days later, he returned to continue filming. Such is the life of a big-name Hollywood celebrity.

My duties as technical advisor were to array the uniforms and lockers in their proper NFL fashion, as they would appear during a real Super Bowl, and to advise the film crew when a certain "look" was not authentic. I worked from eight in the morning till eight every night for two weeks, and the Hollywood crowd was always there when I went home.

Everyone was fun to work with, and if given a chance, I would do it again.

TRADE DEALS

Preseason games were scheduled to coincide with training camp. My first four years in California, the Cowboys were contractually obligated, due to a trade deal made before my time, to play the Los Angeles Rams the first game of preseason. I got tired of seeing the Rams and even sicker of the Los Angeles Memorial Coliseum's dressing room.

Deals are made in every trade, like the one we made with Houston when we traded for veteran Ralph Neely (1965–1977) from the University of Oklahoma. When we traded for the Houston Oilers' 6′-6″, 265-pound tackle in 1965, the Cowboys agreed to play Houston there the first preseason game for the next three years.

Preseason games were played on Saturday nights. As a result, Friday's practice was easier and players did not suit up in full gear. I had the guys' bags packed and loaded on the truck that afternoon. Saturday, the players had their ankles taped at Thousand Oaks, and they remained in their rooms until they boarded the bus for the Coliseum. The team was there by 5:30 p.m., and the rest of the taping was completed at the stadium.

THE STADIUM I LOVED TO HATE

Los Angeles Memorial Coliseum seats upwards of ninety-two thousand fans. Built in 1923, the facility is located three miles southwest of downtown Los Angeles, adjacent to the University of Southern California campus. The coliseum is home to the USC Trojans and former home to the Los Angeles Rams, the Los Angeles Raiders, and the Los Angeles Dodgers.

To access the locker room we had to back the trucks down a steep ramp to unload our equipment. The visitors occupied the first dressing room on your right as you descend the grade.

The home team, headed up by Los Angeles Rams Equipment Manager Don Hewitt, provided four clubhouse staff to help us set up and take down our locker room.

I suppose I should not have disliked the LA Coliseum as much as I did, because the Cowboys won big there—the 1975 NFC Championship Game, 37–7—and the 1978 NFC Championship Game, 28–0.

During my rookie year, Don Hewitt was a legend within the ranks of NFL equipment managers. Don was the Big Kahuna, the senior man equipment managers looked up to. In fact, the first time Mr. Schramm had me fly to Thousand Oaks, he made a special point of scheduling an appointment for me with Hewitt. In retrospect, that two-hour chat set the tone for my successful NFL career as equipment manager for the Cowboys.

After the second loss to the Cowboys in 1978, Don took me aside and said, "Buck, I'm tired of you guys beating us . . . some day, in my lifetime, we're going to win an NFC Championship!"

Don's prediction came close to being fulfilled when the Rams defeated the Cowboys in the 1976 and 1979 Divisional Playoffs. To add insult to injury, however, the Cowboys defeated Los Angeles in Dallas in 1980, the year Roger Staubach announced his retirement, winning the NFC Wild Card Game 34–13 and advancing to the playoffs.

Don Hewitt had a live-wire personality. He was a distinguished-looking gentleman with gray hair and a ton of energy. Don was a former high school coach who was ten years my senior. During our first conversation, he stressed organization, having an eye for detail, and the necessity of getting along with the players as the key ingredients to being a decent equipment manager.

I'm proud to say Don Hewitt was my friend and mentor. His professionalism and attention to detail were reflected every time the Rams took the field—their uniforms and equipment were nothing short of immaculate, no doubt why Mr. Schramm, ever the stickler for neatness, thought so highly of Don.

SETTING UP

I had to be there well ahead of the team to get set up for Game Day. Sporting my handy Game Day checklist I showed our four-man loaner crew a demo cubicle, and I explained how the lockers should be set up. I assigned a man to the Gatorade and the water, and I went over the game-day schedule with the guys.

A retired military man, I was intimately familiar with checklists. I certainly relied on my own to perform my job as equipment manager for the Dallas Cowboys. Players and coaches required a ton of equipment, spare parts, and tools. And they relied on me, in the beginning working alone, for all their equipment, uniform, and spare parts needs.

To ensure that I had everything I needed to equip the team, come Game Day, I developed the Game Day checklist shown on page 116 and I relied on it religiously.

My list included itemized specialty gloves, raincoats, and parkas. Each face mask and helmet had to be cleaned before game time, and the helmets had to be safety-inspected. And, if necessary, the stars and stripes emblematic of the Cowboys had to be changed out on each player's helmet.

I never computed it, but I must have dispensed a ton of chewing and bubble gum to the players—another tradition that has endured to this day.

The Will-call Envelope, midway down the first column, was used to hold game tickets for the team's friends and families. Burdensome at first glance, well into my NFL career with the Cowboys, I could have recited that list in my sleep.

I intentionally left certain items off my list like Copenhagen. For a period of years, wide receivers used that sticky stuff on their hands or gloves, Stick-em, to improve their odds of catching the ball. The league eventually banned the use of such substances. Smokeless tobacco fell out of favor too, and its use, although not banned, was kept under wraps.

In 1975, defensive back Charlie Waters was one of many players who was fond of using Stick-em on his hands to ensure a good grip on the ball. In addition to his defensive back position, Charlie doubled as a field goal ball holder.

GAME DAY CHECKLIST

- ________ 78 Special Gloves
- ________ 92 67 Wilson Gloves
- ________ Toilet Articles
- ________ Players' Bags
- ________ Players' Raincoats
- ________ Rolls - Game; Practice
- ________ Game Socks
- ________ Game Pants
- ________ Game Jerseys
- ________ Coaches' Trunk - Shoes; Socks; Shirts; Caps; Jackets; Belts; Pants; Hair Spray; Clip Board
- ________ Coaches' Rain Gear
- ________ Footballs and "T's"
- ________ Tool and Leather Kits
- ________ Equipment Trunk
- ________ Shoes
- ________ Helmets, Cleaned
- ________ Face Masks
- ________ Valuable Bags
- ________ Will-Call Envelopes
- ________ Shoe Trunk - Turf and Grass
- ________ Back-up Game Uniforms and Socks
- ________ Quarterback Shirts
- ________ Electric Pump
- ________ Gloves - Players and Coaches
- ________ Extra Socks (24); Thins (12); Jocks (24); Shorts (XL-18, XXL-18); T-Shirts (20); 1/2 Shirts (20); Wrist Bands
- ________ Half Towels
- ________ Shoulder Pad Strings
- ________ Hot Packs
- ________ Cleats - 1/2 Male; 3/4 Male
- ________ Sweats for Practice
- ________ Chalk
- ________ Bench Location
- ________ Small Blackboard; 2 Big Blackboards
- ________ 24 Game Balls; Extra Box; 2 Brown Ball Bags
- ________ Visitor's Gum and Cups
- ________ Tape for Socks
- ________ Alcohol
- ________ Ball Boy's Vest
- ________ Check Time (Game Day)
- ________ Stop Watch
- ________ Destroyer Shoes
- ________ 22 Thigh Sleeve & Practice Pants
- ________ 98 Franklin Gloves
- ________ 28 Forearm Pad
- ________ Shoulder Pad Bag
- ________ Signs - Home; Official's Room
- ________ Texas Stadium, 438-7676
- ________ Sideline Jacket Trunk
- ________ Jaw Pads
- ________ Parka Trunk
- ________ Cold Weather Gear - Long Johns; Dickies; Mittens; Saran Wrap; Overshoes; Stocking Caps
- ________ Coaches' Parka Trunk
- ________ Shoe Strings - Black & White
- ________ Coffee Maker
- ________ Extra Helmet Trunk
- ________ Extra Rain Gear
- ________ Kicking Net
- ________ Cleat Cleaners
- ________ Number Board
- ________ Shoe and Hat Stretcher
- ________ Drill
- ________ Cup of Junk, bLUE bAG
- ________ Ice Towels
- ________ Gatorade
- ________ Water
- ________ Ice
- ________ Half Time Set-Up
- ________ Extra Locks
- ________ Spray
- ________ Extra Travel Bags
- ________ Girdles
- ________ Steel Inner Soles
- ________ OL Two-Way Tape, 92,77,98,40, 96,90
- ________ Lace OL Jerseys, 67,77
- ________ Winter Jerseys
- ________ Tea
- ________ Assign Lockers for Players
- ________ Call for Weather Report
- ________ Strings for Pants
- ________ Broomball Shoes, 41,47
- ________ Thins - 31,34,41,47 Short - 67,26, 28,42,24,80-S
- ________ Strings - 71,77,78,94,70,95,44,98, 89,40,55,50
- ________ Scissors
- ________ 77 - K and Reebok Gloves
- ________ Nike Gloves - 88,80,24,41,55, 40,47
- ________ Empty Hamper for Return
- ________ 84 - Special Girdle
- ________ 8 - Birch T-Shirt
- ________ 37 - Forearm Pads & Knee Sleeves
- ________ 60 Black Belt
- ________ QB Caddies

Prior to the play, Charlie would run to the sideline, and I would extend a shower towel to him. The fans had no idea the white towel had been soaked in tape remover.

Charlie would extend his hands and wipe the Stick-em off before returning to the huddle. After the field goal attempt, Charlie reached for the insides of his cotton socks—covered in Stick-em—and he was good to go for the next defensive play.

I maintained constant interaction with my counterpart on the home team or the visiting team, and I was responsible for communications between our coaching staff.

I liaised with the trucking guys, the airport loaders, and the laundry support staff, and had to field a constant barrage of questions on the fly:

What was our bench location?

Where did the trucks have to go?

Who was driving that day?

Where was the team spending the night?

What was the weather forecast?

To avoid the obvious nightmare I kept one key to open every lock.

After the movers had unloaded the equipment, and our support crew had put everything in its proper place, I made certain every player had his locker ready prior to game time.

Transcribed on my trusty clipboard was the roster of players and coaches. A back-up blackboard stood at the front of the locker room with the pregame warm-up schedule.

The locker room had a meeting room and a dressing room. The latter was honeycombed with cubicles. I put the offense and the defense on opposite sides of the visitors' partitioned dressing room, and I assigned no more than two linemen per cubicle.

Each cubicle had two benches, and before the players arrived, I made sure each had a game roll placed on his bench. Otherwise known as the game-day sanitary, game rolls consisted of socks, shorts, and jock, all neatly rolled in a white Cowboys T-shirt and taped with the player's number written on the tape.

I put the player's knee, hip, thigh, shoulder, and any specialty pads on his designated bench and his helmet on the floor beside his shoes. Because of the cramped quarters, players often had to hang their clothes on rusty hooks sticking out from the wall.

After the team arrived, I collected the valuables and placed them in night deposit bags, compliments of the Cowboys' bank, Park Cities Bank. I maintained the lockable Valuables Trunk with a catchall bottom and partitions matching the players' numbers.

In addition to wallets, Super Bowl rings and assorted jewelry, the Valuables Trunk was the repository for Coach Landry's priceless Game Plan. After each game, he would hand me that invaluable document, containing all the team's game plays.

Cubicle assignments were based on seniority; I never placed more than two veterans in one cubicle. The rookies, however, had as many as three players per cubicle.

Using a black magic marker, I penned each name and number and displayed it above the appropriate cubicle. Try fitting three oversized Americans and their wardrobes and briefcases in an area the size of a small closet. Consider a pair of 350-plus-pound linemen, and their full complement of equipment, crammed into that same space.

It's not easy.

With eighty-plus players and just one door leading into and out of the Coliseum's dressing room, bedlam reigned. After the game everyone was anxious to get back to the dorms, and whether we won or lost had a lot to do with the team's post-game attitude.

I collected the team's laundry, returned the valuables, and got everything out the door and loaded onto the trucks after the team left on buses.

Before leaving the dressing room, I conducted a thorough inspection of the premises to ensure nothing was left behind. And after I shed my game-day apparel, showered, and dressed, it was back to Thousand Oaks and an appointment with the laundry folks.

Such was the glamorous lifestyle of an NFL equipment manager in my heyday.

During my career at the Cowboys I never lost any player valuables. We did lose a dozen jerseys in the crowded post-game dressing room after our 1975 first-round Hail Mary playoff win against the Minnesota Vikings. In that packed celebratory dressing room, where everyone was bundled up in heavy winter wear to counter the harsh Minnesota cold, an inept thief could have made off with the British Crown Jewels.

And there was the thwarted attempt by those kids in California to steal Cowboys jerseys at Thousand Oaks. Such a record was difficult to maintain given the conditions at many of the stadiums we played in. Antitheft measures often required my sleeping overnight on a cot in away-team locker rooms.

We had security, but security wasn't always secure.

During a game in Miami at the Orange Bowl, Rams equipment manager Don Hewitt lost four helmets, and his offensive and defensive guys had to share headgear during that contest. Don was awarded a Game Ball by his players at the conclusion of the game because of the innovative fashion with which he handled the loss of those helmets.

NFL uniforms fetched a handsome price on the street, a factor that weighed heavily in Dallas team owner Jerry Jones' decision years later to sell old Cowboys equipment at the memorabilia store at Texas Stadium.

PRESEASON

Drive time from Thousand Oaks to LAX took about an hour and a half, and I had to be at the plane two hours before takeoff. I worked with Mr. Bailey to determine flight designation and departure, and I had a crew standing by to load the hampers, footlockers, trunks, video, and football equipment into the cargo hold of the team's special charter.

We played the Rams and the Raiders at their home stadiums. When we played Los Angeles, we trucked the equipment to the Coliseum and bused the players and coaches. When we played Oakland, I flew in the night before and the team flew in the next day—Game Day.

In six preseason contests in 1973, the Cowboys won four games and lost two. We won the first game in Los Angeles, 24–7. We commuted to northern California and lost the second game to Oakland, 26–27. Our third preseason game was in Dallas where we beat New Orleans, 24–14, before an enthused home crowd.

Despite Ralph Neely's contribution, we lost to his former Oilers, 24–27, in Houston. In our fifth preseason contest we won in Dallas against the Kansas City Chiefs, 27–16. And in the preseason finale, we bested the Miami Dolphins at home, 26–23.

The 1973 preseason presented Coach Landry with a preview of the team's tremendous talent and winning potential. Although preseason isn't always the best litmus test for a winning season, that year it was.

We managed to make it through preseason without any serious injuries, and we were off and running toward a regular season winning record.

In retrospect, it wasn't the long hours that wore me out, but the long hours and the traveling back and forth, often at great distances. My first year in training camp, I averaged fifteen hours a day, on the job. I have no idea how many miles I logged.

Beginning with that season, I looked for every shortcut I could find to save time and improve my system. And as equipment manager I did find several. But no matter how hard I tried and no matter how innovative I became, the job always required grueling work, complicated logistics, and long hours. There was no other way around it.

OFFICIALS

More often than not, NFL officials get a bum rap. It is one thing to be a spectator, seated in the stands or before a TV, drinking beer, eating hot dogs, and booing and cursing the decisions made by the officials on the field. It is altogether different working with and knowing the men who proudly wear the NFL official's uniform each Game Day.

I have worked with sports referees and field judges since my early days in Ballinger, and I've met my share of jerks. But for the most part, the officials I knew and worked with in collegiate sports, and later within the NFL, were generally exceptional personalities—professionals like Pat Haggerty, Ben Dreith, and Bob Pool.

Pat and Ben worked Big 8 basketball and football as well as games at the Air Force Academy during my eight years there. Over time I got to know them very well.

Bob lived in California and worked the PAC 10. He and I worked Cowboys scrimmages with the LA Rams and the San Diego Chargers during training camp at Thousand Oaks.

I was responsible for the officials' dressing room set up at Texas Stadium. In 1973, we had five officials—one referee, one umpire, one field judge, one head lineman, and one back judge—assigned to each game by then–NFL supervisor of officials Art McNally.

While they were in Dallas, the NFL put the officials up in a hotel and our video department supplied them with video equipment to study game footage the night before the game. They arrived at the stadium by limousine two to two and a half hours before kickoff, and were escorted by an armed NFL security guard—former FBI special agent Ben Nix.

Prior to the game they inspected the field and game equipment, and the field judge came by our dressing room and informed me of the official time. I was notified two minutes before we left the locker room, and I was notified two minutes prior to the second-half kickoff. I kept a stopwatch to inform Coach Landry of the time remaining.

I was also responsible for taking the required twelve game footballs to the officials to be inspected ninety minutes before the game. The balls were inspected to ensure they were new and that they had the league-mandated 12.5 pounds per square inch of pressure. In later years, the number of footballs required per game rose to twenty-four, then thirty-six.

After the game, the officials were fed sandwiches and drinks. They showered and dressed and left together in a limousine, and their assigned NFL security man stayed with them until they were safely loaded into their vehicle.

Most NFL officials were class acts. They wore suits and ties to and from the game, and the guys I worked with during my career at the Cowboys were quality men, professionals moonlighting as NFL officials. It was a pleasure to have known them.

ROCK 'EM, SOCK 'EM FOOTBALL

During the 1970s the NFL witnessed some of the hardest-hitting, grittiest, down-in-the-dirt, gut-wrenching football ever witnessed before or since. Driven by a conservative, single-minded coach with a tremendous work ethic and like-minded assistant coaches, carried on the backs of athletes of iron will and dogged determination, the Cowboys came to be known, loved, and admired as America's Team.

Somehow the team seemed impervious to the external pressure cooker American society found itself immersed in—the radical, hippie days, an unpopular war, and a country gone mad with the excesses of drugs, sex, and the if-it-feels-good, do-it mindset.

From 1973 to 1985, the Cowboys backed up their claim as America's Team with a phenomenal winning streak. My first twelve years were highlighted with eleven playoff appearances. We played in seven championship games and won three. And we were in three Super Bowl contests, of which we won one—Super Bowl XII.

In 1972, on the heels of our Super Bowl VI win, 6′-4″, 227-pound running back Calvin Hill became the first Cowboy to rush for over a thousand yards. On December 9, 1972, he carried the ball for 111 yards in Texas Stadium in our 34–24 win over the Redskins. Calvin ended the season with 1,036 yards gained and a record 245 carries.

In 1973, Calvin led the Cowboys in rushing with 273 carries and 1,142 yards gained. In receptions he led the team with 32 completions for a total of 290 yards. A Yale graduate, Calvin left the Cowboys in 1974 after six spectacular seasons (11–2–1; 10–4; 11–3; 10–4; 10–4; and 8–6).

In a game with the Redskins at RFK Stadium on October 8, Calvin broke one of his leather shoulder pad straps minutes before kickoff. Most straps are made of heavy elastic or canvas. Calvin asked if I could mend the shoulder strap, and I said that I would try.

In my tool kit, I had a leather punch. I repaired Calvin's shoulder strap in much the same fashion as a farmer might repair a horse's leather reins. I overlapped two and a half inches of the strap and punched three holes to which I fastened the strap with a shoelace.

"Man, I never would have thought of that," Calvin said.

My rookie year, the Cowboys celebrated their one-hundredth victory with a 40–3 drubbing of the New Orleans Saints at Texas Stadium. Coach Landry ended the season with a career mark of 108 wins, 80 losses, and 6 ties to rank ninth on the NFL's all-time winningest coaches list.

We regained the NFL Eastern Division title with a 10–4 season and broke our own NFL record by reaching the playoffs for the ninth consecutive year.

Coach Landry was a constant force set against a backdrop of radical social change. A handful of new players came onboard, added to a core of incredible veterans, infected with a single purpose—winning.

Unaffected by free agency the Dallas Cowboys fielded a rock-solid, hard-hitting powerhouse team loved and admired by Americans, feared and hated by our opponents.

I don't know if there will ever be another Cowboys dynasty like the one I found myself working for in 1973, but for the sake of every American sports fan, and Texans in particular, I sincerely hope there is.

REGULAR SEASON—1973

The Cowboys had a raft of seasoned veterans on the roster that year. Roger Staubach was our starting quarterback and 6′-4″, 214-pound Craig Morton (1965–1974) was his backup. Roger completed more than 60 percent of his passes that year for twenty-three touchdowns. Craig completed 40 percent of his passes for three touchdowns.

Toni Fritsch was the Cowboys' field goal and extra point kicker. In that department, the 5′-7″, 185-pound Austrian converted every one of his forty-three points after touchdown and made eighteen of his twenty-eight field goal attempts.

Our third-string quarterback was an old-guard player, Jack Concannon, who had distinguished himself with the Chicago Bears. Jack's job was to run our opponent's plays during practice, thus preparing the Cowboys defense for Sunday's contest.

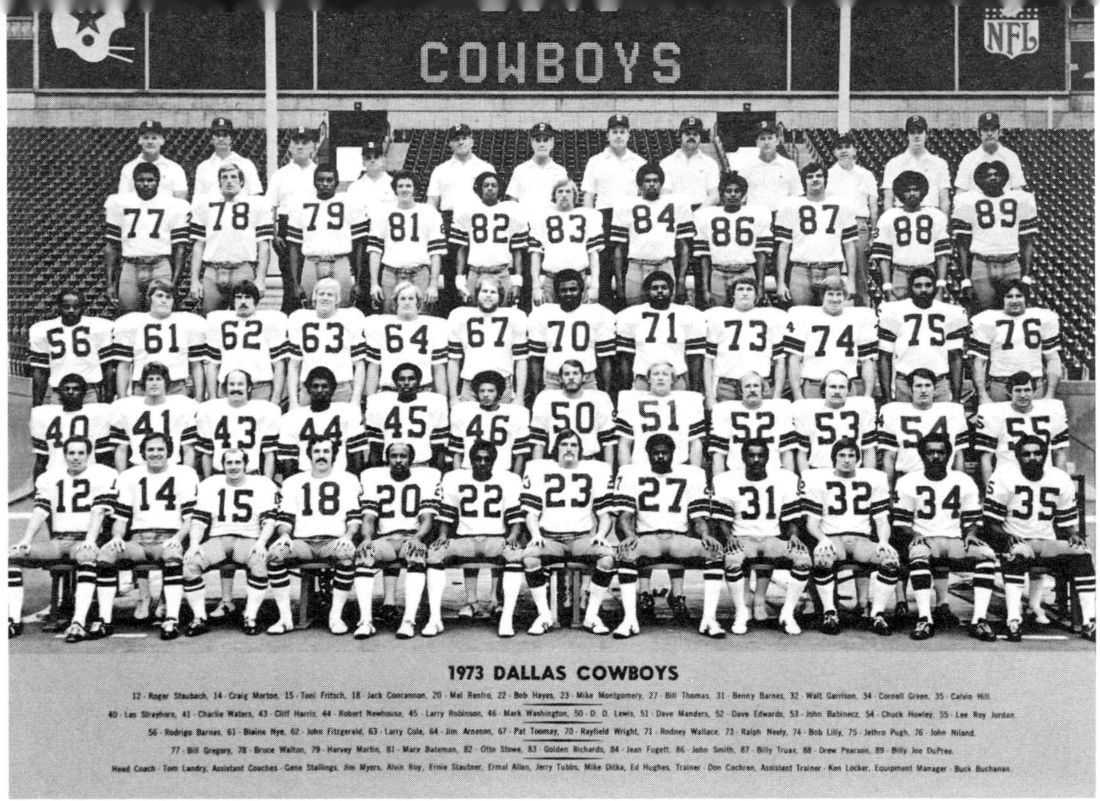

1973 Team Photo

Craig Morton consults with coaches Ditka, Landry, and Myers. Jack Davis looks on.

Yet Jack never played a single down, ending his illustrious career in 1973.

TAXI SQUADS

Getting ready for game one against the Chicago Bears at Soldier Field, I first became familiar with the term taxi squads. At that time, we could suit up forty-six players, but we had fifty-plus on the regular season squad.

Four or more of those guys weren't going to the away game in Chicago. Coach Landry said he'd let me know which ones weren't going so I could pack the appropriate gear.

In the old NFL, tryouts who didn't make the team were retained in their position, but allowed to double as taxi drivers.

Then, if a member of the regular squad got injured and a coach needed to call up a reserve player, he could go to his "taxi squad" reserves.

Coach Landry held his last-minute meeting with the players on Saturday before leaving for the game. And after the meeting, he went to the field for his routine jog.

About that time, my truck had pulled up to load our equipment. I still did not know which players would not be accompanying us to Chicago, so I improvised by jogging a lap with Coach Landry.

Realizing his mistake, he apologized for his memory lapse, "Man, I forgot all about that, Buck." As we ran, Coach Landry provided me with the names of the players who were not going to Chicago.

As luck would have it, Coach Landry's memory was as keen as his coaching and that slip was one of his rare omissions. That oversight proved imminently beneficial for me as Coach stayed in tip-top shape, jogging a mile and a half nearly every day.

THE DRAFT AND FREE AGENCY

Years before in 1965, the Cowboys drafted 5′-11″, 185-pound wide receiver Bob Hayes (1965–1974) in the seventh round. There were those who thought Brandt was crazy and that he was taking a huge chance drafting the collegiate sprinter. Others, however, believed Brandt was a genius and that the deal was a sure bet for the Cowboys.

Bob was the U.S. Olympic gold medal sprinter from Florida A&M who electrified crowds at the 1964 Olympics. He won the gold medal in the 100 meters, tying the world record. Bob anchored the men's 400-meter relay team, ensuring victory for the Americans, setting a new world record and earning another gold medal.

Robert Lee Hayes made the conversion from track and field's "World's Fastest Human" to the NFL's World Champion Dallas Cowboys in 1972. In his rookie season at the Cowboys, Bob gained a thousand yards and scored a dozen touchdowns, leading the NFL with an average of 21.8 yards per reception. Because of Bob's blinding speed, our opponents had to radically alter their defenses, forever changing the game of football.

In 1973, Bob racked up twenty-two receptions and gained 360 yards, placing him sixth on the Cowboys' receiving stats *that year* behind Calvin Hill, Billy Joe DuPree, Walt Garrison, Otto Stowe, and Drew Pearson. The 1973 Cowboys had that much depth!

Most athletes have one nickname, if they're lucky. Bob had three that I'm aware of—Bullet, Speedo, and the World's Fastest Human—a credit to his remarkable talent.

At Dallas the Bullet set a number of records that remain unbroken.

Yet Bob was denied a berth in the Football Hall of Fame.

In large part due to drug and alcohol-related problems and a brief, drug-related prison term, Bob was passed over for induction into the Football Hall of Fame and the Cowboys Ring of Honor, disheartening the Florida speedster and his loyal fans. To his credit, owner Jerry Jones reversed the Ring of Honor decision, admitting Bob in 2001.

After Bob retired, he lived in Dallas for several years before returning to Jacksonville, Florida. I was with him on the sideline when he was admitted to the Cowboys Ring of Honor, and we spoke briefly before he was inducted.

Bob was a gentleman and one of this country's premiere athletes. He died at the untimely age of fifty-nine on September 18, 2002. During the short time we worked together, I came to know Bob as a humble loner. He wasn't outgoing in the locker room, and his closest friend appeared to be defensive lineman Jethro Pugh.

Hoping for a repeat performance of Bob Hayes' brilliant transition from track and field to football, Dallas drafted world-class sprinter John Smith (1973) from UCLA, with the intent of converting the track star to wide receiver.

Smith had a condition known as "alligator arms."

When he ran across the middle of the field, for fear of taking a bone-jarring hit to the midsection, Smith would tuck his elbows in at his sides to protect his ribs. With those arms tucked tight, he lacked the mobility necessary to catch passes. More interested in protecting his body than catching the football, he had speed but lacked the fearlessness necessary to become a great receiver.

Walt Garrison (1966–1974), the 6′-0″, 205-pound running back from Oklahoma State University, is a Cowboys' cowboy; a native of Lewisville, Texas; and a Dallas veteran of nine seasons.

A real practical joker off the field, Walt was all business when it came to the game of football. Walt is a shining example of a low-maintenance player and a guy who played through the pain.

In the 1973 Divisional Playoff Game against Los Angeles at home, Walt suffered a severe contusion to his right shoulder. In the next playoff game, the 1973 Championship Game versus the Minnesota Vikings in Dallas, I used a redundant pad—a donut-shaped pad with the center cut out that fit beneath Walt's regulation shoulder pad.

Time and again, Walt went out and made the same bone-jarring blocks, only to get up gritting his teeth. It was obvious from my sideline perspective that he was hurting, but Walt went back and did it again—and again.

We lost that game, but not from lack of effort or intensity on Walt Garrison's part.

I heard TV commentator Don Meredith (1960–1968), former Cowboys quarterback and Garrison's long-time friend, say about Walt, and I paraphrase, "Walt Garrison is probably the best fullback in the NFL. If you have fourth and two, you give it to Walt and he'll get four. If there is a fourth and three, give it to

Walt and he'll get four. If there's a fourth and six, give it to Walt and he'll get four."

A two-time All-American from Southern Methodist University, Meredith led the Cowboys to their first winning season and first NFL Championship Game in 1966.

That same year, "Dandy Don" was named NFL Player of the Year. Don played in two Pro Bowls, and after his retirement, was added to the Cowboys Ring of Honor in 1976.

Puddin', as Walt Garrison was nicknamed by his teammates, a handle reportedly given him by Cowboys linebacker Dave Edwards (1963–1975) from Auburn, had a knack for whittling wood. More than once I watched Walt use an old pocketknife, whittling on a stick for hours, only to stop after he had carved an unbroken chain from that piece of wood.

To this day, Walt Garrison is a fan of sharp, well-made knives. During this book's writing, I joined Randy White at his Frisco, Texas, barbecue restaurant to commiserate about old times. During lunch, Walt walked in with a friend and it was like old times at the Cowboys.

Walt had commissioned Randy to make him a knife, and Randy had to go to his pickup truck to retrieve a handful of samples—seven knives in all.

When he returned to the crowded restaurant, the former Cowboys defensive tackle (Randy still works out, and he doesn't have an ounce of fat on him) turned quite a few heads in the restaurant. At fifty-two, I believe Randy could still suit up in the NFL.

Like my Dad, Walt rode the rodeo circuit, and rodeo fans throughout North America adored him, waving to the rodeo star as he appeared atop his faithful steed in the parades and rodeo performances Walt loved to participate in.

The ruggedly handsome Garrison appeared in commercials, especially endorsements for the smokeless tobacco we both used. I was always careful to keep a fresh can of Copenhagen around just in case Walt ran out.

Walt rushed 105 times for 440 yards and six touchdowns my rookie season.

Dave Edwards must have had a knack for nicknaming players. As the story goes, he gave kicker Mike Clark (1968–1971, 1973) from Texas A&M the dubious handle "Onside," when Clark missed a Dallas onside kickoff altogether.

Dave proved to be a calming influence on this rookie equipment manager.

In a regular season game at Texas Stadium, he asked my help in repairing his face mask. I nervously bobbled the screwdriver and screw in my feeble attempt to reattach the face mask to No. 52's helmet, when he asked, "Buck, are you a little nervous?"

"It shows?" I asked.

Dave laughed and told me all eyes were on No. 12, Roger Staubach, not on me.

6′-3″, 208-pound Cornell Green (1962–1974) was an All-Star basketball player from Utah State who never played a down of football before coming to the Cowboys. Cornell was one of Mr. Brandt's success stories—a basketball player turned successful NFL defensive back.

For all his talent Cornell was quiet and laid back in the Cowboys' locker room. When I came onboard, Cornell, like so many of the other 1970s-era Cowboy greats I came to know and admire that first year, was nearing the end of a successful NFL career.

HIGH-MAINTENANCE AND LOW-MAINTENANCE PLAYERS

The decade of the 1970s was characterized by low-maintenance players, independent guys who seldom asked for help. On the other end of the spectrum were those rare high-maintenance players who needed help doing most everything, whether it was modifying their equipment or just getting packed for a game.

We didn't have many high-maintenance players in my day, but those we had kept us busy. Cornell Green was a good example of a low-maintenance ball player. He'd bring his own shoes, always one size too small, and cut slits along the side to make room for his toes.

Today, I would have to call a vendor and special order custom footwear.

6′-6″, 251-pound Cowboy guard Bruce Walton (1973–1975) is the brother of Bill Walton, the UCLA/NBA basketball great. Bruce wasn't as tall as Bill but that hamburger was big. Bruce was a tremendous athlete and another example of a low-maintenance Cowboy player—dependable, neat, fiercely independent, and resourceful.

Most receivers didn't require high maintenance. 6′-3″, 219-pound tight end Jean Fugett (1972–1975) verged on being the exception. Jean complained to me one day about returning his game roll with the socks turned inside out. I told him that if he would turn the socks right side out when he gave them to me, I might return them that way. Despite his quirks, Jean was a solid guy who made nine receptions and gained 168 yards in 1973.

Receivers like their ankles taped tight, and their shoes to fit snug. Defensive backs are no different. Charlie Waters liked his shoes and ankles wrapped tighter than a drum. It certainly made sense. Defensive backs, tight ends, running backs, and receivers must make hairpin moves, and require solid ankle support.

Charlie gained 112 yards from five interceptions my rookie year. And he rang a lot of our opponents' bells in 1973 and in the years that followed. Despite insisting that his ankles be tightly taped, Charlie Waters was far from being a high-maintenance player.

Fullback Robert Newhouse (1972–1983) from the University of Houston was a low-maintenance player with a high-maintenance physique. At 5′-10″, 202-pounds, Robert was built like a fireplug. His low center of gravity made it tough for defenders to bring him down.

When we went to camp that first year his size ten-and-a-half grass shoes were adequate, but Robert's 4-E shoe width presented me with a dilemma. Our shoe manufacturer had cleated shoes that wide, but in the Astro Turf footwear the widest it offered were 3-Ds.

Robert approached me in the locker room one day, holding his shoes at arm's length. "Buck," he said, "my shoes are too tight."

Thanks to Walt Garrison, I was familiar with a method of stretching shoes that always worked. Walt's method was simple, yet ingenious: Pour a bottle of alcohol into the undersized shoe and wait a few seconds before pouring it out. Put the Hoke & Ball Stretcher in and stretch the shoe.

Walt swore the shoes would never return to their original shape. And who was I to argue with success, or Walt Garrison? In the end, we used Walt's shoe-stretching process and Newhouse couldn't have been happier.

Newhouse was one stocky dude, with thighs as big around as my waist, and I had to special order his pants. But he wasn't a high-maintenance player by choice, only by reason of his extraordinary physical dimensions. My rookie year Robert dazzled the fans with 436 yards on eighty-four carries.

Just because a player required extra help did not make him high maintenance. Running back Emmitt Smith (1990–1996) and fullback Daryl "Moose" Johnston (1989–1996) liked to change pants at halftime. EM and Moose, as the players were nicknamed, saw their share of the action, and their pants showed it. They had their shoes taped, so changing their pants was labor and time intensive.

Before the game, I put knee pads and thigh pads in another pair of game pants and hung them in their lockers. When the guys came in at halftime, I helped them strip off their soiled pants and don the fresh pair. Half-time wardrobe changes provided them scant minutes to hear Coach Jimmy Johnson's comments before returning to the game.

6′-1″, 225-pound center/linebacker D. D. Lewis (1968, 1970–1981) was one tough hombre from Mississippi State who was selected NFL Man of the Year in 1981.

D. D. is credited with having played in the most play-off games—twenty-seven—an NFL record. Our first game in Chicago, he made a bad snap on an attempted field goal, and Charlie Waters bobbled the ball. Toni Fritsch made the conversion, and we beat the Bears 20–17.

The following Monday, D. D. was back at linebacker, and the Cowboys recalled 6′-2″, 250-pound center Dave Manders (1964–1966, 1968–1974) to replace him. D. D. served as a backup to Chuck Howley until Chuck left in 1973. He also played on special teams.

When the Cowboys drafted D. D. in the sixth round in 1968, he had two linebackers ahead of him, players who had been taken in the third round. As D. D. likes to tell it, "One of them got drafted into the Army, and I made the Cowboys squad through the backdoor."

D. D. wasn't sneaking in the backdoor that preseason game we played Pittsburgh.

"Pittsburgh had run a great screen play with three linemen in front of Franco Harris, and I was the only (Cowboys) player between them and the goal line. I drove under the linemen and made a literal shoestring tackle on Franco. How lucky can it get!"

Skill, not luck, stopped Franco Harris on that down.

After retiring, D. D. and I both remained in Plano, Texas, where we occasionally reminisce about the good old days.

Defensive lineman Jethro Pugh (1965–1978) was nicknamed "Buzzy."

When the 6′-6″, 250-pound tackle came in to sack a quarterback, he came in with his arms flailing like a buzzard's outstretched wings. Years later, as a rookie equipment manager, I heard tales of Jethro's misfortune at Green Bay's Lambeau Stadium.

Buzzy was lined up head to head on the Cowboys' goal line with Green Bay guard Jerry Kramer at the infamous Ice Bowl on December 31, 1967. Famed Packers quarterback Bart Starr scored the winning touchdown with a quarterback sneak over Jethro's position. The football classic ended in a score of 21–17, Green Bay.

Jethro was fond of saying, "I wish they would stop showing that play on the highlights. They're going to make me a legend in my own time."

Jethro had this huge head, size eight or better.

One day, he complained, "My neck's killing me, Buck. Have you got a collar I could use?"

"I'll put one on for you," I told him.

"No, that's okay," he said. "Give it to me, and I'll take care of it myself."

Jethro was another low-maintenance player.

6′-5″, 260-pound defensive lineman, Bob Lilly, a.k.a. "Mr. Cowboy" (1961–1974), is a glowing example of a low-maintenance player. Due to his outstanding collegiate play at Texas Christian University, where he was picked not once, but twice for All–Southwest Conference, Bob was understandably the Cowboys' first draft choice in 1961.

After his first year with the team, Lilly was named Rookie of the Year, and in the succeeding years of Bob Lilly's brilliant football career, the towering defensive lineman set the bar for aspiring players.

Bob was the first to be named to the prestigious Ring of Honor in 1975, and he was the first Cowboy inducted into the Pro Football Hall of Fame in 1980. Bob was a seven-time All-Pro player, named to eleven Pro Bowls—a club record. But he never let his fame go to his head—or did he?

Lilly had a peculiarly shaped head, and his helmet rode low on his forehead. No doctor of anatomy, I knew when a player's equipment was not functioning as it should. I could see it registered on his face, hear it in his comments to the trainers—or find out firsthand, when he approached me with a frown in the locker room.

Often I took preemptive measures during my regular inspections of the team's equipment. Working on Bob's helmet, I noticed an old knee pad wedged into the lining, at the top.

"That thing really work?" I asked him.

"You kidding?" Bob replied, "I couldn't be happier."

When I had a defensive back needing a similar helmet adjustment, I concocted a rig like Bob's, wedging a trimmed knee pad inside the player's helmet. Some time later, 6′-1″, 203-pound defensive back James Washington (1990–1994) walked into my office and asked, "What'd you do to my helmet, Buck? It fits great!"

When James went to the Washington Redskins, their equipment manager, Jay Brunetti, called and asked what I had done to make Washington so happy.

During halftime, in a game played at Texas Stadium against the Philadelphia Eagles on November 23, 1975, Bob Lilly was recognized for his outstanding career. In fourteen years, Mr. Cowboy had not missed a single game.

Bob was and still is an institution in Dallas.

We played the Denver Broncos at Mile High Stadium on December 2, 1973.

The weather during the first half was beautiful. But weather in Denver, at more than five thousand feet elevation, can change in a heartbeat. Before the game ended, it began to snow.

The Broncos fumbled late in the game, before fifty-one thousand screaming fans, and Bob Lilly and Cliff Harris dove to recover the fumble. Bob secured the ball on the ground, as Cliff came barreling in. The ensuing collision resulted in Lilly's torn hamstring.

We won that game 22–10, but Bob didn't suit up again for several games. He played the 1974 season, but I think that injury speeded up Mr. Cowboy's retirement.

Bob Lilly was one of those 1970s players I wish I had gotten to know better.

During the brief time I worked with him, I came to know Bob as a gentleman's gentleman. He was always down to earth, never puffed up. Bob Lilly was a once-in-a-lifetime defensive lineman, a real joy to work with, and a truly decent human being.

We had a throng of reporters at the locker room door after that game in Denver. As was his custom, Coach Landry allowed the press ten minutes before letting them in.

We finally got loaded up, and the snow was coming down in buckets. We had a Denver trucking company at the time, and the windshield wipers on their truck didn't work worth a flip. When we finally got to the airport, the players had already boarded, but the baggage handlers took another thirty to forty minutes to load the equipment on the plane.

When I boarded, the first person I saw was Coach Landry. He was glaring at me, squinting in that customary fashion that only meant one thing—he wasn't happy. But he never said a word to me about being late to the airport.

Mr. Schramm was seated beside Coach, and he too was squinting at me.

Gil Brandt was seated not far away, and when I locked eyes with him, seeking some relief from the scowls of the others, he glared at me too.

I never said a word about the truck or the new company's performance to anyone.

The coaching staff, Mr. Schramm. and Gil Brandt flew first class.

The players flew coach, and I always sat at the rear of the plane, on the aisle, to ensure I was the first off the aircraft to meet the equipment handlers in Dallas.

Before taking off, goody bags filled with snacks were passed out, and after we were airborne, a delicious meal was served.

Days later, during a practice session at Forest Lane, I had an opportunity to speak with the Cowboys' pilot, Wally "Sky King" Nicholson. Wally was a frequent sideline visitor, and he and I spoke often. I mentioned the squinting episode aboard the flight, and Wally explained the reason for my universal unpopularity that night.

"We were the last plane out of town, Buck. In fact, the tower stopped arrivals and departures because of icing shortly after we took off. Mr. Schramm and Coach Landry were sweating bullets that we might not get out of Stapleton. And we barely did."

What constitutes a high-maintenance player? Much of it, from my experience, has to do with his mindset. Does he work hard? Does he complain and whine? Does he play through the injuries? Is he a team member—or an individual out for his own gain?

Today's high school prospects are often high-maintenance players before they ever reach college. When they enter the college ranks, they receive more coddling, only at a higher level. And when they reach the pros, they are high-maintenance players expecting everyone to cater to their every whim. What a shock it must be for such athletes when, for whatever reason, they are forced from the game early in their career.

NEAT GUYS AND NOT-SO-NEAT GUYS

6′-5″, 255-pound defensive lineman Bill Gregory (1971–1977) from the University of Wisconsin was the exception to the rule.

With Danny Noonan

Typically, defensive players had the messiest lockers in the league. But when I walked by Gregory's locker, everything was neat and tidy and in its proper place.

Bill was smart and low key, not at all flamboyant.

He had extremely high cheekbones and a very narrow face.

After several games, I noticed that his jaw pad, the leather padding that kept the helmet off the player's face, was not providing Bill maximum protection.

In a storage cabinet at the back of the equipment room at Forest Lane, I kept an assortment of helmet parts. Digging through the old equipment, I found an unworn Wilson universal jaw pad that could be used on either the player's right or left jaw.

Bill immediately expressed his satisfaction.

"It's much more comfortable than the old pad, Buck," he said.

Defensive lineman Danny Noonan (1987–1992) from the University of Nebraska was one of the messiest players I've worked with. A reporter from the *Dallas Morning News* interviewed me in the Dallas locker room and asked to see the Cowboys' messiest locker. Without hesitation, I immediately escorted him to Noonan's locker.

When the story aired, Noonan's wife called me and lamented, albeit humorously, "Danny's that way at home!" You would have to have seen Noonan's locker—everything was crammed in and piled sky high to the rafters—dirty socks, shorts, sweats, and shoes.

Bill Gregory and Jethro Pugh were among the tidiest players I've known. After practice, each picked up his dirty laundry and deposited it in the nearest clothes hamper.

Thomas Henderson's locker was always in total disarray. One day Thomas lost his car keys and we emptied his locker before locating the keys in one of his shoes.

Thomas had an aisle locker that we had to pass on our way to the field.

"I would always say something to Coach Landry as he walked by," Thomas reminisced. "Nothing rude, but I wanted to say something interesting like, 'What's going on, Coach?' or 'What's up, dog?' Of course, he never answered me and he never stopped. Coach was no-nonsense, and far too serious. Thirty years later, I recognize Coach Landry for being what he was—the greatest man I have been around."

My all-time messiest player's pick would have to go to Cowboys offensive guard Larry Allen (1994–2005) from Sonoma State. God love ya', Larry, but your locker was the worst I've ever seen. But then, the franchise doesn't pay Allen to be neat and tidy. To the contrary, Larry is paid to open holes, protect his quarterback, and annihilate defenders.

And Larry does that better than most.

I really liked tight end Billy Truax (1971–1973). Billy was a good kid from Louisiana State. I fell in love with him when we played the Raiders in preseason.

The baseball stadiums we played in never seemed to have enough locker space, and we always had to double up at Oakland. I had to hang several of the rookies' uniforms on pipes sticking out from the wall, and shoes were scattered on the floor.

Billy came in, and he must have seen the look on my face as I was sizing up the mess. "Welcome to the NFL, Buck," he said. "Hang with us, dude, it's gonna work out."

Thanks, Billy, it sure did.

ROOKIE HOPEFULS

My first year in the NFL was marked by an influx of sizzling rookie prospects that bolstered the team's seasoned, battle-hardened squad of veterans.

From Tulsa, there was free agent wide receiver Drew Pearson (1973–1983), and NFC Pro Bowl tight end Billy Joe DuPree (1973–1983) from Michigan State.

From East Texas State there were defensive end Harvey Martin (1973–1983), who shared Most Valuable Player with Randy White against Denver four years later in Super Bowl XII, and guard Bruce Walton.

We had a pair of short-timers: linebacker Rodrigo Barnes (1973–1974) from Rice and center/guard Jim Arneson (1973–1974) from Arizona, and by way of the University of Hawaii the Cowboys signed wide receiver Golden Richards (1973–1978).

Golden's rookie year was highlighted by twenty-one punt returns for 139 yards, six receptions for 91 yards and one rushing effort for a gain of 2 yards.

We went to the Division Playoffs that year with a 10–4 record. Although we had lost to the Rams during the regular season, 31–37, that first playoff game against LA, played on December 23, 1973, at home, went to the Cowboys 27–16.

We were pumped, but our enthusiasm and our season were nearly over.

On the heels of the victory over the Rams, we lost the NFC Championship Game in Dallas to the Vikings 10–27, sending Minnesota to the Super Bowl.

In the fourth quarter of that losing effort, a controversial Minnesota field goal infuriated Dallas fans and Tex Schramm in particular. Loyal Cowboys fans were devastated by that loss, and there were those who vented their anger at the officials.

Officiating may have played a role in that loss and the team's failure to advance to the Super Bowl, but isn't that what everyone says when they lose the big game?

I know Mr. Schramm considered that possibility, because he swore the football swerved outside the uprights on the Vikings' field goal attempt.

Because of that play, Tex pushed the NFL to raise the uprights ten feet in case there were any doubts *next* time. And Mr. Schramm was successful in getting the rule changed.

The official who called that losing effort against the Vikings also missed a fumble, according to Schramm, and that official never worked another Cowboys game.

Tex Schramm had considerable sway within the ranks of the NFL. He was at the Los Angeles Rams before coming to the Cowboys, and his public relations man in LA was a gentleman by the name of Pete Rozelle.

After Tex Schramm came to Dallas, the NFL posted a vacancy for the position of commissioner, and Mr. Schramm was instrumental in helping Rozelle land the job. As long as Rozelle was NFL commissioner, Schramm's vote carried weight.

The Cowboys had won Super Bowl VI in 1971, and had lost the NFC Championship Game to the Redskins in 1972, the losing effort that denied us a trip to Super Bowl VII.

After our NFC Championship loss to Minnesota, some of the wind was knocked out of our sails. We had the impetus and the resources to come back and enjoy another winning record, and the team dynamic was much the same my second season as it had been my first. But 1974 proved to be less than stellar for the Dallas Cowboys.

THE PRO BOWL

At the conclusion of my rookie year, after losing the championship game to the Vikings, Coach Landry and his staff were selected to coach the National Football Conference (NFC) team against the American Football Conference (AFC) team in the AFC-NFC Pro Bowl in Kansas City.

Cowboy coaches who accompanied Coach Landry to that Pro Bowl contest were Myers, Allen, Ditka, Hughes, Stallings, Stautner, and Tubbs. Noncoaching staff included trainer Don Cochren and myself. Cowboy players in that contest were Calvin Hill, Lee Roy Jordan, John Niland, Mel Renfro, and Rayfield Wright.

During his career at Dallas, Mel Renfro was selected to ten consecutive Pro Bowls. Calvin Hill attended four, Lee Roy Jordan went to five, and John Niland and Rayfield Wright both attended six consecutive Pro Bowls.

Tight end/tackle Rayfield Wright (1967–1979) from Fort Valley State was one of Coach Myers' protégés. Myers converted Rayfield from tight end to offensive tackle.

Always a sharp dresser, Rayfield might have been mistaken for a CEO.

At Coach Landry's memorial funeral service, Rayfield recounted a story that took place during his rookie year. Lined up opposite All-Pro Los Angeles Rams defensive end Deacon Jones, Rayfield was reminded of his rook status by the imposing veteran. When the ball was snapped, Deacon blew right by him without Rayfield laying a finger on him.

Rayfield looked at the bench and noted Coach Landry staring at him, squinting.

Prior to leaving for Kansas City, I asked Don Cochren, "What do I do? I've never been to a Pro Bowl."

Walt Garrison and Rayfield Wright block for Calvin Hill

Don answered in his typical, reassuring manner.

"Buck," he said, "It's no different than training camp. Just pack the players' stuff and the coaches' stuff, and we'll be alright."

I packed and shipped the team's gear to Kansas City a week early.

We were scheduled to leave Dallas on Saturday morning for Kansas City, but hours before our departure Coach Landry called me at home.

"Buck, the league has advised me there will be drizzle and near-freezing conditions in Kansas City all week. There's no way we're practicing there. We're going to San Diego."

My heart sank.

I reminded Coach Landry that our equipment was in KC.

"Can you get the stuff to San Diego?" he asked.

I told him I'd make some phone calls and see what I could do.

The Kansas City Chiefs equipment manager, Bobby Yarborough, was a trusted friend, and I told Coach Landry that I'd call and see what Bobby could do to bail us out.

"Great," Coach Landry said, "Then our equipment will be there Sunday night."

Coach Landry's remark wasn't a question as much as it was a statement of fact. Sunday night was the following evening. The team wouldn't practice till Monday, so I had little time to get everything shipped from Kansas City to the West Coast—and set up.

"Yes, sir," I said.

"Good. Then I'll see you in San Diego Sunday," Coach Landry said.

"Okay, coach," I said.

I had Bobby's work number, so I immediately placed the call and relayed my concern. "Only thing we can do," he advised, "is ship everything to California air freight. Don't worry about it, Buck. I'll take care of it. I'll have it shipped out today."

"Thanks, Bobby," I said. "I owe you big time."

"Damn right," he said.

I left Dallas Saturday morning for San Diego with Don Cochren. The two of us checked into a hotel there, and I caught a cab to the Chargers' field.

Bronco Hennek, another good friend, was the assistant equipment manager for the San Diego Chargers. When I got there, I told him, "I need a special favor, Bronco."

"You name it," he replied.

"I need our stuff picked up at LAX *tonight*," I said.

Bronco acted as if I'd asked him for a ride across the street.

He told me not to sweat it.

As it turned out, our stuff was late getting into Los Angeles International Airport. Fortunately, the drive to the stadium in San Diego, with traffic, was only about four hours.

Bronco dropped by my hotel early Sunday morning with our Pro Bowl equipment. He woke me up and we hightailed it to the Chargers' stadium.

By 4:00 p.m., we had the NFC gear set up for the first practice session on Monday.

It's amazing what a man can accomplish with just a little help from his friends.

We were blessed with balmy weather all week, and the Chargers took great care of us. That first afternoon in San Diego, I changed out the face mask of the Los Angeles Rams' great defensive lineman, Merlin Olson. The darned thing was all busted up.

"Hey, Buck," Merlin asked later, "what did you do to my face mask?"

I told Merlin I had changed his face mask because it was broken.

"Well, let me have it back," he said, "I liked it that way."

Some of the old guys in the NFL preferred to do things their way.

When we got to San Diego, I had my first opportunity to compare other NFL teams' equipment with ours. It gave me a shot of confidence when I saw firsthand how well maintained our equipment was compared to most.

After that Pro Bowl, I formed a new sense of pride in our equipment program.

I had changed 6′-6″, 265-pound Cowboys tackle Ralph Neely's face mask earlier that year, about midseason. The rubber had been worn down, and the metal on the side was exposed. I changed it, but I kept the old piece, just in case.

Ralph later asked, "What in the world did you do to my face mask, Buck?"

"That exposed metal could have cut someone," I told Neely.

"Why do you think I rubbed it on concrete?" he asked.

Without hesitation, I located the original piece and put it back on for him.

A lot of NFL equipment managers wait till a player asks or complains before they change a piece of equipment—not me. But I learned early never to throw anything away.

Ralph was a great offensive tackle known for holding. In the mid-1970s, NFL defensive linemen voted him the best holding offensive lineman in the league.

In a practice session at Thousand Oaks, the towering Neely got into a fight with a Cowboys rookie defensive lineman who made the mistake of pulling off his helmet and squaring off with the veteran. Ralph chastised the rook, "If you're going to get into a fight, keep your helmet on!"

With just one practice each day, I had all morning to get organized and make sure our NFC San Diego locker room was squared away. The league had taken care of our hotel accommodations, our flight arrangements, and our equipment transportation from Dallas to San Diego to Kansas City, so I had relatively few hassles to contend with.

During that week, I was able to interact with a squad of veteran players like Roman Gabriel, John Hadel, Merlin Olson, Jack Youngblood, and Dave Wilcox, professional athletes, celebrities I might only have seen on TV, but for my job.

I have never been an Eagles fan, but Gabriel was all right—personable and a lot of fun to be around.

Hadel was your typical quarterback—serious and always steeped in thought. He was considerate, too. On the flight from San Diego to Kansas City, John brought me a tip from the players—five hundred dollars he collected.

Wilcox was shy and retiring, but he was one mean motor scooter on the field. I've not seen a harder-hitting player. He could knock the opponents' jocks off, but he was always happy and relaxed in the locker room.

With Bob Lilly hurt, Merlin Olson found himself playing in the 1973 Pro Bowl. Merlin was a joy to be around, when he wasn't grousing about my fixing his face mask.

One of the youngest players in the group, Jack Youngblood could not have been happier to be playing in that game. Jack made the Pro Bowl when Vikings defensive lineman Carl Eller decided not to play.

Youngblood made my day when he said, "Buck, yours is a hell of a good looking dressing room. It might even top Don's." Rams Equipment Manager Don Hewitt was my inspiration, and Jack made my day when he offered that compliment.

By week's end, after a successful six days of melding a disparate band of talented athletes into a cohesive football team, Coach Landry blew the whistle, and we reversed the order. I got everything packed and ready to be shipped aboard a charter flight to Kansas City, and I made plans for our 1974 Pro Bowl appearance in Arrowhead Stadium.

We left San Diego for Kansas City on Saturday, and we landed there around four that afternoon. Feeling pretty good, I kicked back for the bus ride to Arrowhead, without a doubt the cleanest stadium I have ever visited.

Arrowhead Stadium was absolutely beautiful.

The turf was perfect and our Kansas City crew couldn't have been more helpful.

But the weather was less than accommodating—a chilly 30 degrees.

Kansas City Chiefs equipment manager Bobby Yarborough, was there with his guys to help us unload, and we immediately began setting up for Game Day.

After we had finished setting up the NFC team's lockers, I caught a cab to the hotel to check in. At the front desk, I identified myself as Buck Buchanan.

The young hotel desk clerk stridently disagreed.

"No, sir. You're *not* Buck Buchanan. I *know* Mr. Buchanan."

"There must be a mistake," I insisted. "I'm Buck Buchanan with the Cowboys."

We bantered back and forth for several minutes, my insisting who I was, and the desk clerk insisting I could not be who I claimed to be—Buck Buchanan. I even showed the guy my Texas driver's license. As it turned out, Kansas City had an All-Pro defensive lineman, Buck Buchanan, and *that* Buck is in the Chiefs' Ring of Honor.

After a curious crowd had formed in the lobby, the manager was alerted and the red-faced desk clerk pitifully relented: "I'm so sorry, Mr. Buchanan."

I wasn't in my room long before I fell asleep atop the bed, fully dressed. The hotel's wake-up call rousted me out of bed at four the next morning. It was Game Day, January 20, 1974, and according to the weatherman on TV, it was a chilly 35 degrees.

By streetlight, I could make out the light drizzle that dampened the streets outside my Kansas City hotel room. The wintry conditions persisted throughout much of the day, and the AFC bested our NFC squad 15–13 in a lackluster offensive showing.

The game was marred with fumbles, our NFC squad suffering a record-breaking ten, of which the AFC recovered four. Buffalo Bills star/AFC running back O. J. Simpson had a good day and set a Pro Bowl rushing record with nineteen attempts.

Miami's Garo Yepremian scored all fifteen of the AFC's points, to include a well-placed, undisputed field goal at the end of the game. But as Garo followed through with his game-winning boot, Dallas/NFC defensive back Mel Renfro hit him, and Yepremian went down like a shot. Yepremian broke Pro Bowl records with his record-setting five successful field goals—a record that has endured to this day.

Mel helped Garo up, and he escorted the dazed kicker to the AFC sideline. That day Fro showed the world what a class act he is, Yepremian was voted the game's Most Valuable Player, and equipment manager Buck Buchanan ended his rookie season.

ENDORSEMENTS

In my humble opinion, media exposure and commercialization have reduced today's game of football to a giant swap meet. Everything from T-shirts and caps to pennants and dolls is sold. In 1973, most players wouldn't even wear a baseball cap.

Several years into my career, around the late 1970s, the manufacturers got into the act and started paying players to wear caps, shoes, shirts, and jackets emblazoned with their logos. Because of the lucrative endorsements, Cowboys players would come up to me on the sideline and ask for a particular piece of clothing to make a few extra bucks.

Shoot, players could wear a baseball cap and make five thousand dollars, so it is no wonder caps became so popular. Today, most receivers and quarterbacks wear caps because it's customary—not only because they're paid the big bucks to advertise someone's product.

You can't blame the players. My first Super Bowl game in Miami, Super Bowl X, two manufacturers paid a couple of our guys a reported five thousand dollars to wear their shoes.

During that Super Bowl contest, defensive end Harvey Martin hailed me on the sideline. Harvey was grinning and waving this shoe, its separated sole flapping.

"Buck, I sure hope you have my old shoes packed away somewhere."

Harvey was limping on one shoe.

"Harvey, I sure do," I said. "Why, what happened?"

Harvey held up one of those expensive shoes with the sole torn and dangling. He was flapping that expensive shoe at me, as we stood there laughing like a couple of idiots.

Manufacturing endorsements got out of hand before the NFL stepped in and established NFL Properties. I remember Buffalo Bills quarterback Jim Kelly wearing a certain jacket on the Bills' sideline that Kelly was reportedly paid ten thousand dollars to be seen in.

When NFL Properties came into existence, the league wrested control of all endorsements, and after that, only NFL-recognized deals approved by NFL Properties were condoned. There was big money to be made, and the league was not to be denied.

Hey, in the '60s and '70s, the Super Bowl was a super contest, a clash of titans, often played in an uncovered stadium, on a muddy, snow covered, natural-grass field.

Today's game is more civil, and football has taken a back seat to commercial enterprise. Tents are set up everywhere, and vendors hawk every trinket and piece of junk under the sun. At halftime entertainers make noise, that stuff that passes for music, jump around on a platform at midfield, shoot off fireworks, and expose themselves to fans.

Don't get me wrong, I love good music and I like to be entertained. But more than anything, I love the game of football. Given a choice, I'll take the game that was played in the 1970s over today's game, with all its commercial hype, any day of the week.

Call me old-fashioned, because I am.

FIGHTS—EVEN THE BEST FAMILIES HAVE THEM

During my career, I probably witnessed a half dozen NFL fights—off the field. Customarily I intervened lest anyone get hurt. Most fights were little more than a pair of oversized kids venting. After it was over, the players went their separate ways.

Heck, the guys were used to bashing each other's heads in on the field, so a little scuffle seldom amounted to much. There were, however, the rare occasions when a fight meant a bruised ego and hard feelings, or worse yet, termination of an athlete's career.

In 1977, we had an offensive lineman and a defensive back get into a fight in the Forest Lane dressing room after practice. The altercation took place beside Ed Jones' locker.

As always, I left the equipment cage to break it up, but before I could get there, the defensive back, a muscular macho guy, had the offensive lineman pinned on the floor. The fight, if you could call it that, was over shortly after it began.

Ed just sat there quietly watching the spectacle. He used massive amounts of baby powder after showering, and after the fight was over and the combatants had moved on, Ed sprinkled a liberal dose of baby powder on the floor. With that massive, gnarly lineman's index finger, Ed drew the outline of a human body.

Intrigued with the scene, I inched closer for a better look.

I asked him, "Ed, what the heck are you drawing?"

"Where the body was," he said with a grin. Ed had drawn a chalk line like those murder scenes on TV. Off to one side, he had drawn another, smaller circle.

"And what's this?" I asked.

"The guy's wig," Ed chuckled.

The offensive player wore a wig, and although he kept his coif secured during the brief scuffle, Ed illustrated his take on the action—on the floor—in baby powder.

Henderson vs. White

The fight that had me most concerned was the clash between 6′-2″, 223-pound linebacker Thomas "Hollywood" Henderson and 6′-4″, 240-pound defensive lineman Randy "The Manster" White.

Both men were about the same age, less than two months apart, with Randy being the oldest. Perhaps with their age equivalency, their impressive athletic skills, and their relative strength, a confrontation between the pro athletes was inevitable.

This happened during the off-season in 1978.

Conditioning Coach Bob Ward (1976–1989) was in the middle of the action when things heated up on the Forest Lane practice field between Thomas and Randy.

A practitioner of the Filipino martial arts, a brilliant mind who was interested in training the whole athlete, Coach Ward had divided the team into pairs, each duo fencing with elongated sponge wands.

The purpose of Coach Ward's exercise was to improve the players' speed and reflexes, but for Thomas and Randy, the pugilistic contest became personal. When Thomas bested Randy and landed several well-placed blows, Randy had had enough.

In seconds, Randy had Thomas on the deck, at which point, Coach Ward separated the players and sent them to the showers.

When Thomas and Randy got to the locker room, there was a lot of bad-mouthing and pushing still going on. And neither man was backing down an inch.

I was in the equipment room when I heard the noise. And by the time I managed to work my way to them, the players were chest to chest, cursing in each other's face.

Spittle was flying, and both men's carotids and nostrils were flared. I could see this was no ordinary shouting match and events were fast getting out of hand.

In seconds I was beside the warring gladiators as I attempted to wedge my left shoulder between their heaving chests. All the while, neither seemed aware I was there.

The cursing and spitting had reached a crescendo when I roared, "Be cool, you guys!" I mustered all the bravado I could, with my slender frame wedged between a quarter-ton of beef, and roared once more, "Now, break it up!" Fortunately, Thomas and Randy backed off cursing, and went their separate ways.

By his own admission, Thomas is a very lucky man despite a rocky start: "I was the luckiest guy. . . . I was the No. 1 draft choice; I got off drugs; I won $28 million on the lottery and I played in three Super Bowls—and won one. And I have changed my life."

Staubach vs. Longley

It was clear there was trouble brewing in paradise. There was Roger Staubach, and there was Clint Longley. The two Dallas quarterbacks could not have been more starkly contrasted.

Roger was the starter until he got hurt, or until he was ready to leave. He was the franchise quarterback. That fact was indisputable. At best, Clint knew he'd always play second or third fiddle to Roger, because we were always getting new backup quarterbacks.

Clint had to know his life span was likely to be short at the Cowboys.

Roger was conservative and mature. He didn't cuss or drink. He didn't run around, and he was, and still is, married to the same girl. He was a solid all-American.

Clint was single. He'd been married and divorced. He was a party animal.

Roger was an older, mature Vietnam veteran and a decorated naval officer.

And lest we forget, that *was* the period known as the radical '70s.

Clint gravitated to the wild side.

Roger was . . . well, just Roger.

Clint attended his third and last Cowboys' training camp that year.

Competition between quarterbacks can be good, but Clint and Roger's beef was personal. Roger didn't like the way Clint came down on their receivers, and he insisted Clint was attaching blame to the receivers and not where it belonged—to himself.

On the practice field, scuttlebutt has it Roger came down hard on Clint. I wasn't there to witness the initial exchange, but several players later confirmed what transpired.

Clint wisecracked back to Roger, and Roger said something to the effect that "If you want to settle it now, Clint, let's step off the field into those bushes."

As the story goes, Clint turned and walked away.

We were at our Thousand Oaks dressing room with those tiny, basketball-style lockers. Not having personally witnessed the exchange the day before, I still had the feuding quarterbacks dressing side by side. I knew they didn't care for each other, but I didn't know the extent or the depth of their hostility.

The next morning Cowboys starting quarterback Roger Staubach and backup quarterback Clint Longley both came in early.

Clint quietly sat down.

I was in the equipment cage, looking out at the dressing room. The two quarterbacks were in front of me, slightly to my left. Clint sat down on Roger's chair and started putting on his uniform in front of Roger's locker.

Whatever the reason, Roger leaned over and mumbled something in Clint's ear. From where I stood, the expression on Clint's face said it all—he was definitely pissed off.

Clint jumped up and delivered a powerful right hook to the side of Roger's head.

It was a good lick, and the force from the blow sent Roger's head smashing into the corner of the wall. Several linemen were dressing nearby, and they immediately jumped into the fray.

Randy White grabbed Clint, and at that point, the fight was all but over.

Roger was escorted out of the building to the K Building, where the training room was located. The trainers had no more than put stitches in Roger's head, when Roger wanted to go back over and get Clint. When Roger left the dressing room, Clint collected his suitcases, headed out, and went back to Corpus Christi, Texas, never to return.

A reporter from the *Fort Worth Star Telegram* asked me about the incident the following day. "I didn't see a thing," I said, "and I don't have a clue what happened."

Clint Longley left the Cowboys without any notice, breaking his contract. The next year, he came back to football and played with the San Diego Chargers a short time.

SEASON'S END

1973 was a roller coaster ride for the team and the team's new equipment manager. For me, it represented a once-in-a-lifetime experience, accentuated with a Herculean work effort and a tremendous learning curve I managed to work through.

America's Team had been favored to regain the NFC Championship title wrested from us by the Washington Redskins on December 31, 1972, but that was not to be. And a year later, at home, we were unable to get past the equally determined Minnesota Vikings.

Without knowing it then, the mid-1970s, especially 1974–1975, marked a major turning point in the history of the Dallas franchise—a gradual changing of the old guard.

Midway through that season, I came home one night and crashed on the sofa.

Jerry joined me in our living room.

"Looks like you've had a bad day, Tom," she said.

"Mom," I said, "I've had a bad year, and it's only half over. I don't know if I'm coming or going. And I'm still not completely convinced we made the right decision."

"I can understand that, Tom," she said, "the kids and I hardly ever see you."

That midseason conversation with Jerry was the first of many heart-to-hearts we shared concerning my NFL career. There were days in 1973 that I seriously considered throwing in the towel, but I've never been a quitter. Somehow the Buchanans survived that very difficult year without a divorce and without my quitting the Dallas Cowboys.

Thus ended my rookie year.

Shortly after the Kansas City Pro Bowl in 1974, during the off-season, I began to think it hadn't been all that bad after all, that I might tough it out another year. Mr. Schramm and Coach Landry were terrific to work for, and in February I got a call from Coach Landry.

Jerry answered the phone. "It's Coach Landry," she whispered.

"Good season, Buck," he said.

Coach Landry paused.

"Buck, we're increasing your pay."

I was in shock. We'd had second thoughts about the job, and now I was getting a pay increase. I couldn't believe it. By season's end, in addition to my annual salary, my Pro Bowl attendance check, and my playoff bonus, I was being handed a pay increase!

Suddenly, those negative feelings about the long hours, the separation from family, and the pressure of meeting Coach Landry's rigid schedule paled. I had been flying by the seat of my pants, but by year's end, the job had become easier, almost routine. By 1974, I had graduated to the big time. Buck Buchanan was no longer a rookie.

5

THE 1970s—A FOOTBALL DYNASTY

The Dallas Cowboys were unrivaled in talent and popularity during the decade of the 1970s. We lost games, we lost conference titles, and we lost Super Bowl contests. But without a doubt, America's Team was the preeminent powerhouse of the decade.

We had our ups and downs and our disappointing losses, but Coach Landry's squad, Mr. Schramm's "Boys," and Mr. Brandt's draft offerings had greater universal appeal than any other team in the NFL—bar none. There are those who will disagree.

1974—VETERAN SEASON

At the outset of the year, I was feeling pretty good about my status on the team. I was, after all, a veteran with a winning season beneath my belt. But as training camp careened into preseason and preseason into regular season, my enthusiasm waned.

The Cowboys traded quarterback Craig Morton (1965–1974) to the New York Giants and veteran linebacker Chuck Howley (1961–1973) retired after a phenomenal thirteen-year career at Dallas.

Running back Calvin Hill (1969–1974) left for greener pastures and the World Football League (WFL), and tight end Billy Truax (1971–1973) left after two seasons.

The Cowboys managed to win half our preseason games, and we beat the Atlanta Falcons our first regular season opener. But we lost the following four contests.

Contrary to expectations, we suffered through a ho-hum year with an eight-and-six record, marking the first time in nine seasons the Cowboys had not made it to the playoffs.

On the positive side of the ledger, we had a terrific first-round draft choice in Tennessee State's defensive end, Ed "Too Tall" Jones (1974–1978, 1980–1989).

Ed is 6′-9″, but he often wore platform heels in public, making the 265-pound lineman even more menacing. Contrary to news reports, I don't believe Ed ever minded the nickname "Too Tall." He had a penchant for flashy clothes and jewelry, but Ed was quiet in the locker room, seldom saying much—unless the subject involved boxing.

Ed Jones loved boxing. When and where he became obsessed with the sport, I do not know. He left the Cowboys for two years to try his hand at the pugilistic art, but returned to Dallas and football after a lackluster career as a pro boxer. Ed was strong and tall and he had a good reach, but his boxing acumen never compared to his football skills.

Three defensive greats—Toomay, Cole, and Lilly

In 1974, I had more time to interact with the players and coaches and observe the action on the field from my sideline perspective. Even then, however, I was not consumed with the actual play-by-play as much as I was with the way the players moved and the way they carried themselves. After the game I would have friends ask me about a particular play, and I would have to honestly say, "I never saw it. I was too busy."

I was ever alert to any sign of trouble—whether with the players' equipment or with the players themselves. In 1974, I was no longer reacting, rather I was anticipating.

One thing I observed about new draft pick, Ed Jones, was that he was neat both on and off the field. When the defense came out of the game, Ed joined us on the sideline.

We had two benches, one for the offense and one for the defense. There were tables in the middle with the Gatorade, towels, and the coaches' communications gear.

Ed grabbed a towel and sat on the bench. He pulled his helmet off and wiped out the inside. He wiped his face and arms, and undid his pants. Ed tucked in his jersey, nice and neat, pulled his socks up, drank water or Gatorade, and waited to get back in the game.

In uniform, Ed Jones was the archetype for every pro football player. His dimensions were ideal, and Ed's tailored uniform was immaculate. In lockstep with Mr. Schramm's uniform and player appearance expectations, Ed Jones was a model player of gigantic proportions. Both on and off the field, Ed "Too Tall" Jones was an inspiration.

Candlestick Park—Another One of Those Stadiums

After our big win in Atlanta (24–0), the Cowboys suffered four back-to-back defeats, at the hands of the Eagles (10–13), the Giants (6–14), the Vikings (21–23), and the Cardinals (28–31).

Bad as it was to have lost those contests, they were close games that could have gone either way.

On the heels of those losses, the team gathered steam and tacked on three impressive wins, redeeming our reputation against the Eagles (31–24), the Giants (21–7), and the Cardinals (17–14). Again, other than the drubbing of the Giants, they were all close games.

Our ninth regular season game was played against the San Francisco 49ers in Candlestick Park on November 10, 1974, and fifty thousand fired-up California fans were there to root on their team.

A huge baseball fan, I was disappointed with Candlestick. The stadium was in disrepair, and the fans could not have been more raucous. Candlestick is a baseball field, and the dressing room was small, certainly inadequate for NFL players.

In several cases, I had to put three coaches in one locker. The coaches' room lacked showers, and the players and coaches had to shower together. It was a mess.

The stadium was old and dirty. It was some distance from the field to the dressing room, which meant the twelve-minute half-time intermission was cut short, denying the players, coaches, and trainers much-needed time to regroup before the second half.

Candlestick had that baseball Astro Turf that didn't run from sideline to sideline, as is customary at stadiums designed for football, but at 45-degree angles *across* the field.

To make it worse, the stadium is below sea level, on San Francisco Bay, and the surface is always damp. For the players, the footing was horrible. Still, we managed to eke out a 20–14 win.

The Mad Bomber

Clint Longley joined the team in 1974. Nicknamed "The Mad Bomber" by his teammates in college, Clint sometimes lacked control passing and managing his temper.

Yet Clint was one heck of a player who came to the Cowboys by way of Abilene Christian College. At ACC, Clint had a reputation for having touchdowns called back.

Clint was the master of the Belly Series, a quarterback fake where he would take the snap, bury the ball into his gut, and fake handing the ball to a running back.

When the running back smashed through the line and was tackled, the referee whistled the play dead. Meanwhile, Clint had the ball, and he often scampered into the end zone untouched. That play was so good, it faked the defense and the college officials.

As a Dallas Cowboy, Clint was fond of going on rattlesnake hunts in Oklahoma. One time he brought a live rattlesnake in a paper sack into our dressing room. Otis Jackson, my assistant and fields caretaker, had been bitten by a rattler years before.

Otis came back to the cage, wide-eyed.

"Buck, that crazy Clint brought a rattlesnake into the dressing room."

I went back, and confronted Clint.

The telltale bulge in the sack was writhing.

"You know you can't have a snake in the dressing room."

"Okay, okay," Clint said, "I'll get rid of it."

As Clint left, he ran into Cowboys' safety Cliff Harris.

Cliff asked Clint, "What have you got in there?"

"A rattlesnake," Clint replied. I think Cliff hated snakes about as much as Otis.

He took a step back. "Get that thing out of here," Cliff yelled.

Clint said, "I'm going."

I don't know what Clint did with that rattlesnake, but he put the empty sack in Cliff Harris' car. After that day's workout, when Cliff was ready to go home, he showed up in front of my desk.

"Is that crazy Clint gone, Buck?"

"He left several hours ago, Cliff."

"That son of a bitch left that sack in my car, and I don't know where the snake is."

"I like you, Cliff," I said, "But I'm not looking in your car for some snake."

Cliff said, "Me either."

Cliff caught a ride home that night, and he left his car in the parking lot.

Short Timers

That year we had a promising center, Jim Arneson (1973–1974).

The team was in need of a good snapper, and Jim was both a good blocker and a talented snapper. A resident of Phoenix, Arizona, he attended the University of Arizona.

For some reason, Jim just never came on that strong, and his stay with the Dallas Cowboys was short-lived.

At one of our reunions, I asked Jim, "Do you still have that star?"

"You're never going to let me live that down, Buck," he said.

In a 1974 home game, the Cowboys were backed up to our 5-yard line, and we had to punt. Jim snapped the ball so hard it went over the punter's head and hit the wall, knocking one of the Cowboys' stars off.

In retrospect, the incident was funny, but it didn't do much for Arneson's career.

That year the roster remained virtually unchanged from my rookie season. Coach Landry wasn't one to change, and we didn't have free agency, so turnover was minimal.

Efren Herrera (1974, 1976–1977) from UCLA, another soccer-style kicker, replaced my pal, Toni Fritsch. A pair of running backs, Doug Dennison (1974–1978) from Kutztown State and Charles Young (1974–1976) from North Carolina State, joined the team, and running back Larry Robinson (1973) from Tennessee retired.

Linebackers Louie Walker (1974) from Colorado State and Ken Hutcherson (1974) from Livingston State and guard Gene

Killian (1974) from Tennessee came aboard. All would be gone by year's end. Linebacker Calvin Peterson (1974–1975), another rookie from UCLA, would be gone after just two seasons.

Longevity was rare, enjoyed by only a handful of truly great and durable players—men like defensive backs Mel Renfro, Dennis Thurman, and Charlie Waters.

Every year there were those who were Cowboys one season and history the next. Curiously, defensive backs often had shorter NFL life spans than kickers.

Running back Dennis Morgan (1974) from Western Illinois was nicknamed "Strawberry" because of his hair color. He was a good player, although eccentric.

In a game in Philadelphia, he walked out on the field laughing—to himself.

Dennis strayed into the Eagles' end zone and got tangled up in the extra-point netting. Our guys had to free Dennis from his embarrassing entanglement.

Dennis returned the Cowboys' longest punt return—98 yards against St. Louis on October 13, 1974, for a touchdown—but was a one-year man, a phenomenon not that uncommon in the NFL.

The Cowboys had a schedule board hung on the wall in our dressing room listing every regular season game. In 1974, Bob Lilly and Dave Edwards were standing before that board, discussing the likelihood of our winning—or losing—to teams on that season's schedule. Their discussion centered on "must wins" and games the Cowboys could afford to lose—and still make it to the playoffs.

Coach Landry overheard the speculative discussion and called me into his office.

"I want that board changed out today, Buck," he said.

Coach didn't like losing, and he sure didn't like his players entertaining any thoughts *but* winning. By the end of the day, the board displayed Sunday's opponent and our previous wins and losses, but every opponent for each game beyond Sunday was blank.

By year's end, after the first truly unremarkable season record since the first six years of the franchise, a number of the older veterans were poised for retirement. And in the months to come, the Cowboys witnessed an exceptional draft and a major rebuilding.

1975—DOWN AND DIRTY

Before the season began Bob Lilly, Cornell Green, and Walt Garrison retired and Bob Hayes was traded. We won ten games and lost four that year with twelve sizzling rookie prospects—the Dirty Dozen. And we made it to Super Bowl X.

On December 28, 1975, the world witnessed Roger Staubach's Hail Mary Pass to Drew Pearson, culminating in the Cowboys' 17–14 Divisional Playoff win over the Vikings in Minnesota. Almost everything we did that year turned out right with the exception of the season finale Super Bowl X loss to the Pittsburgh Steelers.

The key to our success during the 1970s, in my humble estimation, was clearly defined job assignments. The big dogs knew what was expected of them, and they all excelled at what they did. President and General Manager Tex Schramm did what franchise presidents and GMs do best—expertly manage the affairs of the team.

Head Coach Tom Landry was committed to leading his players and coaching staff. In football parlance, Coach Landry was a player's coach. Again, that's what Coach did best.

And Vice President and Director of Player Personnel Gil Brandt with his scouting department was always ready for Draft Day. Together, these three linchpins sustained a well-oiled

Cowboys machine, a winning operation unrivaled throughout the 1970s—and the 1980s.

Coach Landry spent much of his time in the Cowboys' War Room during the draft, and he had his input when it came to drafting players. But Brandt had no equal insofar as compiling and assimilating draft information.

Brandt's success was due in part to his pioneering efforts in cataloguing talent via the computer and his charismatic association with coaches, trainers, and equipment managers. As a result of his efforts, we were light years ahead of the NFL draft pack.

And with a successful draft in place, Cowboys players were unlikely to jump ship.

But there were exceptions—those who left or who were asked to leave.

NFL football can be cold and unforgiving, as defensive back Rolly Woolsey (1975) from Boise State learned during a home game against the Green Bay Packers.

On October 19, 1975, we were ahead with less than two minutes remaining to be played. Rolly was on the Cowboys' return team when he fumbled a Packers punt and Green Bay regained possession. The Packers converted a field goal, and we lost a game that we should never have lost—17–19.

Woolsey was traded before the 1976 season. Another rookie that year, Thomas Henderson, recalls an earlier kickoff return play involving Woolsey. "Rolly handed me the ball on our 3-yard line, and I ran 97 yards for the score. After crossing the goal line, I slam-dunked the ball over the goal post."

One rookie survived, and one was cut.

Had the play gone the other way, might Woolsey have remained?

Brandt was masterful at securing basketball players and seeing them converted into winning football players. Most of his selections were tall and strong, and all of them exhibited superior athletic ability. Defensive back Cornell Green from Utah State

Percy Howard

was one such Brandt pick who set records at Dallas during his thirteen-year tenure with the team.

Free agent wide receiver Percy Howard (1975) from Austin Peay made the leap from hoop ball to wide receiver and kickoff return man.

In our first preseason game against the Rams, Percy returned a kickoff and got clobbered. When he stumbled to the sideline, his helmet cockeyed on his head, Percy said, "Man, it's rough out there Buck." To which I replied, "Those are just rookies."

But Percy was tough and determined, and he wore the Cowboys uniform one year and scored a dramatic touchdown in Super Bowl X against Pittsburgh—immortalized on film in the Hollywood classic *Black Sunday*. He was muscular and he had powerful legs, but Percy damaged his knees and ended his career running pass patterns.

That year marked our first Super Bowl contest against the Pittsburgh Steelers. It was also a banner year for Gil Brandt's scouting department culminating in the best draft in NFL history with twelve of the finest rookies in memory—before or since.

Those eleven draft choices, and one free agent, came to be known as the Dirty Dozen. They were Burton Lawless (1975–1979); Randy White (1975–1988); Thomas Henderson (1975–1979); Mitch Hoopes (1975); free agent Percy Howard (1975); Scott Laidlaw (1975–1979); Randy Hughes (1975–1980); Bob Breunig (1975–1984); Kyle Davis (1975); Pat Donovan (1975–1983); Herb Scott (1975–1984); and Roland Woolsey (1975).

In the beginning, the Dirty Dozen were just kids playing their hearts out. With time, the twelve were integrated into a veteran Dallas powerhouse, ensuring a 10–4 season and an appearance at the Super Bowl.

Herb Scott was a quiet guy and an outstanding blocker. His rookie year, I picked him to make the team. Mr. Schramm was emphatic about having new stars put on the Cowboys' helmets when they became marred. Herb Scott's helmet required a pair of new stars every other day, which meant he was putting that helmet on somebody. I remember remarking to trainer Don Cochren that "Herbie" would definitely make the roster as "I had never changed so many stars before for any one player."

During the decade of the 1970s, the Cowboys played Super Bowl V in Miami (1970) where the Baltimore Colts beat us 16–13. The following year (1971), we won Super Bowl VI in New

Preston Pearson

Orleans, beating the Miami Dolphins 24–3. We missed getting into Super Bowl VII (1972), and I was hired in 1973.

We made it to the 1973 NFC Championship Game, losing in Dallas to the Vikings, 10–27. And in 1975, after the Dirty Dozen made their NFL debut, we made it to Super Bowl X, losing a heartbreaker to the Pittsburgh Steelers, 17–21.

Despite a rocky 2–4 preseason, the Cowboys were well on their way.

We picked up 6′-1″, 208-pound running back Preston Pearson (1975–1980) from the Pittsburgh Steelers, and we were contenders once more. But Roger Staubach was tackled in our December 13 game against the Redskins and suffered bruised ribs, and in only his second year with the Cowboys, backup quarterback Clint Longley came into his own.

In the NFL, play calls were called with odd and even numbers. Preston Pearson was a great third down receiver but he had difficulty adapting to the Cowboys' play calls.

Every team in the NFL, other than Dallas, used even numbers to designate right offensive plays and odd numbers to designate left offensive plays.

Because Coach Landry was a former defensive player and coach, he saw things in reverse when it came to play calling. Consequently, when Cowboys plays were called, they were called in the reverse fashion of what Pearson was accustomed to at Pittsburgh.

His first year at Dallas, I used a black magic marker to write "O" on Preston's white right wrist band—designating odd numbers—for right movement, and "E" on his left wrist band—designating even numbers—for left movement.

By the end of the year, Preston was familiar with Coach Landry's system and we eliminated the "O" and the "E" wristband markings altogether.

We were in the running with expectations of going to the Super Bowl but found ourselves behind in our mid-December contest at Texas Stadium with the Redskins. Compounding our problems, Roger Staubach got knocked out and had to leave the game.

Clint came in and threw a touchdown pass that put us ahead. He made several completions, to include one for more than 60 yards, and we defeated the 'skins 31–10.

There were those who said Clint didn't know enough about our offense or the Redskins' defense to foul up that game. The truth is, he saved our bacon that day and put us that much closer to Super Bowl X. The game was nationally televised, and that pivotal win, and Clint's brilliant performance, catapulted him into the national limelight.

Following our win over the Redskins, Roger remained sidelined. Our next game was against the New York Jets in Shea Stadium, another baseball field with a tiny locker room.

Coach Landry preferred that his quarterbacks locker in close proximity to him.

Clint was slated to start the game against the Jets, and Roger's injury ensured that he had to sit it out. So I put Clint in a locker by himself not far from Coach Landry's locker, and I put Roger, who was not playing, in a locker with a kicker.

Roger had been around since 1969. *He was the man.* But when he came in and saw the set-up, with him doubled up, he looked at me and shook his head. "All you have to do around here is get hurt—you lose your starting position and you get doubled up."

On a cold and nasty overcast day, Clint Longley led the Dallas Cowboys to a 31–21 win over the crowd-favorite New York Jets. Winning that game catapulted us into the 1975 NFC Divisional Playoffs a week later against the Minnesota Vikings.

We played the Vikings in Metropolitan Stadium on December 28, 1975, in a game that marked a milestone in my career—I nearly busted my butt on the sideline.

Metropolitan Stadium was another one of those baseball stadiums with an open dome. The field was covered prior to kickoff, and the sidelines had space heaters, but the weather conditions were trademark Minnesotan—cold and miserable. But despite the sorry weather, I was pleasantly surprised to see that the field was actually in pretty good shape.

The Cowboys won that contest before forty-eight thousand fired-up fans in a fiercely contested 17–14 game, immortalized by Roger Staubach's Hail Mary Pass to Drew Pearson.

Roger provided the following firsthand narrative of that famous play:

"The Cowboys went to Minnesota as a wild card after making the playoffs as the underdog. We hung in there all through the game and all of a sudden, the game was almost over and the score was Minnesota 14–Dallas 10. We got the ball on our own 20-yard line and got into a fourth and 18. I threw a corner pass that Drew Pearson caught just as he was hit and couldn't get his feet inbounds. It was a referee's judgment call—in our favor that Drew was pushed out of bounds. He made the first down with thirty seconds to go! Drew was obviously out of breath, so I asked him, 'What can you do?' He responded, 'Well, I don't want to do anything right now, I want to rest.' So I threw the ball off to Preston Pearson, but he dropped it. If he had caught it, the time probably would have run out—but he dropped it.

"Immediately, I said, 'Drew, what if everybody blocks and you just go deep and I'll try to look off Paul Crause?' He said, 'Okay,' and that was the play! It was just 'Drew Pearson—Go Deep!' I pumped to keep Crause from double-teaming over with Drew. He took a step towards where I pumped, and then I came back and intentionally underthrew Drew. I guess I pumped too long because I didn't get it there, but Drew caught it on his hip, and I got hit right as I threw it. At the same time, Nate (Wright) slipped and something happened, but Drew caught it and went in the end zone, and we won 17 to 14!

"After the game, the press asked me, 'What were you thinking about when you threw the ball?' I replied, 'I closed my eyes and said the Hail Mary!' That was the official coining of the term 'Hail Mary.'"

I concocted a bodysuit—a combined rib and shoulder pad system that afforded Roger's bruised ribs more protection and allowed him greater freedom to pass. And Captain America did what every Cowboy did in the early days—toughed it out and played through the pain.

After the game, the media swarmed that tiny locker room like locusts. I couldn't walk around or pick up after the team, much less pack the trunks for the return trip home.

Between the players, the throng of media, and guests, I could barely move.

There were a lot of unfamiliar faces there that day—friends, family members, associates, and hangers-on—who swelled the ranks on the sidelines and filled that tiny locker room to overflowing.

The mood was ecstatic as guests, in winter coats, streamed in from the cold.

Our next game was in Los Angeles against the Rams, which meant warm weather.

I was relieved, because when I got back to Dallas and conducted my equipment inventory, I was missing twelve cold-weather jerseys. There had been a souvenir-collecting frenzy in that Minnesota locker room and all those heavy winter coats had made it easy.

Every NFL team has warm-weather and cold-weather uniforms. Lucky for me, the jerseys that came up missing after Minnesota were our winter uniforms, and we were headed to a balmy NFC Championship Game in southern California. Normally I can't stand to lose anything, but I was thrilled that we had only lost the cold-weather jerseys.

I reported the loss to Mr. Bailey in an After-Action Report when we got home. "What the hell is an After-Action Report?" he yelled. "We got a war going on, or what?" I didn't write any more action reports, and in the next eighteen years, I never lost another jersey.

We returned to Los Angeles, and before eighty-five thousand fans soundly defeated a very tough Rams' squad 37–7 for the 1975 NFC Championship. Running back Preston Pearson (1975–1980) caught three Staubach touchdown passes that day, and the victory catapulted Dallas into Super Bowl X contention against the Pittsburgh Steelers in Miami.

On the sideline, when it was certain that we would defeat the Rams, I asked the more experienced Don Cochren, "How do I prepare?"

Don said, "Treat it just like you would a mini–training camp."

And I did.

After the win over the Rams, I had two weeks to prepare for Super Bowl X, and the players had a light practice week before reporting for Super Bowl training in Florida.

The Cowboys held training camp at Yankee Stadium in Ft. Lauderdale, Florida, home of the Yankees' spring training camp. The staff there could not have been more helpful, and they had everything set up when I arrived. The Orange Bowl's field was in good shape, but the dressing room had no lockers. At least we had plenty of space.

In an earlier game, the AFC Oakland Raiders played the Pittsburgh Steelers for a chance to meet the NFC champion in the Super Bowl. Stick-em was a pasty substance used by receivers and running backs to secure a better grip on the football. It wasn't officially sanctioned, but it wasn't exactly illegal. Yet most teams used the stuff liberally.

In the 1975 AFC Championship Game, the Raiders' center attempted to snap a Stick-em–covered ball to his punter. The snap was bad, and the Steelers recovered on the Raiders' 20-yard line and subsequently scored. That bad snap, compliments of the Stick-em, sent the Steelers to Super Bowl X where Pittsburgh later defeated Dallas 21–17.

Security in Miami on Game Day was poor to nonexistent. To get from the dressing room to our truck, security had to line the route to allow us to navigate the phalanx of crazed Miami fans. Mounted police scoured the grounds, alert to signs of trouble—and there was plenty to be found.

If we dropped anything, it was gone before it hit the ground.

We lost to the Steelers before a crowd of eighty thousand screaming fans. It was a terrific game that would have been even better had we won. Cowboys punter Mitch Hoopes had a punt blocked in the second half, and the Steelers scored a safety. That safety was the turning point and Mitch never suited up again as a Cowboy.

The Pittsburgh fans were incredibly rowdy that day, some would say out of control. Mr. Schramm's secretary was there, as were the players' wives and my wife, Jerry. Many of the team's family and friends were there—aboard three crowded buses.

The police escorted the buses to the stadium. Jerry said that when they got there, the Pittsburgh fans ran up to each bus, cursing the Dallas contingent. She said they were the worst she had ever seen. I don't know—I've been to Pittsburgh and they can be crazy.

Super Bowl X served as the backdrop for the Hollywood movie *Black Sunday* that many of the Cowboys, including Coach Landry and Staubach, unwittingly starred in. The irony of that Steelers win and the film's dark title was not lost on the Dallas faithful.

At the conclusion of Super Bowl X, "Miami's Finest" allowed us thirty minutes before the media was allowed into our locker room. If there was an upside to that loss, that was it. Crime aside, Super Bowl X on January 18, 1976, was an outstanding contest.

Immediately after the game, we had three players scheduled to fly to New Orleans to play in that season's Pro Bowl in the Louisiana Superdome—quarterback Roger Staubach, free safety Cliff Harris, and tackle Rayfield Wright. I was responsible for getting their gear packed and loaded onto a bus—no easy task given the throng of fans.

Roger was upset when I volunteered to help him pack for the game in New Orleans. "Buck, I can't believe we just lost the Super Bowl, and you're asking to pack my stuff for the Pro Bowl." I left for five minutes, returned, and packed his bags by myself. My son Bucky and his cousin, Mike Cole, helped me with the other Cowboys' bags.

A handful of key Cowboys veterans left in 1975, but we were blessed with an influx of incredible rookie talent, thanks to Gil

Brandt. Despite a season many believed would be a rebuilding year, our momentum took us close to the top of the NFL charts.

The dynamic that had begun in 1975 with the acquisition of twelve sensational rookies, the Dirty Dozen, propelled Dallas to an unprecedented eight winning seasons.

Those seasons were highlighted by six Divisional Playoff titles ('75, '77, '78, '80, '81, and the '82 Super Bowl Tournament); three NFC Championship titles ('75, '77, and '78), three Super Bowl bids (SBX, SBXII, SBXIII), and one Super Bowl win—Super Bowl XII—on January 15, 1978.

1976—THE YEAR THAT SHOULD HAVE BEEN

The season record for 1976 was an impressive 11–3, and the games we lost were close. Two of those losses came at the hands of the St. Louis Cardinals and the Atlanta Falcons, contests determined by fewer than seven points. Our largest point disparity came at the hands of the Washington Redskins, 14–27, in our last regular season game.

On December 19, we suffered a heartbreaking Divisional Playoff loss to the Los Angeles Rams, 12–14, in a real nail-biter, ending our season and any Super Bowl hopes.

That year, Clint Longley punched Roger Staubach and left the team for good, and the Dallas Cowboys drafted cornerback Aaron Kyle (1976–1979) from Wyoming.

I didn't notice the social changes within the Cowboys that were sweeping the country in the early 1970s. Even at the end of that decade, it wasn't obvious. I guess I was too busy.

I've heard about hippies, but we didn't have many in Texas at that time.

Thomas Henderson heads for the end zone

A year earlier, in 1975, I did learn a thing or two about interracial relations.

As Thomas Henderson recalled during the development of my story, "My rookie year as a Cowboy, I had a big Afro haircut. I exited the showers at Forest Lane, wrapped in a towel, and approached the equipment cage.

"'Buck,' I said, 'you have Vitalis and all the other hair-care products for white players, but you don't have any for us black athletes. That Vitalis doesn't work on a black man's hair—it makes our hair turn hard and feel like a broom. Where's the Afro Sheen, the Glycerine, the hair picks, and the rakes?'

"Next day, the bathroom had everything the Cowboys' black athletes needed for grooming. That was one reason Buck was so admired and loved by the players—it took one request, and any player, rookie or veteran, had what he required with Buck Buchanan as our equipment manager."

During a preseason practice at Forest Lane in 1980, a skinny streaker entered the field on the north end and ran 100 yards before making his exit, escaping through our parking lot.

That streaker was fast, and had he stuck around, we might have signed the guy.

Defensive Coordinator Ernie Stautner (1966–1988) turned to me and said, "If I didn't have more to show than that, Buck, I believe I would have kept my shorts on."

Coach Stautner was one of the toughest coaches on staff, and he was a great defensive line coach whom outsiders would have been well advised not to joke with.

Stautner was an All-Pro defensive end and tackle for the Pittsburgh Steelers (1950–1964) and was elected to the Pro Football Hall of Fame in 1969, his first year of eligibility. In 1982, he was voted to the Steelers' fiftieth anniversary team.

Coach Stautner has huge lineman's hands, and he speaks with a stutter. According to defensive back Charlie Waters, team meetings might have been cut from fifty minutes in duration to thirty-five, had it not been for Coach Stautner's halting speech.

Under the direction of tough guy Ernie Stautner, another former U.S. Marine, the Cowboys consistently fielded excellent defenses and All-Pro defensive linemen like Bob Lilly, George Andrie, Harvey Martin, Randy White, Ed Jones, and John Dutton.

Harvey Martin leads the Cowboys in all-time quarterback sacks per season with 23 in 1977. George Andrie made 18½ sacks in 1966, and Randy White had 16 sacks in 1978.

The Cowboy all-time career sacks leaders are Harvey Martin with 113, Randy White with 111, and Ed Jones with 106. But

Coach Stautner wasn't satisfied with Martin's play. "You don't play hard enough," he said. "Harvey, you have to get mean."

The Dallas Doomsday Defense began to emerge shortly after Coach Stautner arrived as the Dallas defensive line coach in 1966, and Ernie was instrumental in fashioning Doomsday II that carried Dallas to its second Super Bowl title in 1977. Coach Stautner was the master of the head slap, a defensive tool banned in the mid-1970s.

Only years later, in 1985, did I begin to notice a perceptible change in player attitudes. It was shortly after we moved to Valley Ranch—the facility I helped design. The kids from college didn't have the dedication to the game the earlier vets had exhibited. It seemed they no longer saw football as a job, unlike the old guys.

By and large, most vets were responsible. They seldom got fined for team infractions, and I could see the difference in the little things—like players complaining and preparing their game equipment, or not.

A plumber has to be familiar with the tools of his trade. By necessity, he must know how and when to use those tools. That wasn't always the case with many of the players I worked with in the 1980s, and beyond. It seemed the newer players were far less concerned with the details and more concerned with the fame and the glamorous lifestyle.

The Cowboys certainly could have used a plumber after an incident that took place in our locker room prior to a regular season game at Texas Stadium. The mood was serious as Coach Landry prepped the Cowboys before kickoff.

Coach was finishing up his comments when there was a booming crash and the ceiling tile above running back Doug Dennison gave way, showering the meeting with debris, soiling No. 21 with water that had been pooling overhead in the acoustical tile.

Those players who avoided their second shower of the day swiftly moved away from the soiled Dennison as the room broke out in laughter. Doug sat there in shocked disbelief, and Coach Landry stared at the scene without blinking or missing a beat.

"Now let's go out and do what we have to do," Coach concluded. Coach turned to Dennison and said, "Get cleaned up and join us on the field." I stayed behind and helped Doug out of his soiled uniform.

Certainly, during the decade of the 1970s, players took the game seriously, as the job most of us agreed it was. Sure they had fun and showed emotion. But they generally took care of themselves and were a different breed of player than those that followed.

In 1976, we drafted 6′-1″, 187-pound wide receiver Butch Johnson (1976–1983) from the University of California at Riverside. Butch was an outstanding receiver, but he was one of a new breed of players. After scoring a touchdown pass against the Broncos, Butch performed an end-zone dance for the crowd—a first for the Cowboys.

Coach Landry wasn't big on end-zone celebrations. We never had anyone do much more than flip the ball to the official or spike it after scoring. Butch liked to dance a jig after scoring, a Western shuffle, where he pulled a pair of imaginary pistols from imaginary holsters and fired those *pistolas* into the stands. The crowd loved it.

Coach didn't care for it, but to his credit he never stopped it. Thus began a new episode of TD revelry and a new mindset for players. The trend has continued to this day.

One of my favorite Cowboys was Russell Maryland. For defensive tackles, the second most coveted prize is tackling the quarterback. But scoring is their greatest thrill.

Russ achieved every tackle's dream when he scored in Chicago in 1992.

"I broke through the Bears' line during the quarterback handoff," Russ later confided. "The running back bobbled the ball—all the way into my hands—and I ran 30 yards into the end zone. During the run, a million things went through my mind, like what kind of dance do I do? I was going to dunk the ball over the goal posts, but I didn't get all the way up and realized it wasn't going to happen. So I slipped the ball over my back and fell on my gut—like a beached whale."

Russ had an opportunity years later to celebrate with the Packers. Believing he had scored a touchdown before a penalty called the play back, clutching the ball for dear life, he tried to climb the green end-zone wall in Lambeau Field. In his attempt to scale the high end of the wall for a celebratory leap into the stands, he ran flat into the wall. "My guys had to help me over the wall,"

Applying eye black to Butch Johnson

#67 Russell Maryland

Russell laughed. "I came close to scoring on that quarterback fumble, but it was called back. Still, I did the whole dance, just in case."

The team drafted 6′-3″, 250-pound center Tom Rafferty from Penn State that year. Tom was a guy I never had to worry about when it came to caring for his equipment.

When he retired in 1989, Tom had the same pads I issued him in 1976.

Over time, Tom had broken his equipment in, and I guess he never saw the need for switching it out. I had everything reconditioned each year—the league required as much. But when we played away games, I was always careful to carry Tom's gear because I was too embarrassed to have another team's crew unpack that ratty equipment.

Rafferty was an all-around good guy and an especially good offensive player.

During one practice session, Coach Jim Myers had him lined up against some of the Cowboys' defensive linemen during a pass protection drill—one of the toughest.

It must have been Tom's day, because he did quite well for himself. I told Tom the Cowboys should have made an instructional video of that day's performance.

"Wait till tomorrow, Buck," Tom said, "and they'll have to burn my tapes."

According to Tom, his most memorable play was a block he threw during the January 3, 1983, Minnesota game resulting in Tony Dorsett's fabled 99-yard TD run.

"I had to make a fold or a back block on Vikings' defender James White—not one of my stronger blocks—but I got lucky," Tom explained, during the production of this book, "and that block helped clear the way for TD's record-breaking touchdown run."

Tom Rafferty played in the same Cowboys jersey—No. 64—for four years. I got that jersey to where it fit him perfectly, and he didn't care to trade it for another.

When players left the team, they had to turn in their equipment. If they wanted to keep their jerseys, however, I'd usually let them, but few ever asked.

We got new jerseys each year, and we played preseason in the previous season's game jerseys. But beginning with the new regular season, we'd use brand-new jerseys. In the 1970s, we kept old jerseys as backups. Today, they are sold at the Pro Shop.

1977—HOW SWEET IT IS!

New York City experienced a twenty-five-hour blackout, Jimmy Carter replaced Gerald Ford as president of the United States, *Star Wars* opened in America's theaters, and the Cowboys won Super Bowl XII by beating the Denver Broncos 27–10 in New Orleans.

Former All-Pro linebacker Chuck Howley, a Cowboy from 1961 through 1973, became the fourth member of the Cowboys

Ring of Honor. Chuck was honored during half-time ceremonies at Texas Stadium in our October 30 contest with the Detroit Lions.

When Chuck retired, Coach Landry said, "I don't know that I've seen anybody better at linebacker than Howley." A six-time All-Pro, Chuck was the Most Valuable Player in Super Bowl V. He was drafted by Chicago in 1958 and traded to Dallas in 1961. He was an All-America center at West Virginia and a six-time Pro Bowl selection.

We got off to our best start that year with eight wins and no defeats, eventually dropping back-to-back games to the Saint Louis Cardinals on November 14, 17–24, and a week later to the Pittsburgh Steelers, 13–28.

The Cowboys ended the year 12–2, the best season record since 1968.

The Steelers and the Cowboys had one of the fiercest and most hotly contested rivalries of the 1970s—one that has endured in its bad blood to the present.

From 1975 to 1979, we played them four times—and lost every game—Super Bowl X, the 1977 regular-season loss on November 20, the 31–35 Super Bowl XIII loss on January 21, 1979, and the October 28, 1979, 3–14 loss at Pittsburgh.

As a result of such "history" many Dallas fans have visceral feelings about the Pittsburgh Steelers. Conversely, Steelers fans have never concealed their utter contempt for the Cowboys. Thirty years later, the Pittsburgh faithful still get rankled whenever Dallas is referred to as America's Team—in their minds, a totally unmerited moniker.

We beat the Chicago Bears 37–7 in Dallas to cinch the Divisional Playoffs and a week later beat the Minnesota Vikings at home, 23–6 to take the NFC Championship title.

That year we drafted one of the premier running backs of all time, Tony Dorsett (1977–1987), from the University of Pittsburgh. Before coming to the Cowboys, Tony was

1977 Team Photo

Tony Dorsett evades defenders

instrumental in helping his alma mater win the National Collegiate Athletic Association championship in the New Orleans Superdome.

Tony played in New Orleans and helped Pitt win the NCAA championship. Months later, he played in the Superdome and helped Dallas win the NFL Super Bowl.

After guiding the University of Pittsburgh to the 1976 national title and claiming the Heisman Trophy, Tony captured Rookie of the Year honors in 1977 at Dallas.

Tony holds the NFL record with a 99-yard touchdown run, and he was inducted into the Ring of Honor in 1994. He was also selected to the Pro Football Hall of Fame in 1994.

Coach Landry was averse to playing rookies. He believed they made crazy mistakes. That philosophy held true with Tony Dorsett—TD to his teammates—in the beginning. Coach barely played Tony the first third of the season, but when he did and when he saw what a great player Tony was, he kept him in for the remainder of the year.

Tony impressed everyone—including the Philadelphia Eagles—at Texas Stadium on December 4 before sixty thousand delighted fans when he carried the ball twenty-three times and gained 206 yards.

There may never be another running back like Tony Dorsett. He was so agile, so sure-footed, and so amazingly fast that defenders never got a clean shot on him. Tony's ability to burst through the line and his blinding speed were nothing short of incredible.

Two steps and TD was gone.

Tony finished his career as the second-leading rusher in NFL history, and he played in five NFC Championship Games, two Super Bowls, and four Pro Bowls.

Like running back Emmitt Smith (1990–1996) from Florida, Dorsett and the other great running backs have uncanny peripheral vision. They see things on a wide, panoramic scale, unlike the rest of us mortals. If ever, defenders only got a decent shot at Tony and Emmitt when they were slowed by incidental contact.

Fortunately for both running backs, that seldom happened.

Eccentric players come in all shapes and sizes, and defensive back Randy Hughes (1975–1980) from the University of Oklahoma certainly had his peculiar ways.

Randy started a tradition that year with his propensity for sweets.

After every Friday's practice, the Tom Thumb Grocery Store near Forest Lane delivered a sheet cake sufficient to meet the sugar requirements of all the team.

Randy loved icing. After the cake was delivered, the lanky player knelt down before the table on which the cake rested in the

Emmitt Smith gains yards

players' lounge, and dove into the tasty treat, mouth first. After Randy had eaten his share, he got up with his face covered in icing and headed for the showers.

Before every game, Randy insisted on drinking a half-dozen Diet Dr. Peppers. As he explained, "Diet Dr. Pepper has the highest caffeine content, Buck." I don't know if the sugar or the caffeine did the trick for Randy, but he always played with intensity.

We drafted a pair of quarterbacks that year—Glenn Carano (1977–1983) from Nevada–Las Vegas and Steve DeBerg. We kept Glenn, and Steve went on to play for the San Francisco 49ers. Steve DeBerg later coached at San Francisco.

During the off-season, Otis and I were moving weight machines when Glenn dropped by and asked if he could help. He was that kind of guy—always personable.

"No, thanks," I told the Dallas quarterback.

I could only imagine what Coach Landry would have said upon learning that his backup quarterback was helping Otis and me rearrange the weight room. I made a point of asking Glenn if his hands were insured, and he said that they were not.

Glenn was released in 1983, but his life after football was anything but ho-hum. His dad was a big shot in Reno, Nevada, and I learned Glenn landed a lucrative job there.

Key to our success that year and our win in Super Bowl XII over Denver were offensive players Roger Staubach, Tony Dorsett, and wide receiver Tony Hill (1977–1986) from Stanford. Equally instrumental was the Cowboys' indomitable defense, anchored by tackle Randy White (1975–1988) from the University of Maryland and defensive end Harvey Martin.

The sight of Martin swooping into the backfield from his right end position was a fearful sight for NFL quarterbacks. Harvey was the Cowboys' all-time quarterback sack leader and led the club in that category for ten straight seasons.

Beginning in the 1960s and 1970s, the Cowboys were known for their swarming Doomsday Defense—spearheaded by defensive end George Andrie (1962–1972) from Marquette, defensive tackle Jethro Pugh, tackle Larry Cole (1968–1980) from the University of Hawaii, and defensive lineman Bob Lilly.

Such Dallas defenders anchored the defense, making life for offensive players a living hell in the time frame preceding the Dirty Dozen. To their advantage, Dirty Dozen rookies had a raft of seasoned defensive vets from which to learn—notably Jethro Pugh.

Fullback Robert Newhouse (1972–1983) was a strapping kid from east Texas who played at the University of Houston. In 1977, Robert was a seasoned Dallas veteran. He was smart, with short, stocky thighs and large, powerful legs.

During his twelve-year career at Dallas, Robert rushed 1,160 times for 5,009 yards—an average of 4.3 yards per attempt. His longest gain was 54 yards, and Robert scored thirty-one touchdowns, placing him in the top ten all-time Cowboys rushers.

In 1971, the Cowboys won Super Bowl VI in New Orleans. At that time, the Super Bowl winner went on to play the college All-Stars in an off-season exhibition game. Before the 1972 regular season, the Cowboys got it on with the All-Stars at Chicago's Soldier Field. We won that game and collegian Newhouse scored a touchdown against the Cowboys. Weeks later, suited up as a Dallas fullback, Robert was busy scoring touchdowns against our NFL competitors.

Robert was a family man with twin daughters. Today he works as a player counselor with the Cowboys. In 1977, he liked that Stick-em the players put on their hands to keep from fumbling the ball. It had an orange tint, and the texture was comparable to adhesive grout with the viscosity of honey. Players liberally applied it to their socks for game-time application to their hands. The league finally banned the stuff.

In Super Bowl XII, Newhouse broke from the huddle frantically licking the Stick-em off his hands. I had seen the phenomenon before in practice, and I thought to myself, "That

Staubach hands the ball to Robert Newhouse

hamburger's going to pass." Sure enough, Staubach handed Robert the ball. Robert faked a handoff and threw a touchdown pass to Golden Richards in the end zone.

When Newhouse joined me on the sideline, I said, "I hope you don't get sick."

"Buck," Newhouse replied, "I just hope I don't get constipated."

I'm still amazed the other team didn't pick up on Robert's Stick-em–eating antics.

Teams keyed in to the habits of their opponents.

Every NFL team studies hours of game film, and the Washington Redskins were no exception. Veteran Redskins defensive tackle Diron Talbert could spot the run when Robert had his mouthpiece in. If it was out, Diron knew we were going to pass. Teams are quick to key on such habits, and smart coaches teach players to avoid telltale routines.

That year we were quarterback rich, with Roger Staubach as our starter and backups Danny White and Glenn Carano. Danny was our primary backup, and Glenn served as the offensive quarterback during the Cowboys' defensive practices.

We enjoyed a sweet season, and we secured first place in the NFC East with our 14–6 home win over Denver in the season finale. That year's Divisional Playoff was at home against the Chicago Bears, and the Cowboys won hands down, 37–7.

The NFC Championship Game followed a week later with a runaway 23–6 win over the Minnesota Vikings in Texas Stadium. We played the Broncos again in Super Bowl XII in a lopsided 27–10 rematch in New Orleans. In that Super Bowl Game, the Cowboys made history when two players—Randy White, defensive tackle, and Harvey Martin, defensive end—received the Most Valuable Player Award.

Middle linebacker Bob Breunig often sang with fellow teammate Thomas Henderson. The pair was crooning to the Temptations song "Just My Imagination" when the press corps caught their act. Enjoying the two musically inclined Cowboys, sports reporter Dick Schapp offered the guys air time and asked Bob if they had a guitar. They did not. Schapp handed Bob a one-hundred-dollar bill and said, "Go buy one."

Musicians Waylon Jennings, Willie Nelson, and Jimmy Buffett often graced Cowboys postgame parties. After Super Bowl XII a number of Cowboys, including Bob Breunig on guitar, enjoyed the company of Willie Nelson and friends in New Orleans.

1978—THOSE "DAMNED" STEELERS

Much of the core Cowboys' squad was intact, and the mood that year could not have been more elevated after coming off our Super Bowl XII win. With a season record of 12–4, 1978 was nearly as successful as the Super Bowl–winning season before it.

The Cowboys had a good draft year with defensive lineman Larry Bethea (1978–1983) from Michigan State and running back Todd Christianson (1978).

Christianson always gave 110 percent in practice. His life's ambition was to be a running back, and he definitely did not care for the tight end position. But Coach Landry thought he'd make a good tight end due to his size, and tight end Coach Ditka agreed.

Todd gave it a go at tight end for the Cowboys, but he was never happy there. When his contract expired, he signed with the Raiders and later made All-Pro with Oakland—as a tight end. Todd's ambitions of being a running back never materialized.

That year the league lengthened the regular season to sixteen games from fourteen by reducing the number of preseason contests from six to four. The move was primarily done for television and the enhanced box-office revenues.

Rookie defensive back Dennis Thurman (1978–1985) hailed from the University of Southern California. You talk about ego and confidence—when Dennis came in he said, "Get a number ready, Mr. Buck, because I'm making the team."

Dennis wasn't that big, 5′-11″, 170-pounds, but he was one tough hamburger, and he went on to make good his claim to fame. In a win over Philadelphia, Dennis said of talented Eagles wide receiver and former Cowboy Harold Carmichael, "I'm going to break his pass completion streak." At that time, Harold had an impressive consecutive game streak of completed passes.

And I'll be darned, if Dennis didn't do just that.

Tight end Billy Joe DuPree got hurt midway into 1978, and the team brought Jackie Smith, formerly of the St. Louis Cardinals, out of retirement to fill Billy Joe's shoes. Jackie was an old-school player. He was the nicest guy in the world and never asked me for anything. He did his job, worked out, and played hard.

In the fourth quarter, we were in the Steelers' red zone with short yardage, and Roger called the play with Jackie Smith as his

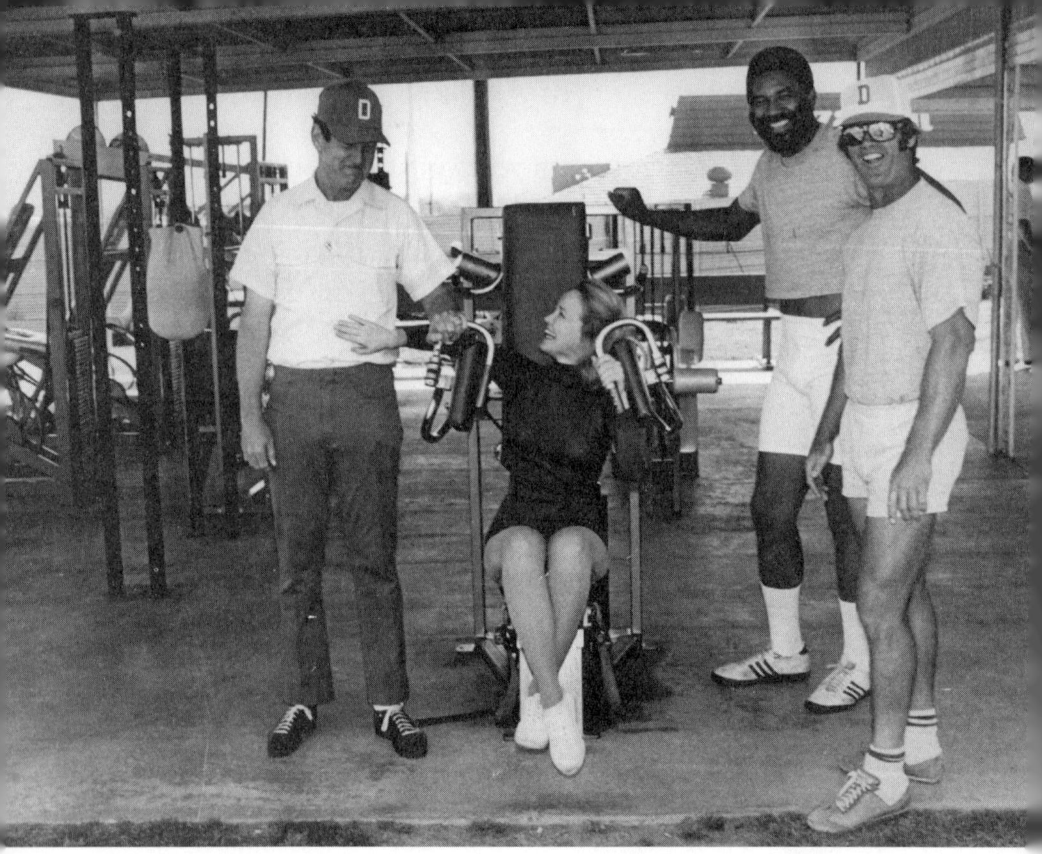

Hamming it up with Cathy Lee Crosby, Jethro Pugh, and Coach Ward

primary receiver. Roger hit Jackie in the end zone with a picture-perfect pass, and Jackie dropped the ball.

Devastated, he lay on his back in the end zone, motionless, his arms outstretched.

To show how professional both Jackie and Roger are, in the postgame interviews Jackie said, "Roger's pass was perfect, I should have had it."

Roger said, "It was a poor pass, I should have led Jackie more."

Two plays—and possibly an equal number of bad calls—cost the Cowboys Super Bowl XIII. Cornerback Benny Barnes (1972–1982) covered Pittsburgh Steelers receiver Lynn Swann, undoubtedly the NFL's premier receiver at the time.

Bob Breunig jams with Willie Nelson after Super Bowl XII win in New Orleans

An official made a questionable pass interference call on Benny, giving Pittsburgh the ball on our 20-yard line. Arguably there was contact, but it appeared there was more contact on Lynn's part than on Benny's. In all fairness it should have been a no call. Both players were going for the ball, but the official had the last word—or so we thought.

Pittsburgh went on to score a touchdown and successfully kicked the extra point.

On the ensuing kickoff there was a bad kick and the ball went to Ring of Honor inductee Randy White. Randy was a nine-time Pro Bowler during his fourteen years at Dallas. He established a club record with eight straight All-Pro selections, and he was co-MVP with teammate Harvey Martin in our Super Bowl XII victory over Denver.

The Manster, Randy White

Randy was a consensus All-America defensive end for Maryland in 1974.

He won both the Outland Trophy and the Vince Lombardi Award, and Randy was elected to the Pro Football Hall of Fame in 1994. But the Cowboys' defensive lineman had his hands heavily taped, as linemen do, and he couldn't hang on to the ball.

Randy fumbled, Pittsburgh recovered, and the Steelers scored their second touchdown in less than four minutes. That series took the wind out of our sails, and the rest, as they say, is history. We lost 31–35 to the Steelers in Super Bowl XIII. Those who saw that game insist it was one of the best, most fiercely contested football games the Cowboys ever played.

1979—A LEGEND'S SWAN SONG

In a game against the St. Louis Cardinals on October 21, 1979, the Cowboys celebrated their twentieth anniversary season at halftime. Coach Landry and Cowboys stars from each of those twenty seasons were introduced to the Dallas faithful in Texas Stadium during half-time ceremonies.

On December 16, the Cowboys' last regular season game, a funeral wreath was sent to Dallas, ostensibly by a Washington Redskins fan. That wreath was delivered to our Forest Lane facility, and Coach Landry told me to leave it in our dressing room.

The Saturday before the game, Harvey Martin asked me to have the ominous flower arrangement delivered to Texas Stadium. I told Harvey that I would, and the wreath resided in the Cowboys' equipment room throughout the contest on Sunday.

After we defeated the Redskins in a fiercely contested 35–34 battle, during which Roger Staubach threw a touchdown pass to Tony Hill and Rafael Septien kicked the winning point after, Harvey asked me for the funeral wreath. He grabbed it and exited the equipment room, turned right, and walked directly to the Redskins' locker room.

Harvey opened the door to the Washington locker room as the Redskins players undressed, and unceremoniously pitched the flowers into the room with several choice remarks I choose not to print.

When Coach Landry learned of the incident, he chastised Harvey and demanded he apologize to the 'skins organization. Harvey later confided to me that he would have refused the apology but for his respect for Coach Landry.

That winning touchdown pass from Staubach to Hill was considered by Roger to be his second-best NFL effort, second only to his famous Hail Mary Pass of 1975.

In 1979, we won our last three games to finish with an 11–5 record, our fourteenth consecutive winning season. Unfortunately we couldn't follow through in the playoffs.

Our first and last postseason game, the 1979 Divisional Playoff Game, was played on December 30 at home against a determined Rams team. Los Angeles squeaked out a 21–19 victory over Dallas that afternoon to end the Cowboys' hopes.

The last pass of the game, the season, and Roger Staubach's professional career was an illegal pass to Cowboys guard Herb Scott (1975–1984). Roger threw the ball to the first Cowboys jersey he saw, and that completed pass to an illegal receiver ended our prospects for Super Bowl XIV and Roger's brilliant career.

That loss was especially painful when we learned it was Roger's swan song—Captain America's last season at Dallas. Roger had been with the team since 1969, even though it seems like he had been a Cowboy forever. Staubach was the undisputed starter at the quarterback position through the decade of the 1970s.

After graduating from the U.S. Naval Academy, Roger was drafted by the Cowboys despite his four-year military obligation

Roger looks downfield

to the United States Navy. Tex Schramm and Gil Brandt tossed the dice in that landmark decision, betting that Roger would be a healthy quarterback contender after his four-year Navy hitch.

That Roger began his NFL career after a four-year sabbatical, one year of which he served as a combat officer in the Republic of South Vietnam, is a testament to his physical and mental strength.

Without a doubt the mold was broken after Roger Staubach was born, and a leadership and talent void quickly formed after his departure from Dallas.

About two weeks into that year's training camp, Tony Dorsett took a big hit during live drills, and everything came to a screeching halt on Coach Landry's practice field. The normally loud practice became deathly still as players milled around and waited.

On the sidelines, Tex Schramm had been speaking with Cowboys' business manager Joe Bailey. After Tony got hurt, both men immediately shut up and focused their attention on the fallen running back from Pitt, and a pair of Cowboys doctors raced over to check Tony out.

The initial diagnosis was favorable, and X-rays were ruled out. The doctors paid considerable time and attention to Tony's bruised knee. Cowboys orthopedic surgeon Dr. Marvin Knight confirmed that Tony was okay, but his practice session was over for that day. The incident proved how important major players like Dorsett were to the Cowboys. Tony had only been with us two years, but his worth was already incalculable.

That year, the Cowboys learned of the nefarious activities of our nemesis, the Washington Redskins. According to the "reports," prior to a game, 'skins head coach George Allen would call a friend in Dallas and have him rent a room on the third floor of a nearby motel. The motel was adjacent to and just north of our Forest Lane practice field, and the elevated perch provided a commanding view of the Cowboys' practice sessions.

To avoid intelligence leaks the Cowboys considered renting the third and fourth floors of the motel prior to each game with Washington. The idea proved cost prohibitive so a young man from our scouting department was assigned to monitor the alleged activities. Coach Landry gave our scout instructions to confront any and all offenders.

For days everything went without a hitch. Finally, a burly gentleman stepped onto the third floor balcony overlooking the practice field. Immediately, our scout flew into action. Prior to his leaving on his first mission, I urged the young man to use diplomacy.

Our man ascended three flights of stairs, dashed the length of the hallway and stopped shy of the suspect and his door. Breathing heavily, he confronted the interloper.

Several hundred yards removed, I stood on the sideline shading my eyes from the sun, as I witnessed our man arguing with a very large and menacing fellow on the third floor. It was clear they were involved in heated debate.

In short order, the "spy" lifted our scout, the smaller man, by the collar, our man's feet dangling a foot above the floor. When the spy put him down, the scout wisely bolted for the safety of the Cowboys' practice field.

"How did it go?" I later asked the visibly shaken young man.

Perspiring badly, he blurted, "He's just a truck driver, Buck. His rig is parked next door. He rented that room, and he isn't going anywhere. What do you think I should do?"

"If you want to live," I said, "don't go back up there. Let him watch."

6

THE 1980s—A FACELIFT

On March 31, 1980, Dallas quarterback Roger Staubach announced his retirement at a press conference in the Texas Stadium Club. After eleven record-breaking seasons, Roger held all major Cowboys passing records and was the all-time leading NFL passer.

During the preparation of this book, Roger said, "One of the most memorable days I recall was filled with mixed emotions. The day I announced my retirement, it was like leaving a 'special family.' The parting, while it was the right decision, was really painful in the moment. I'm grateful for all the people I came to know and care for during those Cowboys years, especially Buck Buchanan. We've stayed in touch throughout the years."

There wasn't a dry eye in the room when Roger spoke of his days with the Cowboys and his love for Coach Landry, "that guy with the hat." Roger is a gifted communicator, and he's seldom at a loss for words, but he had a hard time finishing.

1980—THE DANNY WHITE YEARS

March 30 marked the end of an era and the beginning of the Danny White reign. Behind Danny, the Cowboys rolled to our fifteenth consecutive winning season with a 12–4 record, tied for

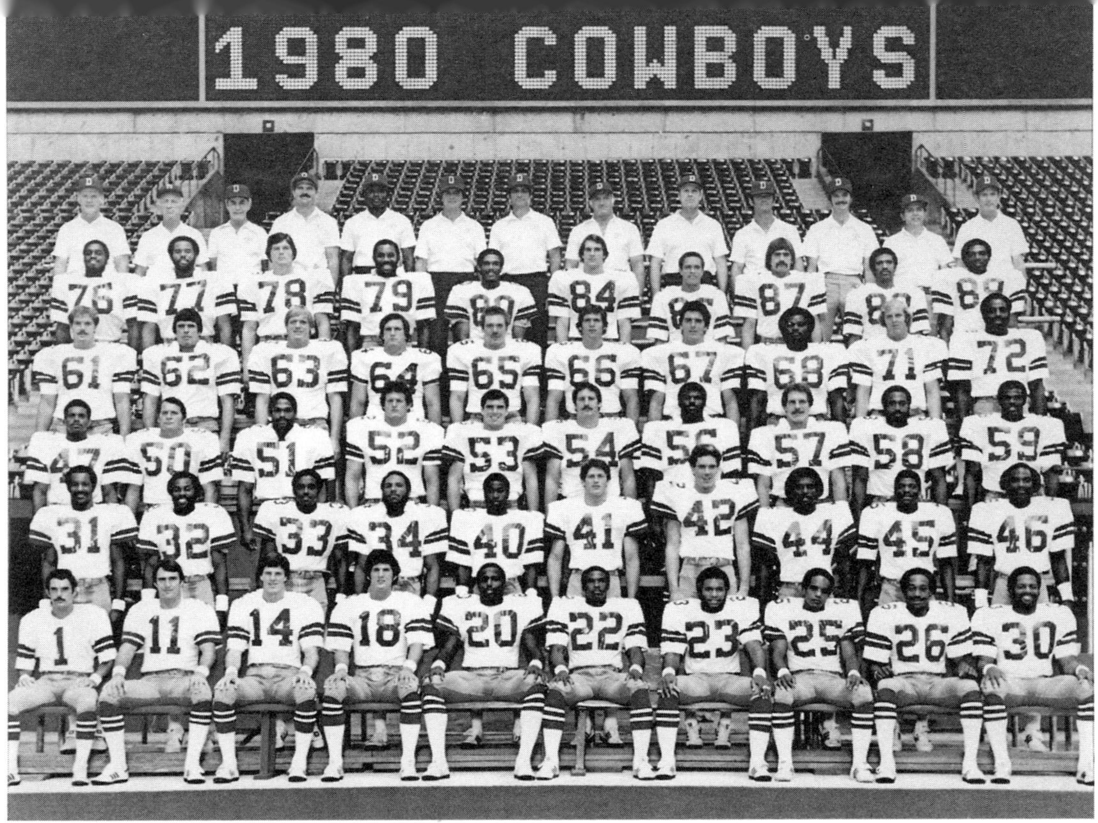

1980 Team Photo

Danny White scrambles

best in the league with the Philadelphia Eagles and the Atlanta Falcons.

The Cowboys traded their No. 1 and No. 2 draft choices to the Baltimore Colts for highly touted defensive end John Dutton (1980–1986) from the University of Nebraska.

John played seven seasons for Dallas, and we made it to three NFC Championship games. John filled out his uniform much like Ed Jones, and kept it neat like "Too Tall," which certainly must have pleased Tex Schramm.

That year's rooks included linebacker Bill Roe (1980) from the University of Colorado and running back James Jones (1980–1985) from Mississippi State. We had offensive lineman Kurt

Petersen (1980–1985) from the University of Missouri, quarterback Gary Hogeboom (1980–1985) from Central Michigan, running back Timmy Newsome (1980–1988) from Winston-Salem State, and guard Norm Wells (1980) from Northwestern.

Hogeboom was a successful college quarterback who was seriously being groomed by the coaching staff as the heir apparent to Danny White.

Gary was a smart player who was both tall and strong, but who ultimately fell short of the Cowboys' expectations. You could tell he was from a small school because he didn't have a big head. Hogeboom got married the year after signing with the Cowboys, and he played for the St. Louis Cardinals after leaving Dallas.

James Jones received the dubious nickname Kool-Aid, an inferred reference to Jim Jones and the Jonestown mass suicide in Guyana in 1978.

"Jonesey," as I called him, was a quiet kid from Vicksburg who always had a big grin. He was a homebody who never seemed to mind the guys calling him Kool-Aid.

In our last preseason game on August 30 with the Pittsburgh Steelers, toward the end of the third quarter, Billy Joe DuPree ran to the sideline and asked me for a plug of chewing tobacco. I asked Joe if he had chewed before, and he replied, "A little."

"If you get hit," I warned the Cowboys tight end, "you could swallow the stuff."

Joe was insistent, and I gave him a plug of tobacco.

Two series later, he ran a pass route across the middle and took a big hit, compliments of Steelers linebacker Jack Hamm, forcing the Cowboys to punt.

Joe came to the sideline looking bad.

"Buck," he said, "I should have listened to you. I feel terrible." Somehow Billy Joe was able to finish the game, but he never asked me for another plug of chew.

We won the 1980 NFC Wild Card Game over the Rams in Dallas, 34–13, to advance to the 1980 Divisional Playoff Game in Atlanta against the Falcons, which the Cowboys pulled out 30–27.

In the win over Los Angeles, Coach Landry set another milestone—his two-hundredth victory—raising his record to 200–119–6, regular season and playoff games inclusive.

In the 1980 NFC Championship Game in Philadelphia we lost to the Eagles 7–20—quashing the Cowboys' bid for a sixth Super Bowl appearance.

Danny White had been the Cowboys' backup quarterback since 1976, shortly after former backup QB Clint Longley had punched Roger Staubach and quit the team.

There wasn't the bad blood between Roger and Danny that there had been between Roger and Clint. The two had more in common, and they seemed to get along. Both are conservative with religious backgrounds—Roger is a Catholic and Danny is a Mormon.

I made sure there was always an ample supply of soft drinks, water, Gatorade, and coffee in the dressing room, depending on the time of year and the temperatures.

One winter's game, Danny said, "Buck, I can't drink coffee. Can you get me some hot chocolate?"

"That stuff has more caffeine than coffee," I said.

Beaming that Danny White toothpaste smile, he said, "I'd still prefer some hot chocolate."

I got Danny what he wanted, and made sure we always had an ample supply of hot chocolate on hand.

Danny was an all-round athlete and good guy who attended the University of Arizona on a baseball scholarship. With the Cowboys, he excelled at the quarterback position as well as a number of sports the players engaged in during their spare time.

During the off-season Danny headed up a Cowboys baseball team, and he won most of the racquetball and Ping-Pong tournaments he joined in. In training camp, after two-a-day workouts, he often retired to the rec center to play piano "for a little R&R."

Rafael Septien, Danny White, and I setting up the kicking net

In my opinion, Danny White (1976–1988) was one of the finest quarterbacks Dallas ever fielded. Certainly, he ranked up there with Roger Staubach (1969–1979) and Troy Aikman (1982–2000) from UCLA as one of the three all-time best Dallas QBs.

Troy holds the Cowboys' career passing record with 2,898 completions to Danny's 1,761 and Roger's 1,685. But then Troy's passing attempts totaled 4,715 to Roger's 2,958 and Danny's 2,950. Troy leads Dallas quarterbacks with a career record of 165 touchdowns to Danny's 155 and Roger's 153.

Danny was a talented punter and extra-point and field goal kicker.

On fourth down, after our offense had left the field, Danny would remain behind to punt. As such, White posed an added threat to Dallas opponents who never knew if he was going to kick or run a sneak offensive play. Danny carried a special square-toed shoe from college that he was capable of kicking field goals with out to 30 yards.

Amazingly, Danny holds the punting record at Dallas with 612 punts to Mike Saxon's (1985–1992) 591 and Toby Gowin's (1997–1999, 2003) 338.

In our September 23, 1984, game at Philadelphia, Danny set another Dallas record with eleven punts in that game with the Eagles. On the other side of the ledger, he holds a Dallas career high five punts blocked to Saxon's four and Micah Knorr's (2000–2002) three.

However, Danny holds the Cowboys' record of most consecutive punts with not one blocked, 341, to John Jett's (1993–1996) 253 and Saxon's 204.

During the NFC Championship Game in Philadelphia, the temperature was 10 degrees with a wind chill factor of 10 below. I packed everything I could in the way of cold-weather gear—long johns, turtlenecks, and gloves. I even packed a full complement of those black scuba gloves divers wear. Those gloves worked well for our receivers who were on the field briefly, but they failed our linemen miserably.

Randy White came to the sideline in the first half and tossed his pair of black gloves at me. "These sons of bitches aren't going to cut it, Buck," he said. I discovered the reason for Randy's frustration—the gloves made his hands sweat, and the perspiration had nowhere to go, forming frozen ice cubes in his fingertips.

Randy had a reputation for being the meanest and toughest defensive lineman in the NFL. But when he brought his infant daughter Jordan White to Forest Lane, I saw an altogether different side of "The Manster." Randy called his little girl "Bumble Bee," and it was revealing to observe Randy's gentler side, especially when little Jordan's daddy could demonstrate such intensity and ferocity on the gridiron.

Before that game I received dozens of phone calls offering remedies for everything from improved traction on the frozen Astro Turf to warmer winter gear.

One caller insisted basketball shoes worked better on frozen Astro Turf, so I called Converse and ordered shoes for every player on the team. Converse shipped the shoes to Philly on Saturday, the day we were due to land, and I alerted our truck driver, Jack O'Malley.

"I'll be damned, Buck," he groaned, "I don't have room for a load of tennis shoes." Before I could protest, Jack stopped me in midsentence. "I'm just kidding, dude. I'll pick up the tennis shoes for you."

Jack was an itinerant Irishman who would just as soon cuss a cop as spit.

Fortunately, the stadium crew had done a yeoman's job on the field, and the Cowboys players never needed those basketball shoes.

For cold-weather conditions like those in Philly, the NFL employed heated fiberglass benches on the sidelines. The benches were solid, fore and aft, and were warmed by gasoline-powered heaters. Special louvers situated at the base of each bench, facing the field, allowed players to toast their feet and ankles—when they were used properly.

Facing the stadium seats, defensive lineman Larry Bethea from Michigan State (1978–1983) inserted his feet into the louvered bench and stood up during that game in Philadelphia. When we turned the ball over on fourth down, the cry rang out, "Defense!" but Larry did not step forward—the big lineman could not extricate his feet.

I heard someone hollering on the bench, and I ran over to see what was going on. Larry's feet were trapped, and he was about to fall ass-backward. To his embarrassment, to the amusement of the Eagles fans, and to the consternation of the Dallas defensive coaches, I had to free Larry from his restraints before he joined our defense on the field.

We lost that Eagles game and it proved to be the first loss in a series of three failed NFC Championship bids for Danny White. That first loss was heartbreaking. The ensuing NFL Championship losses in 1981 and 1982 had the fans in Dallas grumbling and talking about a Super Bowl Curse.

The defeats were especially hard for the team, but Danny took them even harder. In spite of those setbacks, he held onto his starting position as quarterback and remained there until his retirement—and the end of the Tom Landry Era—in 1988.

1981—PANTYHOSE AND THE CATCH

For the second straight year, the Cowboys had another winning record of 12–4. Danny White returned as sharp and as healthy as he had been his first year at the starting quarterback position. We played some of the better teams that schedule, and if our QB was experiencing any lapse in confidence or physical ability, it didn't show in his play.

Former All-Pro defensive back Mel Renfro, the Cowboys' all-time leading pass interceptor, became the fifth member of the Cowboys Ring of Honor. Mel was honored during half-time ceremonies at the Cowboys-Dolphins game at Texas Stadium, October 25.

We regained the NFC Eastern Division Championship, our twelfth division title since 1966, and in the process tied Oakland's mark of sixteen straight winning seasons.

We suffered away losses to the Cardinals, the Lions, and the Giants, but they were squeakers we lost by a margin of only three points. Our only significant loss was an away game, a major drubbing by the San Francisco 49ers, 14–45.

Ring of Honor member Mel Renfro on an early punt return

The year before, on October 12, 1980, we had trashed the 49ers 59–14, and San Francisco exacted its revenge in a payback showing on October 11, 1981, at Candlestick Park. In his typical manner, Coach Landry never showed emotion, win or lose, and he never complained. He always gave the Cowboys a postgame briefing followed by, "Let's load 'em up and start again next week."

The game in San Francisco was so lopsided and boring, the TV station that carried the contest left in the fourth quarter to broadcast another, more exciting event.

Tex Schramm knew his job and he performed it well. Generally, he let Coach Landry coach without any interference. However, I vividly recall one exception.

On December 13, 1981, Dallas led the Philadelphia Eagles at Texas Stadium. We had the ball on the Eagles' 5-yard line with thirty seconds remaining. Coach Landry ran a play and let the time expire—without attempting a field goal or a touchdown.

After the game, Tex came into the coaches' locker room where I was straightening up, and I overheard him say, "Tom, you should have gone for the score."

The team with the highest cumulative points determined playoff tiebreakers. There were no tiebreakers that year, but Tex had a valid point.

He repeated his admonition.

"Next time, Tom, go for the score."

"I can't do that, Tex," Coach Landry dissented.

Coach Landry might have gone for more points against the Eagles, but he didn't believe in "piling on." In 1980, we beat San Francisco 59–14. Although it may have appeared to the 49ers that Coach was piling on points, Dallas played nearly every player on our roster to provide them game time—and to avoid running up the score.

The objective was never to pile on points or embarrass San Francisco. A year later, in 1981, the 49ers returned the favor and thumped us good at Candlestick Park.

Quarterbacks Coach John Mackovic (1981–1982) joined the Cowboys that year when Dan Reeves went to Denver as the Broncos' head coach. At Wake Forest, Coach Mackovic had turned the school's program around.

Mackovic was meticulous, diplomatic, friendly—and very tough. In fact, he was one of the strictest coaches I have known, and he did a fine job mentoring Danny White.

He was released in 1982 and went to Kansas City as the head coach of the Chiefs.

Coach Mackovic in training camp

In our last regular season game with the Giants, Randy White, the dread Manster, "half man, half defensive monster," known and feared by linemen and running backs throughout the league, broke with the dress code that cold day at the Meadowlands.

During an earlier game, the always-flamboyant Jets quarterback Joe Namath had worn and endorsed Big Bertha Pantyhose. Broadway Joe maintained the ladies' nylons kept him warm and toasty on cold winter days.

Not to be outdone, one styling Dallas equipment manager, always eager to help the team, ordered sixty pairs of the Big Bertha Pantyhose in sizes large and extra-large.

The scene in the Cowboys' locker room was hysterical as the Manster made three aborted attempts to slip his muscular frame into the women's hose. Each time, Randy failed, his toenails gouging cavernous holes in the nylons.

We won't print Randy's comments that day, but it's safe to say he wasn't happy.

Several Cowboys receivers and defensive backs, dreading the cold more than the team's razzing, donned the pantyhose that afternoon, but the big linemen shunned them like the plague. At day's end, I threw every pair of pantyhose in the trash, and the subject was never mentioned again.

Entering the playoffs for the fifteenth time in twenty-one years (1966–1981), the Cowboys advanced to the NFC Championship for the ninth time in twelve seasons by destroying Tampa Bay 38–0 at Texas Stadium.

But for the second year in a row, we lost the conference title when San Francisco scored a last-minute touchdown to edge us out 27–28 for a berth in Super Bowl XVI.

We were ahead in that game by six points with less than two minutes remaining.

The 49ers had a fourth and 10 on the Dallas 15-yard line.

Joe Montana dropped back, pursued by Ed "Too Tall" Jones.

Montana made a clutch pass on the run and threw what looked to be an overthrown pass to 6′-6″ 49ers' tight end Dwight Clark.

Dwight was covered by Cowboys defensive back Everson "Cubby" Walls (1981–1989) from Grambling. Clark made a fingertip catch for the touchdown, and the successful extra point put the 49ers ahead by a single point.

The Cowboys got the ball back with a minute and a half remaining.

Danny drove from our 30-yard-line to the 45.

On third down, White passed to Drew Pearson.

Drew held the ball long enough to constitute a completed pass.

Drew got clobbered by two defenders and fumbled.

The 49ers recovered, ending the game.

That loss marked Danny White's second defeat in as many NFC Championship bids. And, to rub it in, the sports highlights continue to air "The Catch" to this day.

Linebacker great Bob Breunig, one of the Dirty Dozen, characterized the Montana-to-Clark last-minute pass and subsequent loss to the 49ers as one of the saddest moments in his illustrious ten-year career.

"We should have gone to the Super Bowl," Bob lamented.

Uncharacteristically, Coach Landry showed disappointment after that loss, quietly pacing our dressing room five or six times with his head bowed. Had we made it to the Super Bowl, we felt confident we could have easily defeated the Cincinnati Bengals.

Not putting the Bengals down, we just *knew* we could beat them.

Super Bowl XVI was slated for Detroit that year, and because the Cowboys were the NFC squad, we would have been lockered at the Lions' plush Detroit facility.

But then, that's the game of football.

Everson Walls grew up in the Dallas Hamilton Park area.

Young Everson lived two miles from our Forest Lane practice facility.

After making the team and being one of the rare rookies to start at the cornerback position for Dallas, he told me, "Buck, when I was a kid, you ran me off the practice field."

Everson walked two miles from his house, climbed the solid tin fence surrounding our practice field, and watched the Cowboys practice. He made the NFC Pro Bowl team his rookie season and again in 1982, 1983, and 1985.

Cubby was always a pleasure to be around.

Another rookie starter that year was defensive back Michael Downs (1981–1988) from Rice University. Michael played alongside Cubby in the defensive backfield as a free safety. Michael was a tall player whom I called "Steady Eddy," because he was always steeped in thought, preparing for the next play, the next series—or the next game.

He was also a low-maintenance player who took the game of football seriously. Downs and Walls provided a solid Dallas backfield that made life perilous for receivers.

1982—THE PLAYERS' STRIKE

That spring before training camp, soccer-style kicker Rafael Septien (1978–1986) from Southeast Louisiana dropped by our Forest Lane facility for kicking practice. With him, Septien brought a parrot. I don't know birds all that well, but Septien's was a multicolored parrot with a topnotch. I am told it must have been a macaw—one of those expensive, exotic birds from South America.

I was a little put out with Septien for bringing a pet to work. I never knew what a player might bring into the Cowboys' locker room. I asked the little guy if he wouldn't mind leaving his feathered pal outside, in the weight area. He did, and the parrot seemed content to roost on a set of weights—and leave his deposits on the floor below.

After practice, Septien took the bird home.

Months later, fishing for something to say to the guy, I asked him, "How's your parrot, Rafael?" To which he promptly and nonchalantly replied, "My dog ate him."

I don't know much about birds, but that had to be an expensive doggy treat.

Like most kickers, Septien was unorthodox. But his contribution to the team is indisputable. Rafael scored the second-highest career point total in Cowboys' history—ninety-four, with forty points after touchdown, and eighteen field goals—second only to running back Emmitt Smith (126).

I signed Brian Baldinger as a free agent that year, and the league went to hell in a handbasket. The Cowboys began the season with a 28–36 loss to the Steelers in Pittsburgh and a 24–7 victory over the Cardinals. After beating St. Louis, the NFL Players' Union called a strike, and every player was contractually obligated to walk out.

Never having been involved in a strike, I was a little uneasy about my employment status. However, Mr. Schramm kept every member of the Dallas Cowboys on the payroll. That's the kind of man Tex was. He knew that in an after-strike world, the Cowboys would need every one of us to resume a winning season.

As a condition of the strike we could not allow players into our facility. To ensure compliance, there were union reps stationed across the street from our Forest Lane facility. Tight end Billy Joe DuPree must not have known the ramifications when he visited our locker room and rang the buzzer shortly after the strike had been called.

"Joe, you can't come in," I insisted.

"Man, Buck, you're hard," Billy Joe said. "I need something out of my locker."

"Let me know what it is, and I'll get it for you. But you can't come in," I said.

The strike of 1982 lasted two months, and eight games were canceled.

The season resumed on November 21 with the Cowboys' 14–9 win over the Tampa Bay Buccaneers at Texas Stadium. We won four more contests in that abbreviated season and lost the final two—20–24 to the Eagles at home and 27–31 to the Vikings in Minnesota.

Defensive back Rod Hill (1982–1983) from Kentucky State was our No. 1 draft choice that year. Rod had a world of athletic ability, and he was a bona fide physical specimen, deemed by Conditioning Coach Ward to be one of the most gifted athletes he had ever coached.

But Rod lacked the mental toughness required to compete in the NFL. He just didn't have the intensity to play professional football, nor the durability to take the licks.

Given our six-win, three-loss regular season record, the Cowboys were eligible for a Super Bowl Tournament bid versus the Tampa Bay Buccaneers in Dallas.

We beat Tampa Bay 30–17 and advanced to a second Super Bowl Tournament bid with the Green Bay Packers, again at home. We beat the Packers 37–26 and advanced to the 1982 NFC Championship Game in Washington against the Redskins.

We arrived in DC the third week in January, and it was bitterly cold. A truck had pulled into the stadium's docking area before we had and destroyed the door. The truck was wedged halfway inside, and we had to wait an hour before the logjam was cleared.

Jerry Fowler and I spent the night in the stadium dressing room to safeguard the team's equipment. Our vigil, however, did nothing to help Cowboys tight end Jay Saldi (1976–1982) from South Carolina.

The 1982 NFC Championship Game was played at RFK on January 22, 1983, and it was uncomfortably cold. I had packed winter jerseys, the kind with the pouches in front for the receivers' hands. The winter jerseys were hanging in the players' lockers when they filed in.

After the team was suited up, before the pregame warm-up, another Cowboy noticed that Jay's name was misspelled on his jersey. Instead of Saldi, the jersey manufacturer had inadvertently spelled the Dallas tight end's name "Sladi."

It was my goof, and I apologized. But Jay was a New Jersey kid, and the cold didn't phase him. "Give me a summer jersey," he insisted, and Jay was good to go.

Saldi was another low-maintenance player.

The following day we lost to the Redskins 17–31.

That NFC championship loss was Danny's third in as many attempts, but the loss made us eligible for a second Pro Bowl appearance in Hawaii. The Cowboys' season was over, and those players selected to the Pro Bowl were relaxed heading to Honolulu.

For the quarterback position, NFL players had cast their votes for Danny White and Redskins quarterback Joe Theismann, to represent the National Football Conference.

Danny and Joe sat beside each other in the Aloha Stadium dressing room in Honolulu, Theismann talking nonstop. On the way home Danny insisted, "Buck, if we ever go to another Pro Bowl with Theismann, put me in a different locker. Better yet, put me in another locker room. My ears are still burning. I like the guy, but he won't shut up."

Coach Landry played Danny the first quarter and Joe the second.

In the third quarter, I was on the sideline beside Coach Landry.

The hitting wasn't as intense, and the players and staff—even Coach Landry—seemed to be enjoying themselves.

A stern Theismann approached Coach and prefaced his Pro Bowl Game Day advice with, "Tom, here's what I think we should do with Danny to pull this game out."

Coach squinted and walked away, leaving Theismann standing there alone.

Coach Neill Armstrong joined the Cowboys in 1982, charged with studying and evaluating NFL players and teams. He took over the reins of research and development in 1984 when Coach Ermal Allen retired.

Armstrong's reports laid the groundwork for the Cowboys' game plans through 1989. He had a 30–34 record in four seasons (1978–1981) as head coach of the Chicago Bears. Before his tenure

Coach Lowry at Thousand Oaks

at Chicago, Coach Armstrong served as an assistant coach for the Minnesota Vikings. A graduate of Oklahoma State University, Armstrong was a low-key, solid guy, in my book, a real class act.

After returning home to Dallas, I spoke with old friend and former Air Force buddy Kirby Sweatt from Alabama. Kirby loved the Crimson Tide and Bear Bryant.

In the January 1, 1973, classic, the University of Texas had beaten the University of Alabama in the Cotton Bowl. UT player Alan Lowry scored a game-winning touchdown late in the game, propelling UT to a 17–13 victory over Alabama. Kirby and his UA faithful claimed Alan stepped out of bounds and that Alabama had been screwed.

In 1982, Alan Lowry (1982–1986) became the Cowboys' special teams coach.

Each Christmas the Cowboys were given holiday greeting cards with a team photo. Before Christmas, I asked Lowry for his help. I told him I would like to send a card to Kirby explaining what had really happened in UT's Cotton Bowl win over the Crimson Tide. Coach agreed and sent Kirby a special holiday greeting that read, "Merry Christmas, Kirby. I *did* step out of bounds in UT's win over the Crimson Tide. Yours truly, Alan Lowry."

Coach Lowry served as the receivers coach for the Cowboys from 1987 to 1988.

He was special teams/tight ends coach in 1989 and tight ends coach in 1990. Coach Lowry fielded a special teams unit that was the best in the league, finishing second in the NFL in kickoff return average and in the top ten in kickoff coverage. That year, rookie James Dixon finished second in the NFC in kick return average and became the first Cowboy to return a kickoff for a touchdown since 1975.

1983—WILD CARD HEARTBREAKER

Dallas began the season by beating the Redskins 31–30 before fifty-five thousand fans at RFK Stadium. In that come-from-behind win, after a 23–3 half-time deficit, Danny White rallied the Cowboys to defeat Washington on Monday Night Football.

The Cowboys enjoyed another terrific winning season with a 12–4 record that took us to the playoffs. Unfortunately, home field advantage did not serve us well in that wild card game with Los Angeles, and the Cowboys fell to the Rams 17–24.

We had several promising rookie prospects, notably defensive end Jim Jeffcoat (1983–1994) from Arizona State. Jim assumed responsibilities as a Cowboys coach upon retiring with the Buffalo

Bills fifteen years later. Linebacker Mike Walter (1983) from the University of Oregon played one year with the Cowboys before going to the 49ers. With San Francisco's Super Bowl wins in succeeding years, that trade turned out well for Mike and the 49ers.

Heated moments on and off the field during training camp were common. Whenever offensive and defensive linemen tangle, there's bound to be hard feelings. After practice, players were dog-tired and the least little thing could lead to a fight.

That year rookie offensive tackle Chris Schultz (1983–1985) from the University of Arizona got into a beef with fellow teammate and defensive tackle Jim Jeffcoat.

Chris and Jim were paired off in practice, and I was headed back to the dressing room early when Chris stormed in and threw his helmet at his locker.

Seconds later, Jim walked in. Chris turned and saw Jim, and without a word, the two linemen charged each other. The ensuing clash was brief. Two blows followed—Jim hit Chris—and Chris hit the floor. After Jim saw that Chris was down, he turned and returned to his locker.

Chris was unscathed, and the two linemen later became good friends.

Offensive tackle Mark Tuinei (1983–1997) from the University of Hawaii was signed by the Cowboys as a free agent and converted from defensive end, with Coach Jim Myers' help, his rookie season.

Mark made the Pro Bowl twice during his career (1994, 1995). He had a great sense of humor and always had a quick retort to his teammates' jokes and barbs.

Anticipating our first Super Bowl game with Buffalo, we knew we had to get past San Francisco in the 1992 NFC Championship Game. One of Mark's friends, a fellow Samoan and a San Francisco player, had said to Mark, a week before the game, something to the effect that "Hey, bra. The way to the Super Bowl is through San Francisco."

After the Cowboys defeated the 49ers 30–20 at Candlestick Park, Mark and his Samoan friend met on the field and Mark replied, "Hey, bra. Thanks for giving us directions to the Super Bowl."

In 1994, my first year of part-time employment with the Cowboys, we were aboard a chartered aircraft, en route to an away game. Mark stopped by my aisle seat on the plane and joked, "Hey, Buck. What part of retirement don't you understand?"

Mark and my son, Bucky, were good friends. The two loved to play jokes on each other. Mark and Bucky bet on the outcome of a golf match. Mark won the golf match and the wager. Had Bucky won, Mark would have paid Bucky's mortgage payment for two months. Since Mark won, Bucky had to wait on Tuinei for the duration of training camp.

According to the arrangement, Bucky was at Mark's beck and call.

That last year of training camp in Austin, Toyota was our sponsor. To promote their product, Toyota had a life-sized inflatable pickup near the practice field at St. Ed's.

With the end of training camp approaching, Bucky was to return to Dallas to prepare Valley Ranch for the team's return. The night before leaving, he enlisted the help of two of his cronies to deflate the large Toyota inflatable and move it into Mark's room.

The three jokers squeezed into Mark's dorm room and inflated the mock pickup truck, escaping through a window. Returning that night from a team meeting, Mark opened the door to his room, and the inflatable pushed the door out of his hand, slamming it into the wall.

One of Bucky's partners in crime was there to record Mark's reaction, and he later reported, "Mark yelled, 'That damned Bucky! Wait till I get him in the morning.'"

But Bucky was already gone.

Early in the season, veteran offensive lineman Jim "Coop" Cooper (1977–1986) by way of Temple University suffered with what NFL players call Astro Turf toe—a strain of the big toe caused by the hard and unforgiving Astro Turf surface.

During our September 11 game at St. Louis with the Cardinals, Jim wore a special metal insole in his Converse Astro Turf shoes to combat the injury. That hamburger was one tough kid, because by the end of the game, the temperatures had soared at Bush Memorial Stadium, blistering the entire front pad of his right foot. Coop never once complained, but then quality players like Jim Cooper were low maintenance.

A year later, again in St. Louis, the Cowboys had the ball on our 5-yard line.

Dallas quarterback Danny White handed the ball to wide receiver Drew Pearson, and Drew faded back and passed to another Cowboys receiver for long yardage. Our receiver made the catch and ran the ball into the end zone for a touchdown.

But the play was called back due to a holding penalty on No. 61—Jim Cooper.

The Cowboys went on to defeat St. Louis 24–17.

After the game, a grinning offensive coordinator and quarterback coach Jim Shofner walked by Coop's locker and sardonically remarked, "I'm sure glad we won the game. I know you're pretty happy, too, Coop."

After making such a mistake, most NFL players prayed for redemption.

The Cowboys were fortunate to win that day, and I'm sure Coop was relieved.

Rookie safety Bill Bates (1983–1997) from the University of Tennessee was a fierce competitor. He wasn't the fastest man on the field, but Bill had a big heart and he was one of the smartest.

Coach Bates (1998–2002) became the Dallas defensive assistant coach (1998–1999), the defensive backs coach (2000), and assistant special teams coach (2001–2002).

What Bill lacked in the way of speed, he made up for by endless hours studying our opponents' game film. As a result, he always seemed to know where to be on the field by reading the offensive alignment.

Before playing the Rams in the NFC Wild Card Game in Dallas, we had six consecutive below-freezing days. It got so cold, Coach Landry decided to hold practice in the Houston Astro Dome. We practiced there two days and came home for more practice at Forest Lane prior to the wild card game.

Bill Bates hung with his friend and roommate, punter John Warren (1983–1984) from Tennessee. The ice kept the duo from getting out of their driveway, and Bill called and asked if I would pick them up and take them to practice.

Coach Landry's players knew better than to miss one of his practices—even if the streets in Dallas were glazed with ice. I picked up Bill and John in my red pickup truck and took them to practice in the bed of that '76 Chevy. Under Coach Landry, the Dallas Cowboys shared the U.S. Postal Service motto: "Snow, rain, sleet, or ice."

That season, Tony Dorsett scored a 99-yard touchdown against the Minnesota Vikings. During that play, the Cowboys lacked eleven men on the play, fielding only ten.

Tony broke through the Minnesota line and within a handful of steps was gone.

The missing eleventh man, running back Ron Springs (1979–1984) from Ohio State, was a friend of Tony's. After the game, Ron maintained he should have received some recognition for having been the missing man on the field when Dorsett made that record-breaking touchdown run. But the glares Ron received from Cowboy coaches were his only reward that day.

After Ron had been with the Cowboys several years, he had a bad habit of razzing me about my somewhat pronounced ears each time we boarded a flight to an away game.

As stated earlier, I customarily sat in the last row of the aircraft on the left aisle seat. Ron generally sat three rows up, on the right-side aisle seat.

The team would be settled in, and the chartered aircraft would be taxiing down the runway, when Ron would lean out of his seat grinning, and holler at me, "Better pin those ears back, Buck. The tower called and complained about the interference."

1984—THE SILVER SEASON

Fourteen games into a lackluster regular season, Dallas defeated the Eagles in Philadelphia to extend the Cowboys' NFL record to nineteen consecutive winning seasons. The 1984 season was, in my opinion, the beginning of the end of the Cowboys' Glory Years.

Dallas endured a 9–7 season, and we did not make it to the playoffs for the first time in ten years. In nineteen years, that was only the second time the Cowboys missed the playoffs.

The wear and tear was beginning to show on Coach Landry.

That season, he was conflicted over a major decision to swap quarterbacks.

Danny White had been the starter since Roger Staubach left in 1979. But Coach was having second thoughts about Danny and was seriously considering replacing him with Gary Hogeboom.

Toward the end of the season, Coach Landry had made a decision: *Hogebloom*, as Coach always mispronounced Gary's name, would start, and White would sit the bench.

In a team meeting on a Wednesday afternoon, Coach Landry made the announcement, but inadvertently said that Phil Pozderac—not Hogeboom—would replace Danny White. The players exchanged quizzical looks before Coach Landry caught his mistake and announced that Hogeboom, not Pozderac, would indeed replace White.

It was clear that Coach Landry was troubled with the quarterback decision and his demeanor and conversation evidenced that uncertainty. But the switch proved only temporary, and White returned after ten games as our starter to replace Hogeboom.

Rookie hopefuls that year included linebacker Eugene Lockhart (1984–1990) from the University of Houston, by way of Crockett, Texas—a real head knocker—and safety/linebacker Vince Albritton (1984–1991) from the University of Washington.

Vince was always cheerful, and he nicknamed me "Buckaroo Bonzai." He was quick enough to be a defensive back and strong enough to play as a linebacker, when needed.

Other rooks that year included tight end Fred Cornwell (1984–1985) from Southern California, linebacker Steve DeOssie (1984–1988) from Boston College, and quarterback Steve Pelleur (1984–1988) from Washington. There were free agent wide receiver Mike Renfro (1984–1987) from Texas Christian, tight end/linebacker Brian Salonen (1984–1985) from the University of Montana, and defensive back Victor Scott (1984–1988) from the University of Colorado.

The University of Washington quarterback had some throwing arm.

Pelleur is credited with one of the all-time longest Dallas forward passes—an 84-yard bomb to Herschel Walker resulting in a touchdown against the Philadelphia Eagles.

That year's rookies included outside linebacker Dowe Aughtman from Auburn; linebacker Billy Cannon from Texas A&M; and free agent wide receiver Harold Carmichael and running back Norm Granger, both from Southern.

By way of Rutgers, there were cornerback Carl Howard, guard John Hunt from Florida, guard Syd Kitson from Wake Forest, wide receiver Kirk Phillips from the University of Tulsa, wide receiver Waddell Smith from the University of Kansas, and linebacker Jimmie Turner from Presbyterian.

All were one-year Dallas men.

1984 marked the team's twenty-fifth anniversary. Prior to training camp we had a Cowboys reunion with players dating back to the organization's inception. At a news conference at Texas Stadium, Tex Schramm announced commencement of the Cowboys' "Silver Season" celebration, highlighted by a reunion at a posh Dallas downtown hotel.

Everything Tex did was first-class, and that reunion was no exception.

Schramm secured every team member's precise clothing measurements and had the players, coaches, and staff outfitted in stylish tuxedoes. We had Dallas owner Clint Murchison to thank for that gala reunion, as Mr. Murchison gave free rein to Tex in such matters.

From the time I came onboard until the time Mr. Murchison sold the Cowboys to Bum Bright, I saw Murchison no more than three times. Reports have it that he made his fortune in oil, construction, and finance. He was a quiet, low-key man, and he was always kind and unassuming in my presence. Murchison owned a golf course in Hawaii that the Cowboys made good use of during our Pro Bowl visits to the Aloha State.

One Saturday, Murchison came in the back door at Forest Lane, looked around for a few minutes, and left. Another Saturday I had the season schedule on my desk when he dropped by. Murchison chatted with me briefly about the schedule and the team's jerseys and left.

By all outward appearances, Mr. Murchison was a gentleman, but he never spent much time at our facilities, and he never had much to say to me when he did.

On March 19, the NFL owners approved Murchison's sale of the Cowboys to an eleven-member limited partnership headed by Dallas businessman H. R. "Bum" Bright at the league's annual meeting in Hawaii. The sale was finalized on May 18.

During a midseason practice at Forest Lane, the infamous motel behind the practice field, the old Days Inn at Forest Lane and Abrams off LBJ, became the scene of another encounter of a humorous kind.

We were halfway through practice and the offense was in the huddle, facing away from the motel. Suddenly, the huddle stood up en masse, and stared back at the Days Inn. Two shapely young ladies had strutted provocatively from one end of the motel concourse to the other, ostensibly to visit their room.

Every Cowboy's head was turned.

I have no idea what the girls were doing, but they came out of their room wearing these skimpy, sexy bras and panties. Maybe they were auditioning to be cheerleaders. If they were, they had definitely come to the wrong place. The girls stood on the balcony overlooking the field doing these shakes and shimmies and dance moves for the team.

Their presence put a serious damper on Coach Landry's practice. Thereafter, the guys went through the motions half-heartedly calling and executing plays and hurriedly looking back over their shoulders to get a glimpse of the girls on the balcony.

This went on for some time before Coach Myers insisted I call the motel manager and have him remove the distraction. "Just go in there," Myers pointed to the locker room, "and call the motel and get those girls off that balcony!"

Another Cowboys coach who shall remain unnamed said, "Yeah, Buck, go call that manager, but give us ten minutes before you do!"

1985—NEW DIGS

Roger Staubach, the Cowboys' "Comeback Kid," was inducted into the Pro Football Hall of Fame in his first year of eligibility. Roger found himself in good sports company when jersey No.

12 was enshrined on August 3 in Canton, Ohio, with noted football greats Pete Rozelle, Joe Namath, O. J. Simpson, and Frank Gatski.

That year we moved to Valley Ranch. We left the old Forest Lane location going into training camp at Thousand Oaks, and when we returned to Dallas everything we had not taken to the West Coast—offices, lockers, spare equipment, and the bulk of the weights—had been moved into our new home. On August 27, players and coaches reported to the team's new headquarters and training facility at Cowboys Center.

Upon returning from training camp, I joined the Dallas coaches for an inspection tour of the Valley Ranch facilities and practice fields. I admit I had mixed feelings. I played a key role in the design of the new facility's locker room, and it *was* a vast improvement over Forest Lane. But we had less than two weeks to get settled into our new digs, and I was concerned that we might not get everything ready in time for the season.

But we did.

Our first regular season game was televised on Monday Night Football, and Dallas defenders intercepted six passes, five from Joe Theismann, defeating the 'skins 44–14.

The Cowboys did their homework preparing the grounds at Valley Ranch. A year prior to our moving from Forest Lane, management had made certain that the turf and the sprinkler systems had been properly installed and adjusted.

Upon moving in, the washers and dryers weren't hooked up, the shelving in the equipment room was unfinished, and the carpet on the dressing room floor was not laid. As I would learn, the place had its wrinkles, mostly small things that would be ironed out over time—but the much-awaited new facility was everything I had hoped for and more.

During the tour I mentioned to Joe Bailey, "There are no goalposts." In fact, both fields lacked goalposts. My son Bucky was there when we toured Valley Ranch.

1985 Team Photo

Years later, after I had retired, he remarked, "Dad, I remember the look on your face that day. I thought you were going to cry."

I have never had much of a poker face.

Much like a prepurchase home inspection, with the building contractor trailing the exuberant new buyers, I realized the bulk of the unfinished work would be relegated to the low man on that pre–move in inspection team totem pole—me. Getting everything prepped and up and running for Game Day would largely be my responsibility.

The equipment room, the training room, and the coaches' offices were nearly completed, but everything else was in a state of construction. I'd left the frying pan—training camp—and had returned to the fire, a brand-spanking-new unfinished facility.

In the beginning, I had to contact a Fort Worth laundry business for our laundry needs. The folks we had used at Forest Lane all those years were in Garland, too far to make it worth their while to remain the official Cowboys launderer.

The guy in Fort Worth ran a reconditioning plant with huge washers and dryers, and he was able to pick up and return our laundry the next morning.

Unlike the smaller Forest Lane facility where we had the one field, we now had two—with twice the upkeep—and the dressing room was larger, at ten thousand square feet.

Each player had an oversized double locker capable of holding all his equipment, replete with a study desk and chair. There was room for a projected computer hook-up, a plan that later fell by the wayside, but all the extra room eventually proved most useful.

Instead of one big area, the dressing room was set up in four sections with a large cubicle in each corner. The offense was on one side, and the defense was on the other.

"Too Tall" Jones, the Cowboys' star defensive end, threw a monkey wrench into the construction works in the beginning and nearly drove our building contractor crazy.

Ed was fond of using baby powder after showering—volumes of the powdery stuff. I don't know if he owned stock in a baby-powder company or if one had signed Ed to a contract. Nevertheless, he used that stuff like it was going out of style. Ed took care of his football equipment, and he was equally fastidious about his personal hygiene.

After showering, the big man would stand in front of his locker and apply a liberal volume of the talc, with the plumes rising to the ceiling. The contractor knew there must be an electrical short in the new system, because every day after practice the fire alarm went off, shutting off the lights, the washers, the dryers—and everything in the building.

After some serious back-engineering, the electrician was able to trace the cause of the timely occurrences. Each time Ed applied his favorite talcum, the fire alarm would go off, shutting down the electricity and leaving the Cowboys in the dark.

After laborious checking, it was determined Ed's enormous frame, together with the vast clouds of baby powder he wafted airborne, had wreaked havoc on the fire alarm's delicate mechanism. An adjustment was made and Ed made the baby-powder company rich.

Conditioning Coach Bob Ward (1976–1989) was track coach for eleven years at Fullerton College in California before joining the Cowboys. He is widely credited for his innovative conditioning regimen, including nutrition, weightlifting, aerobics, flexibility, and martial arts training.

Coach Ward is a graduate of Whitworth College in Spokane, Washington. He received his master's degree in physical education from the University of Washington and his doctorate from Indiana University.

After the NFL banned the head slap, Ward resorted to martial arts training for the team. According to Randy White, "When the rules changed disallowing the head slap, he brought several martial arts instructors to camp to teach us hand fighting. For me, it made a big difference. It was a key ingredient to my success. Ward was ahead of the game."

Coach Ward had asked management for a twelve-thousand-square-foot open weight area.

The only problem with the arrangement was that in the summer it got hot, and during the winter it got cold. Players were at the mercy of the elements—and the legion of birds that loved to roost in the rafters and leave their endearing deposits.

Just outside the Cowboys' weight room stands a maze of aerobics bars and metal structures of Coach Ward's design. I remember the day Tex Schramm questioned the metal bar setup and Ward provided him with a plausible, scientific explanation.

The weird-looking monkey bars—affectionately named "son of a bitch" by Cowboys players—still grace the area outside the Dallas weight room, less the wear and tear from twenty years' exposure to the elements, nearly as pristine as when they were built.

Coach Ward was hired by Coach Landry and shown the door by Coach Johnson, leading him to remark, "I was hired by the best, and I was fired by the best."

By his own admission, sensing the inevitable after the team had been sold in 1989, Coach Ward asked Coach Johnson to fire him, and Jimmy accommodated him.

In his seventies as of this writing, Ward competes in international weightlifting competition, works full-time in the healthcare business, and doesn't look a day over fifty.

The Cowboys improved their record to 10–6 that season, and perhaps the new facility inspired the coaching staff and players. Our playoff game that year was in Los Angeles with the Rams. That game proved to be a major disappointment, with the results of the contest less than what we had all hoped for—a 0–20 spanking. That may well have been the Cowboys' worst playoff showing in history.

Coach Ward in the Thousand Oaks weight yard

The Rams had a running back phenom by the name of Eric Dickerson, a graduate of Southern Methodist University. Eric rushed for over 200 yards in that deciding game and our defense was incapable of handling the Dickerson-led Rams offense.

Midway through the third quarter, Coach Landry was approached on the sideline by two policemen in dress suits. He spoke briefly with Coach Myers and was escorted from the field. The team, the announcers, and the stadium were abuzz with speculation.

Coach Myers assumed head coach responsibilities, and the game went on. Later, I learned there had been a death threat made against our head coach.

That year, returning from an away game we had an offensive and a defensive lineman get into a tussle on the plane coming home. The defensive player was 6′-7″, 266-pound defensive lineman Don Smerek (1981–1987) from Nevada-Reno. The offensive player was 6′-9″, 272-pound tackle Phil "Poz" Pozderac (1982–1987) from Notre Dame.

The veteran linemen wound up wrestling in an empty area between two seats, precariously close to one of the aircraft's emergency exit doors.

I quickly unfastened my seatbelt and waded into the fray.

Randy White stood up, and in Randy's unmistakable, booming voice hollered, "Okay, you assholes, sit down!" I've not seen five hundred pounds of muscle and brawn move so fast. Certainly, the Cowboys coaches yearned for such action on the field on Game Day.

The Manster had some reputation, and nobody was challenging him that day.

Don and Phil broke it up and quietly sat down.

"Were you really going to jump into the middle of that?" Jerry Fowler asked. "You could have gotten hurt."

"We all would have gotten hurt if those hamburgers had kicked open the plane's emergency door," I replied.

In a game against the Giants in the Meadowlands on November 2, Pozderac was called for a holding penalty after we scored what should have been the winning touchdown. The play was called back and the Giants won the game 17–14.

A review of the game film at Valley Ranch the next Monday clearly showed the Giants defensive player grabbing Phil's jersey and falling to the ground, holding on.

The official had obviously made a bad call.

The same New York player, whose name I shall not reveal, admitted in a postgame interview with the *Dallas Morning News* that he had held Poz and had gotten away with holding before. But that's football.

That year, we signed defensive tackle Kevin Brooks (1985–1988) from the University of Michigan as our No. 1 draft choice. Kevin turned out to be a high-maintenance player and a royal pain in the butt for the trainers, notably Ken Locker.

Kevin never jelled with the Cowboys, and he left after three seasons.

Guard Crawford "Big Daddy" Ker (1985–1990) from the University of Florida was of Scottish descent. According to Big Daddy, the Kers moved to Florida from Scotland when Big Daddy was a boy. Big Daddy had the neatest southern Scots accent.

That year, we rented folding chairs for the guys before the benches were installed at Valley Ranch. Big Daddy came by his nickname honestly—he was 6′-3″ and tipped the scales at 283 pounds. After moving to the new facility, he was leaning back in one of those metal chairs, lost his balance, and took a tumble.

Big Daddy missed two games with a back injury. In pregame warm-ups three games later, he reinjured his back and missed yet another game. When asked by a Dallas newspaper reporter what had caused his injury, Crawford opined, "them killer chairs."

Quarterback Troy Aikman remembers his most embarrassing moment in an incident involving Big Daddy Ker: "In 1989, my rookie year," Troy explained, "I lined up under the left guard, Crawford Ker, to get a snap. Big Daddy let me know pretty quickly that my hands were under the wrong guy!"

I always called Troy by his first name.

Cowboys players referred to their starting quarterback as "8-Ball," a reference to Troy's jersey number. Troy was a quarterback extraordinaire. He was a real country kid from Oklahoma, a gentleman who was fond of pickup trucks, blue jeans, and boots.

Today, Troy is a successful Dallas businessman and a widely recognized sports announcer. In the heat of the battle, I never once saw Troy get rattled. I wish I could say the same about his body. Troy eventually had to leave football after one-too-many concussions, the result of the hits Troy took as the Dallas franchise quarterback.

Averse to playing with a new football, he preferred to use a game ball that had been slightly scuffed. In many ways, Troy was a loner, but he hit it off with backup quarterbacks Steve Beurlein and Jason "Red Ball" Garrett (1993–1999) from Princeton.

Troy Aikman fades back to pass

Running back Herschel Walker (1986–1989, 1996–1997) graduated from the University of Georgia. Herschel was drafted by the Cowboys but played briefly for the United States Football League before coming to Dallas.

Herschel was a muscular specimen with a squeaky, high-pitched voice. He was very interested in conditioning, and it was common to see him drop in the dressing room or in the weight room and knock out fifty to one hundred pushups, as many as five times a day.

Herschel stunned the Eagles on December 14 with an 84-yard touchdown run, one of the all-time longest from scrimmage, in our losing 21–23 effort at Texas Stadium.

Fullback Todd Fowler (1985–1988) came to the Cowboys by way of Stephen F. Austin. Todd was an outgoing country kid who loved to hunt deer. He often brought photographs to the Cowboys locker room of his deer to show his teammates. When he told me he had eaten the heart of his first deer, I lost all interest in Todd's hunting stories.

After the Divisional Playoff loss to the Rams, the Cowboys had a five-year dry spell. We did not make it to another playoff until 1991—under Head Coach Jimmy Johnson (1989–1994).

That 1985 loss was the beginning of the end for Coach Landry's brilliant career.

That year, Robert Newhouse had a career high 930 yards rushing.

The 1985 Pro Bowl was played in Honolulu, Hawaii, and four Cowboys were selected to the NFC team—Tony Hill, Everson Walls, Randy White, and Doug Cosbie.

Doug had been to two Pro Bowls, 1983 and 1984, and when his wife called Valley Ranch and asked who was slated to go that year, I told her, "Hold on, let me get the list." I proceeded to deliberately read the names of selectees to Mrs. Cosbie.

"No," I said, "I guess Doug isn't going. I don't see him on the list."

Tony Hill makes an over-the-shoulder catch

I paused. "Hold it, a minute, Mrs. Cosbie. Here he is... Doug Cosbie."

Mrs. Cosbie replied, "Buck, you are a big turkey."

Doug later came in, laughing.

"I hear my wife thinks you're a turkey, Buck," he said.

1986—ALL GOOD THINGS MUST...

The Cowboys held training camp in Thousand Oaks, California, and during the preseason, we played our first overseas game in

London, England, against the Chicago Bears. That year's preseason was the worst showing in team history—we lost all five of those games—tying the dismal preseason record of 1962.

On the overseas flight my assistant Jerry Fowler, the Cowboys' video crew, the trainers, and myself shared the upper deck of an American Airlines 747. The crew treated us like royalty. When Schramm, Bailey, and Dan Warner, Bailey's assistant, visited us topside, they were duly impressed and just a little jealous over our accommodations.

In London, I sent Jerry ahead with the team, and I waited for the bags to clear customs. During that customs check, a British police dog detected a controlled substance in one of the seats on our flight. That led to the officials opening and inspecting each bag.

We were finally cleared to leave, after our innocence had been determined.

Upon clearing customs, I caught a cab to our Crystal Palace practice facility.

After getting the Cowboys' locker room set up for practice, I caught a cab to the London Hilton, the team's plush accommodations across the street from Hyde Park.

That week Britons were treated to American football and a Cowboys walkthrough practice. The Cowboys lost 6–17 in Wembley Stadium before eighty-two thousand English fans, and that game with the Bears proved to be a portent of things to come.

We concluded the season with a 7–9 record, failing to make it to the playoffs for only the third time in twenty-one seasons. The Cowboys' streak of twenty consecutive winning seasons (1966–1985), third longest in professional sports history, came to an abrupt end after losing seven of our last eight games.

By season's end, I could see that the older vets were running out of steam.

Roger Staubach was gone.

Individually and collectively, with few exceptions, the team had lost its stamina, its will, and its direction. It wasn't any one thing but a combination of factors both physical and emotional that precipitated the Cowboys' decline.

That year, we welcomed promising rookie wide receiver Mike Scherrard (1986) from UCLA and tight end Thornton Chandler (1986–1989) from the University of Alabama, but as a team the Dallas Cowboys lacked their former luster.

On November 18 in our last regular season win of the year against the San Diego Chargers in San Diego, we played under the worst field conditions I have ever witnessed.

It was a rainy southern California day when we arrived at the San Diego airport.

It rained all day Saturday, and it continued raining until mid-morning Sunday.

To make matters worse, the stadium had allowed some type of a motorized event to be held on the field we were scheduled to play on. From one 30-yard line to the other, the field was muddied and rutted. When we set up the night before, I told Fowler, "Let's wait and see, but we may have to go with the longer cleats."

And we did. The field was a real mess.

I was at the stadium by 5:00 a.m., and hours before the game my old friend from the Air Force Academy, the equipment manager for the Chargers, Sid Brooks, informed me that I had a long-distance call from my wife. When I took the call, Jerry told me that my mother, Ina Ruth Buchanan, had passed away in her sleep the night before.

Word spread quickly and Coach Landry stopped by the cage before the game to express his condolences. Little was said, but the compassion was evident in his eyes.

"The funeral's on Wednesday," I reported. "I'll be going to Abilene, Coach."

Coach said, "I remember you saying your mother was a Christian lady."

I nodded.

"Then we both know where she is," he said, and walked away.

Coach Landry was a man of faith.

His unwavering priorities were God, family, and job.

We played that game under horrible field conditions and won 24–21. Coach Landry handled the conditions in his typical manner—with grace and composure—and when we returned to Dallas, I read that the San Diego stadium manager had lost his job.

Defensive lineman Don Smerek was a tall, rowdy character who loved to play practical jokes on others. After he was shot outside a Dallas nightclub at the end of the regular season, Don spent the first two months of the off-season recuperating.

When he returned to Valley Ranch sometime in March, Don stopped by the cage and we discussed his near-death experience. Curious, I asked what it felt like to be shot.

"All I felt was this stinging sensation," he said, clutching the left side of his stomach below the ribs. Fortunately for Don, his assailant had used a .22 pistol, not a higher caliber weapon, and the big guy was on the mend a month after the shooting.

Always happy to return a practical joke to another jokester, I took three gray Dallas T-shirts and cut small holes in each one in the approximate area of Don's wound.

I took a red magic marker and highlighted the area around the "bullet hole."

Don got a real kick out of wearing those T-shirts in practice.

After first moving into Valley Ranch, jogging on the new half-mile track, Don discovered and killed a rattlesnake on two separate occasions. The last time, he draped the dead snake over a low-lying tree branch, directly over the track. One of the Cowboys secretaries, enjoying a midday run, nearly came out of her skin when she passed beneath that tree limb—and Don's strategically placed snake.

Her screams could be heard as far away as the weight room.

Smerek and Randy White could not tie a necktie. That or they preferred the way I tied a knot. Given Coach Landry and Tex Schramm's strict dress code, everyone was expected to wear a coat and tie to each away game. Don and Randy always made a point of stopping by my aisle seat on the plane, leaning over and having me tie their ties.

On February 12, 2000, at Coach Tom Landry's funeral, Don and Randy looked for me in the foyer of the chapel and asked me to tie their ties at that most somber event.

1987—THE REPLACEMENT KILLERS

We suffered through a 1–3 preseason. It was rare to have back-to-back losing preseasons. It was even more unusual for the Cowboys to have a losing preseason *and* a losing regular season. That had not happened in more than twenty-five years.

But 1987 was anything but ordinary.

In a less-than-stellar performance, we lost our season opener to the St. Louis Cardinals in St. Louis 13–24. After our second regular season game and a 16–14 win over the New York Giants in New York, the NFL Players' Union called the strike of 1987.

After the NFL Players' Strike of 1982, team owners had agreed that game cancellations were far too costly—in terms of team revenues and the game of football in general. In the event of another strike the owners had opted to go with replacement players—*scabs*, in their terms. After all, they reasoned, why wait for the union to renegotiate a contract while losing revenues?

Why not continue the regular season and the box office receipts with scabs?

I never liked the term scabs.

Replacement players represented a unique challenge. To be sure there were some talented athletes within their ranks. Overall, they worked hard. But they were temps in a real world of full-time professional athletes.

One young man stands out in particular—quarterback Kevin Sweeney—son of San Diego State's then–head football coach. Smaller than most, Kevin was a tough, disciplined kid.

For replacements, the strike was a potential gold mine. After the strike was over, assuming they played extraordinarily well, perhaps they would land a permanent job on the Cowboys' roster, or another NFL team. Wide receiver Kelvin Martin (1987–1992, 1996) from Boston College was one of the fortunate few to return as a veteran Cowboy.

Most replacements, however, faded into obscurity.

With the impending strike I found myself back at square one. A week after our win over the Giants, shortly before noon, the vets and rookies began to stream into Valley Ranch to pack up and clear out. That phase of the strike was accomplished before three in the afternoon.

Two hours later, a pair of buses rolled to the curb and the replacements filed off.

And the process began anew—the fitting of helmets, pads—the works.

We had two short weeks to train and outfit a new team. That meant new jerseys, new pants, new shoes, new nameplates—new everything. Mr. Schramm insisted everything remain the same, that the strike should be treated as though it were a new season.

Since 1960, the Cowboys have had a team photograph taken every year.

Consequently, a second team portrait had to be made of the replacement players.

I worked till two the next morning to get ready.

And that day, the replacements began meeting with the coaches.

It was bedlam.

I was faced with my second training camp in less than a month.

Because of the strike we suffered one home-game cancellation, September 27 against the Buffalo Bills. The strike was in effect, the vets remained off the job, and the replacements played their butts off hoping against all hope that they would land a job.

An erratic series of regular season wins and losses followed with *our* alternates unable to sustain a winning streak against *their* alternates. Finally, Tony Dorsett and Randy White crossed the picket line and broke the strike.

TD and the Manster played in our October 11 game against the Eagles, and we walloped Philadelphia's replacements 41–22 before an enthused home crowd of forty thousand fans.

Two weeks later in a game played in Philadelphia the Eagles put the hurt on the Cowboys and exacted their revenge 20–37 before sixty-one thousand screaming Philadelphia fans. One of those fans was Eagles head coach Buddy Ryan, who was still irritated with Coach Landry for allowing the pair to cross the picket line to beat his Eagles.

Eagles quarterback Randall Cunningham had seconds remaining before calling a time out. Randall walked to his sideline and spoke with Ryan. He returned to the field, the Eagles huddled, and their center snapped Cunningham the ball. Randall knelt down and the Cowboys' defense slowed to a trot, believing the game was over.

Cunningham sprang to his feet and threw a touchdown pass.

The Eagles piled on those extra points with seconds remaining because Buddy Ryan was still fuming at Dallas. In point of fact, the decision to reinstate Dorsett and White was Schramm's—not Coach Landry's.

Ryan exacted his revenge, and the Eagles won by 17 points, not 10.

When asked what he thought of Coach Ryan's decision to go for the touchdown, Coach Landry had little to say. In his typical fashion he handled it as he did every situation—with finesse and a sense of detachment.

After several years as the Eagles' head coach, Buddy Ryan went to the Houston Oilers as their defensive coordinator. In a televised sideline incident witnessed by millions of fans, Ryan threw a punch at one of the Oilers' offensive coaches and lost his job.

1987 marked the arrival of Offensive Line Coach Jim Erkenbeck (1987–1988).

Coach Erkenbeck came to Dallas with a lot of vim and vigor. He was hard to work with at first, until I showed him how the Cowboys' dressing room was managed.

His second year at Dallas, during a televised Monday Night Football game, Coach Erkenbeck stood on the sideline, with a communications set hooked to the back of his pants. An official made a call that Erkenbeck didn't like, and he flew onto the field, ripping his pants from the belt line to below his derriere, exposing his gray shorts.

I said, "Coach, you stopped real fast. Good work!"

The former U.S. Marine joined the Dallas Cowboys after reviving the New Orleans Saints' offensive line. In 1985, the Saints were one of only two teams in the NFL to allow more than fifty-five sacks and average less than four yards per rush.

In 1986, with Coach Erkenbeck coaching the offensive line, the Saints became one of only four teams to allow less than twenty-eight sacks and average more than four yards per carry.

Coach Erkenbeck molded the young Cowboys offensive line into one of the most powerful in the NFL. And by the end of the season, our boys had three new starters with an average weight of 290 pounds.

Erkenbeck left the Cowboys shortly after the pants-tearing incident.

The New York Jets were our first opponents after the strike ended.

That game was in the Meadowlands.

Normally, the Cowboys wore coats and ties, a result of Coach Landry and Tex Schramm's strict dress code. In that game with the Jets, we were advised to wear casual attire because of the potentially volatile nature of the New York fans and local unions.

I dressed like a truck driver, in part because I accompanied the equipment truck to and from the stadium. And what union man would attack a fellow truck driver, I reasoned?

Given the strike we were on the lookout for trouble, but there was none. The only grief we got was from a handful of pickets at the stadium.

We beat the Jets 38–24 before a crowd of twelve thousand and change.

What followed was an erratic series of wins and losses.

Dallas drafted nine players in 1987 who made it to the active roster.

Those players included defensive tackle Danny Noonan (1987–1992) from the University of Nebraska, defensive back Ron Francis (1987–1990) from Baylor, offensive lineman Jeff Zimmerman (1987–1990) from the University of Florida, and wide receiver Kelvin Martin (1987–1992, 1996) from Boston College.

There was No. 5 draft pick wide receiver Everett Gay (1987–1988) from the University of Texas, quarterback Kevin Sweeney (1987–88) from California State Fresno, tackle Kevin Gogan (1987–1993) from the University of Washington, running back Alvin Blount (1987) from the University of Maryland, and linebacker Dale Jones from the University of Tennessee.

Kevin Gogan was very loud and very large. For some inexplicable reason, he called Troy Aikman "Roy." He called me "Buck Wild," probably because he knew I was far from being so. And in return, I nicknamed the 350-pound-plus tackle "Go Wild."

In a particular goal-line series, some years later, the Cowboys tried Gogan, No. 66, at tight end. I will have to admit he made a large and imposing target. So as not to be credited with being an ineligible receiver, Gogan had to report to the official prior to the huddle.

He was furious that quarterback Troy Aikman didn't see him in the end zone.

"I was wide open," the converted tackle complained to "Roy."

That was Gogan's one shot at fame, and it was not to be.

Our season ended on December 27 with a disappointing record of 7–8. We never made it to the playoffs, and just when I'd hoped and prayed it couldn't get worse—it did.

1988—THE END OF AN ERA

Coach Landry handled everything in stride. If it wasn't under his control, he simply didn't worry about it. Nothing ever seemed to shake the head coach of the Dallas Cowboys. Even when he set NFL records.

That year, Coach Landry began the season against the Pittsburgh Steelers by tying a long-standing NFL record. From 1921 to 1949, Curly Lambeau had coached the Green Bay Packers and set an NFL record—*longest consecutive seasons with the same team*.

In 1988, Coach Landry tied Lambeau's record.

We split our preseason games winning two and losing two. But those wins were soon forgotten, overshadowed by far greater losses. The Cowboys won a grand total of three regular season games and lost an unprecedented thirteen. In the two-month period from October 3 through December 4, America's Team lost ten consecutive games.

It's pretty tough when you can remember a season by the handful of wins and not the handful of losses. We beat the Phoenix

Cardinals, the Atlanta Falcons, and the Washington Redskins—all in close contests decided by fewer than seven points.

We lost to every other team that year, and we never made it to the playoffs.

For the coaching staff who had been there with Coach Landry since the early years, the season of 1988 marked the most disappointing chapter in the twenty-eight-year history of the franchise.

Of the Cowboys' management, Schramm seemed most affected by the dire turn of events. My memories with the team are mostly pleasant. But if I had to pick a year that I would just as soon not have been there, it would certainly have been 1988.

Cowboys quarterback Danny White lived in Phoenix, Arizona.

That year, the Cardinals moved from St. Louis to Phoenix.

On September 12, the Cowboys played the Cardinals in Sun Devil Stadium, and Danny's father, a resident of Phoenix, attended the game.

Seated in the Dallas section, behind our bench, a disgruntled Arizona fan unleashed a torrent of verbal abuse at Cowboys quarterback Danny White.

Tired of the assault on his son's character, Danny's dad punched the guy.

It must have worked because the fan shut up.

Days later, in Dallas we read in the paper that the fan was suing Danny's father. I had met Mr. White, and I used the occasion to call him in Phoenix, posing as a lawyer.

"Mr. White," I said, attempting to veil my identity, "I'm a Dallas attorney, and I was wondering if you might need some legal assistance."

To which he replied, "No, thanks, Buck."

I don't have a poker face, and I am lousy at impersonations.

In 1984 and 1985, I was honored when the Cowboys management asked for my help in designing the Valley Ranch locker room. Coming from a military background, I asked for half again as much as I thought we needed.

My tours at the Air Force Academy spoiled me for the NFL.

The Air Force brass never spared any expense in the design of the cadets' athletic facilities in Colorado Springs. Being an old noncom, I knew that if I asked for more than I expected, I might actually get what I wanted. But my calculations went awry, and I discovered that what I asked for from the Dallas Cowboys, I usually got—in spades.

At the outset, the architect had floated a reasonable request: "Since most players are tall, why not raise the shower fixtures?" That made perfect sense to me, and I agreed.

For two seasons I never heard a complaint from any Dallas player. But in 1987, I received my first. For NFL standards, Kelvin Martin was small, at 5′-9″ and 161 pounds.

After showering, Kelvin got all over me one afternoon, "Buck, is it true? Did you really have something to do with designing these showers?" I told Kelvin that I had.

"Then why did you have to put everything up so high, where I can't reach it?"

The new Valley Ranch facility had spacious lockers, and it was common for me to put two players in one locker. Punter Mike Saxon (1985–1992) from San Diego State and placekicker Roger Ruzek (1987–1989) from Weber State shared a locker.

The pair soon came to be known as the Cowboys' Odd Couple.

Mike was messy; Roger was neat.

After two weeks sharing the same locker, Roger came by the cage and asked me for a bottle of alcohol to wipe down his side of the locker. Mike could have cared less.

1988 was a hard year for everyone at Dallas.

When you're winning, everyone walks around with a great big smile on his face. When you're losing, everyone's noticeably subdued, grumpy, and uptight.

Not since the first five years of the franchise, during those critical team-building years, had the Cowboys done so poorly in the conference rankings.

In 1988 we secured fifth place in the NFC East—*last.*

Things went from bad to worse, and the extent of the hemorrhaging was greater than most could have imagined, or were willing to admit. The contagion was endemic, rising up through the organization's ranks to the highest rung—to owner Bum Bright.

It is said Bum made his fortune in real estate and finance. As both began to decline, his empire began to shrink, and the sale of the Cowboys became imminent.

Invisible to the public eye, behind-the-scenes deals were being considered that by year's end would culminate in the sale of the team and the demise of its legendary head coach.

Toward the end of 1988, rumors began to swirl suggesting the potential sale of the Cowboys, but the rank and file—the players, staff, and fans—were unaware of the extent of the crisis. I'm sure Coach Landry knew of the team's predicament. But if he did, Coach wasn't the kind of man to worry or express concern—much less talk about it.

Whether he did or did not know that his beloved Cowboys were headed for the auction block, we may never know. But we know what history has recorded—the end of a football era was upon us—and Coach Tom Landry would soon be out of a job.

1989—THE JONES DYNASTY

At the end of 1988 and early in 1989, celebrity sightings in Dallas put Arkansas oil and gas mogul Jerry Jones and University of Miami Head Coach Jimmy Johnson at a downtown Mexican restaurant—the two principals engaged in animated dialogue.

Jimmy and Jerry had played on the same Arkansas Razorbacks football team, and the men had known each other for years. Reportedly, the two were good friends.

Rumor led to speculation.

Speculation led to the sports page and front-page Dallas news.

Were plans in the works to sell the team?

Was this Coach Landry's swan song?

Was America's team to be auctioned to the highest bidder—worse, a non-Texan?

The news, on the heels of three losing seasons, had Dallas talking. Then it hit town like a bone-jarring Cliff Harris tackle—the team had been sold to Jerry Jones.

Jones reached an agreement to purchase the team from Bum Bright on February 25 and announced that Jimmy Johnson would replace Tom Landry as head coach.

NFL owners unanimously approved the sale on April 18 at a special meeting in New York. At that meeting, Tex Schramm was named president of the new World League of American Football and Schramm announced his resignation as the president and general manager of the Dallas Cowboys, after twenty-nine years.

At Valley Ranch, everyone from admins to coaches speculated as to his or her job future. Anxiety spread within the ranks, and hushed hallway conversations were common.

There may have been a silent few who knew of Bright's dilemma before the news broke—certainly Schramm and Brandt. After the cat was out of the proverbial bag, stories circulated suggesting Tex had made attempts to seek buyers for the team.

I don't know. I will tell you that certain trainers—members of the NFL trainers' union—were the first to know that change was in the wind. It must be a union thing.

1989 Team Photo

Shortly after the change in head coaches had been announced, the Cowboys held a minicamp for the veterans at Valley Ranch. The mood was somber. Coach Landry, Tex Schramm, and Joe Bailey were there. Coach Landry followed the last player into the meeting room and closed the door behind him. That door remained shut for ten minutes.

When Coach Landry opened the door and sped toward his office, I could see the tears coursing down his cheeks. Later I spoke to the players and I was able to piece together bits and pieces of the announcement.

Players say Coach called the meeting to order and spoke to them about their great times together, and his love of football. They said he was unable to finish what he'd set out to say, and that he abruptly left the room.

To this day players and coaches are loath to discuss that meeting.

The hallway outside was crowded with concerned staff members. Coach Landry went directly to his office without speaking to any of us. He had his personal belongings—nearly three decades of memories—cleared out of Valley Ranch by week's end.

After the meeting I saw Coach Landry several times that week—and each time, in his typical fashion, he appeared in good spirits. He shook my hand and wished me well.

I didn't see my mentor, friend, and hero again until 1993, when Coach Landry was inducted into the Cowboys Ring of Honor.

It takes a whole lot to get veteran NFL players down.

During the course of my career there has been the rare occasion where I've witnessed one or two older vets shed a tear or show anything approaching gut-wrenching emotion. After Coach Landry's farewell meeting, the Cowboys took it harder collectively than any single incident I know of.

With Coach Landry

For Tom Rafferty, his saddest Cowboys memory was "The night that Coach Landry was fired and the team meeting the next day."

Tom's sentiment echoes in players' and coaches' conversations to this day.

Coach Landry's sudden loss was especially hard for the assistant coaches who were involved in rebuilding after the dismal seasons of 1986 (7–9), 1987 (7–8), and 1988 (3–13).

Perhaps Coach Ward's sentiments best sum up the mood of players and coaches: "In 1989, we were as ready as any year I was there . . . and boom . . . he (Landry) was gone."

The 'boys had lost their single most stabilizing influence—and hero. The underpinnings of the dynasty were in disarray—and yet more pillars were soon to topple.

Tex Schramm got his walking papers two months later.

Gil Brandt managed the draft of '89, then he too was gone.

Jerry Jones and Coach Johnson held another minicamp shortly after Coach Landry left. Old guard Dallas coaches who had been there since the early days retired, quit, or were replaced with Coach Johnson's staff.

Many seasoned coaches had already left.

Coach Stallings (1972–1985) left in 1985.

Coach Myers (1962–1986) retired in 1986.

No doubt sensing the inevitable, Coach Tubbs (1966–1988), Coach Stautner (1966–1988), Coach Lavan (1980–1988), Coach Erkenbeck (1987–1988), Coach Hackett (1986–1988), and Coach Solari (1987–1988) left at the conclusion of the 1988 season.

Coach Ward (1976–1989) and Coach Armstrong (1982–1989) were released in 1989, and Coach Nolan (1962–1967, 1982–1990) was replaced in 1990.

Linebacker Jerry Tubbs (1960–1967) from the University of Oklahoma wreaked havoc on OU opponents. Jerry was the Cowboys' first starting middle linebacker. As a Linebackers' Coach (1966–1988), he passed those same skills along to Dallas greats Lee Roy Jordan, Bob Breunig, Eugene Lockhart, Chuck Howley, and Thomas Henderson.

Tubbs, Jordan, Breunig, Howley, and Henderson all played in the Pro Bowl.

Tubbs was tough as nails.

He was also a quiet man who preferred to eat his lunch alone in his car.

Jerry Tubbs was an All-American center-linebacker for Bud Wilkinson's unbeaten Oklahoma teams from 1954 to 1956. He was the Walter Camp Award winner in 1956 as the nation's outstanding player. In 1985, *Sooners Illustrated Magazine* rated Jerry Tubbs No. 4 on the list of the ten all-time greatest Oklahoma football players.

Defensive Backs Coach Dick Nolan was another cagey NFL veteran and former Dallas Cowboy safety (1962). From 1962 until 1967, he coached the Cowboys' defensive backfield before taking the job of head coach for the San Francisco 49ers (1968–1975).

Nolan's 49ers won the NFC West championship in 1970, 1971, and 1972.

Nolan and Tom Landry were defensive back teammates with the New York Giants (1954–1955) when Landry was a player-coach. He also played under Landry in 1956, 1957, and 1959 when Landry was New York's defensive coach.

Following a tradition set by Gil Brandt, Coach Nolan converted Cowboy Manny Hendrix (1986–1991), a former Utah basketball star, to cornerback. He was instrumental in converting Robert Williams (1987–1993), formerly a running back from Baylor, into a successful cornerback. And at first, Vince Albritton (1991–1994) from the University of Washington was tried out at linebacker before the Cowboys kept him on as a safety.

Coach Nolan was an old-school coach and a funny guy whose sense of humor helped ease tensions. Today, his son, Mike, is the head coach of the San Francisco 49ers.

The former trainer for the University of Miami, Kevin O'Neil, replaced Cowboys Head Trainer Don Cochren. However, Don was kept on the Dallas payroll, in large part due to his expertise in the area of record keeping—specifically, litigation.

With encouragement from wide receiver Michael Irvin, Coach Johnson gave O'Neil the thumbs-up for head trainer. More than a trainer, Kevin is a very smart guy.

Video Director Bob Friedman (1960–1989) was cut, and in Bob's stead, Robert Blackwell, the former assistant director, was selected to head up our video department.

Many of the old guard who had been there the longest wound up being cut.

Former quarterback Jerry Rhome (1965–1968) agreed to sign as the quarterbacks coach during the transition phase, but was gone after his one-year contract expired.

Special teams coach Alan Lowry stayed through the year and left.

Otherwise, the post-Landry Dallas coaching staff consisted of new coaches brought with Coach Johnson from the University of Miami, or picked up elsewhere.

Coach Hubbard "Axe" Alexander (1989–1997) was Coach Johnson's pick for receivers coach. Under his leadership, the

Cowboys fielded such All-Star players as Michael Irvin, Alvin Harper, and Kelvin Martin.

Alexander's wide receiving corps made immense progress in 1991. Irvin led the NFL with 1,523 yards, sixth most in NFL history, and the NFC with ninety-three catches, seventh best ever in the league. Michael was named Most Valuable Player in the 1992 Pro Bowl.

Harper became a starter in the ninth game of his rookie year and three weeks later caught four passes for 101 yards in our win over Washington at RFK.

Defensive Back Coach Dave "Camp" Campo (1989–2002) came to the Cowboys with University of Miami Head Coach Jimmy Johnson. During his two-year stint with the Hurricanes, Camp fine-tuned the best defensive back in school history—safety Bennie Blades, the 1987 Jim Thorpe Award recipient.

Coach Campo was a perfectionist with as good a player work ethic as I have seen.

Prior to coming to Miami, Campo spent three seasons on the Syracuse coaching staff, culminating in national contention for the Orangemen.

Eight of Campo's Miami players went on to sign NFL contracts.

In the midst of the abrupt coaching shuffle that year, Jerry Fowler and I were wondering if we still had jobs. Coach Johnson visited the equipment cage shortly after Coach Landry's dismissal and relieved us of our concerns. "Thought I'd let you know, Buck," Jimmy said, "there won't be any changes in your department."

Along with the staff changes came fresh, new faces and inspired talent.

Quarterback Troy Aikman was an outstanding contribution to the organization. The Cowboys held the No. 1 draft pick for only the second time in our history, and we announced the signing of Aikman to a six-year contract on April 20.

Troy's backup was quarterback Steve Walsh from the University of Miami.

Guard Mark Stepnoski (1989–1994, 1999–2001) from Pittsburgh and free agent linebacker Jack Del Rio (1989–1991) from the University of Southern California, by way of Kansas City, joined us in 1989. Today, Del Rio coaches the Jacksonville Jaguars.

Defensive end Tony Tolbert (1989–1997) from Texas El Paso had been a linebacker in college. Conditioning Coaches Ward and Woicik oversaw Tony's bulking up and developed Tolbert into an outstanding NFL defensive lineman.

In 1996, Tony had twelve quarterback sacks.

Tony's knees started to go bad toward the end of his career, and it was not uncommon to see the doctors drain fluid from both knees immediately before a game.

Troy Aikman got hurt after eleven games, and Steve Walsh stepped in to fill Troy's shoes.

The only game we won that year was with Steve Walsh at the Cowboys' helm, in a 13–3 squeaker over the Redskins in Washington's RFK Stadium on November 5.

That year the Cowboys placed fifth—last place—in the NFC East.

To top off a shattered year, the Cowboys suffered an inauspicious 1–15 record.

Not since the team's first-year 1960 record of 0–11–1 had the Cowboys suffered through a more embarrassing season.

Given the change in head coaches, the Cowboys were allowed an additional minicamp in 1989. Coach Johnson was intent on making the transition as speedy and as painless as possible.

During the minicamps that followed, Coach had the players run timed 110-yard sprints. A certain asthmatic kicker had the slowest time on the field that first day, and Jimmy had him run the "asthma" field. The kicker was released that afternoon.

Steve Walsh was the No. 3 draft choice in 1989.

Coach Johnson (middle) listens to Coach Jerry Rhome as Coach Wannstedt looks on

Jersey numbers are sacrosanct for most NFL players.

When Steve joined the club he requested the No. 4 jersey, but punter Mike Saxon (1985–1992) from San Diego State had that jersey. Mike extended Steve an olive branch and an offer—five thousand dollars and you can have my number. Walsh declined Mike's offer.

According to Thomas Henderson, "A book could be written on player numbers and how they are assigned."

I agree, Thomas.

Dallas has never retired one.

Defensive lineman Bob Lilly, Mr. Cowboy, is the exception—or is he?

After Bob retired, Schramm issued orders "never to give out No. 74."

Schramm later clarified his statement: "But No. 74 is *not* retired."

No. 74—Bob Lilly's number—has not been worn by a Cowboy since.

Former All-Pro linebacker Lee Roy Jordan became the seventh member of the Ring of Honor when Lee Roy was recognized during the half-time ceremonies of the Phoenix Cardinals' game on October 29.

Despite the tremendous ups and downs associated with that rebuilding season, one highlight stands out. I chatted with former Academy pal and San Diego Chargers equipment manager Sid Brooks before our first preseason game on the West Coast.

Sid was instrumental in my landing the job at Dallas.

San Diego is home to many active service and retired U.S. military personnel. The Chargers were anxious to honor our servicemen and -women by celebrating Uniform Day at Chargers Stadium during the Cowboys-Chargers preseason game halftime.

Sid asked if I still had my Air Force "blues" uniform, and I said that I thought I did. He explained his plan, and I asked Coach Jimmy Johnson what he thought about honoring our service personnel. Jimmy agreed, and I called Bucky in Dallas. I asked my son to search for my boxed uniform in the attic and have it shipped to me in San Diego.

The uniform had been stored in our attic for sixteen years—nothing a good cleaning could not fix. Bucky found the uniform, had it dry cleaned, and overnighted it to me. The cleaning destroyed the coat's lining, but the game—and the military tribute—went on.

In that August 13 game in San Diego, Sergeant Sid Brooks and Sergeant Thomas "Buck" Buchanan stood shoulder to shoulder at midfield during pregame ceremonies. The Cowboys went on to win that game 20–3.

Uniform Day at Chargers Stadium in San Diego

Sid's old uniform no longer fit his new physical proportions. He ended up buying a new, much larger Air Force uniform, and Sid hasn't lived it down since.

That was one record-setting year.

And to top it off, we never returned to training camp at Thousand Oaks.

7

THE 1990s—THE JONES ERA

It is safe to say most of us who remained after the sale of the team to Jerry Jones on April 18, 1989, in New York, had no idea what to expect from our new management.

For almost three decades, Tom Landry had coached the Cowboys.

Tex Schramm had served as the team's president and general manager.

Gil Brandt had served as vice president and director of player personnel.

And, alternately, the Murchison family and an eleven-member limited partnership, headed by Dallas businessman H. R. "Bum" Bright, had owned America's Team. Overnight, all that changed.

When Mr. Jones bought the Cowboys, he made his intentions crystal clear: *There would be no substitute for winning*. Super Bowl triumphs would no longer be just the distant memories of a proud franchise. Returning to the Super Bowl quickly became the daily focus of the entire Cowboys organization.

In the years to come, his contributions would affect the NFL in a significant fashion. NFL Commissioner Paul Tagliabue appointed Jones to the Competition Committee, making him the first owner to serve on that prestigious committee since the death of Cincinnati's Paul Brown. In the years to come, Mr. Jones would serve on the Broadcast, the Management Council Executive, and the Business Ventures Committees.

1990—DOUBLE TROUBLE

Not only was I forced to adjust to a whole new set of assistant coaches, trainers, and players, I had a whole new set of contacts to work with during training camp—both of them.

After dropping our deal at Cal Lutheran in Thousand Oaks, the Cowboys held the 1990 season's training camp—the first of two that year—in Austin, Texas.

On July 18, I settled into the team's new Austin training camp at St. Edward's University. St. Ed's had no football field, no doubt because the school had no football program. But the Austin Chamber of Commerce was pulling for the Cowboys to hold training camp there. They did have a soccer field and a very large uneven field that later doubled for two back-to-back practice areas—but it was no Thousand Oaks.

Joe Bailey's replacement, Director of Operations/Facility Coordinator Bruce Mays, had assigned me to the field project earlier in the year. During the off-season, Bruce had me work with Austin Parks and Recreation's lead architect.

The field required the range of modifications, not least of which included a viable sprinkler system, sodding, and drainage, as well as a major leveling of the uneven playing surface. Bleachers had to be constructed and set in place along the sideline for the fans.

Our first day of practice was held despite heavy rain.

Still, the field held up.

Bleachers were strategically positioned and a campaign was launched to encourage the public to view the Cowboys' practice sessions, free of charge.

Someone once said, "If you build it, they will come."

And come they did, by the thousands.

The bleachers were always filled with adoring fans—consumers with money to buy Dallas souvenirs. All told, our first-ever in-state camp attracted nearly one hundred thousand fans.

It was great holding training camp in Austin. Commuting time from Dallas was a mere three hours, depending on traffic, making the logistics of moving our equipment easier.

But for the players the hot, humid climate was more inhospitable than the dry desert conditions at Thousand Oaks. For those of us who lived in Dallas, family life when it could be found was easier.

We drove to Austin on Wednesday and practiced on Thursday afternoon.

In keeping with the new NFL trend, the Dallas Cowboys franchise had become a brilliant commercial enterprise. Team paraphernalia was offered to the crowds, and our fans were more than willing to snap up every trinket and bauble.

If I had any complaints about training camp at St. Ed's, it would be over the dressing rooms. The university's dressing rooms were tiny, and there were no windows. We had to constantly use large fans to prevent the humidity from rusting our equipment. Everything metal, including the helmets' hardware, rusted out and had to be replaced.

But like every other obstacle, we worked through that, too—until August 10.

Almost settled in, Coach Johnson shook my world with news that we were moving training camp to ritzy La Jolla, California, nestled on the windswept Pacific shore above San Diego.

So I packed and sent three trucks to Valley Ranch and another to La Jolla for the upcoming preseason San Diego Chargers' game.

La Jolla presented me with a whole new set of challenges.

We remained at our West Coast training camp from August 12 through 17, played the Los Angeles Raiders on August 18, and returned to Dallas the following day.

The Cowboys had a great crop of rookies—the No. 1 draft choice, running back Emmitt Smith (1990–2002) from the University of Florida, and the No. 2 draft choice, defensive tackle Jimmie "Swampy" Jones (1990–1993) from Miami of Florida.

Swampy had played for Jimmy Johnson at Miami. The always laid-back lineman had to be pushed to work hard, but Coach Johnson knew the correct buttons to push.

During the 1992 midseason, I heard a God-awful racket out back.

I opened the equipment room back door that led to the loading dock at Valley Ranch and saw a large black foreign automobile rocking back and forth to a rap tune.

After checking with the players, I learned the car belonged to Swampy, and it had been outfitted with a security system that was guaranteed to deafen any would-be thief.

Swampy finally turned off the noise and returned laughing.

We were fortunate to draft cornerback Kenneth "The Shark" Gant (1990–1994) from Albany State that year. Kennie was especially good at getting the fans at Texas Stadium worked up by waving his hands and prancing around on the field.

The Cowboys enjoyed one of our better trades when we nabbed free agent tight end and University of Wyoming graduate Jay Novacek (1990–1996) from the Cardinals.

Cowboys offensive lineman Dale Hellestrae (1990–2000) from Southern Methodist University was one of the best deep snappers in the NFL.

When "Poppa Dale" retired in 2000, he went to Phoenix to live, but was later picked up by the Buffalo Bills when their deep snapper was injured.

I often wonder how Dale fared in the frigid northeast, because at Dallas, before suiting up for practice, he routinely dropped by the cage to inquire about the weather.

Today, Dale lives in Phoenix where he hosts a radio sports talk show.

Other rookie Cowboys included fullback Tommie Agee (1990–1994) from Auburn, linebacker Vinson "Vin" Smith (1990–1992) from East Carolina, and safety James Washington (1990–1994) from UCLA.

Tommie Agee came close to knocking me down in 1993 during a regular season offensive drill. I was spotting the ball on the 20-yard line. Tommie's assignment was to cross the line of scrimmage, cut left, and run a pass pattern toward the sideline.

Middle linebacker Kenny Norton, Jr. (1988–1993) from UCLA was responsible for covering Agee. Kenny gave Tommie a forearm shiver, knocking the large fullback into the Cowboys' scrawny equipment manager.

I took a good shot and lost my hat in the process—not bad for a sixty-year-old.

Lucky for me, Tommie felt contact and stopped on a dime. I received a nasty chest bruise, and Video Director Robert Blackwell captured the precious moment on film.

Robert later said, "Buck, you still have pretty good reflexes."

Tommie was a good kid with a booming voice.

I still think he should have been a Country-Western singer.

Emmitt Smith held out until after training camp to sign—well worth the Cowboys' wait as three seasons later, EM was nominated Most Valuable Player (1993).

Emmitt led NFL rookie running backs that year in rushing yardage and touchdowns and was named the Associated Press NFC Offensive Rookie of the Year.

He went on to a record-breaking Dallas career, securing the all-time number one position for career points (986) and touchdowns scored (164). In rushing attempts, Emmitt surpassed every Dallas player to date, including Tony Dorsett (2,755), with 4,052.

I was charged with spotting offensive drills at Valley Ranch, and I knew after watching his first play carrying the ball that Emmitt was going to be something special.

Dorsett was quick, and faster than Emmitt out to distance, but Emmitt's rocket-like takeoff was faster than Tony's. Unlike Tony, who seemed to gain momentum over the long run, Emmitt's sustainable speed was good to twenty-five yards.

Both are great men, and it was a pleasure to know them and watch them play.

Emmitt Smith and wide receiver Michael Irvin (1988–1999) from Miami, Florida, began a Cowboys tradition, indeed a NFL tradition, of keeping the game balls they scored with.

After their touchdown, Emmitt or Michael would hand me the ball, and I'd write his number on it in black magic marker and place it in my lockable sideline trunk.

TV sportscasters John Madden and Pat Summerall observed the ball-collecting activity and commented on it on air. The practice quickly spread throughout the league.

With Aikman hurt, starting quarterback Babe Laufenberg (1989–1990) from the University of Indiana had a bad day on December 30 at Atlanta's Fulton County Stadium in our last regular season game.

The Falcons defeated the Cowboys 26–7.

After we returned to Dallas I spoke with Babe, who is a Dallas TV sportscaster today, about his performance.

"You really had a bad day in Atlanta," I said.

"How could you tell, Buck?" he asked.

"Come on," I said, "follow me."

I led Babe back to the equipment room where we were getting the team's uniforms ready to be laundered. Babe's jersey was atop the stack of dirty uniforms.

I retrieved the jersey and we studied its front—it was clean, and Babe's No. 15 was clearly discernible. I turned the jersey around and we inspected its back, which was heavily grass stained and covered in mud. Babe's number was barely legible.

Babe nodded and walked away.

That was Laufenberg's last NFL game.

The Cowboys showed only modest improvement that year with a 7–9 record. Enduring a major rebuilding, Dallas finished the 1990 schedule with a fourth-place showing in the NFC East.

We put a string of four wins together in midseason before losing the last two games—routs to Philadelphia and Atlanta—and we failed to make it to the playoffs.

Despite having to rebuild, Jerry Jones and Coach Johnson continued to build one block on top of the other, setting the stage for an impressive comeback and a divisional playoff bid their third year with the team.

The Cowboys picked up Special Teams/Tight Ends Coach Joe Avezzano (1990–2000, 2002) from Texas A&M that year. At A&M, Joe had coached the offensive line and helped lead the Aggies to three Southwest Conference titles and two Cotton Bowl wins.

Coach Avezzano was an outstanding special teams coach and a fierce competitor. In 1991, we led the NFL in points scored on special teams and in kickoff return averages.

That season, Joe was named the NFL Special Teams Coach of the Year.

Today, he is an assistant coach for the Oakland Raiders under head coach Norv Turner, former Cowboys offensive coordinator and quarterbacks coach.

Strength and Conditioning Coach Mike Woicik (1990–1996) took over Coach Ward's job. Mike joined the Cowboys after ten years as the conditioning coach at Syracuse, one of the nation's top football programs during the decade of the 1980s.

From 1990 to 1996, the Cowboys developed into one of the healthiest and best-conditioned teams within the NFL, evidenced by our overall 78–31 record, including eleven playoff victories and three Super Bowl titles.

With Woicik at the Cowboys' conditioning helm, Dallas finished each year strong, going into fifteen playoffs in six consecutive seasons. Woicik also played a role in player rehabilitation.

Working in concert with the Cowboys medical staff, Woicik implemented programs for players to regain their strength during lengthy rehab periods, allowing them to return to practice in a more timely fashion. His efforts were recognized when his peers voted him the NFL "Strength Coach of the Year" after the Cowboys' Super Bowl XXVII victory in Pasadena.

One of Woicik's prize pupils at Syracuse was fullback Daryl Johnston, the Cowboys' second-round pick in 1989. Woicik also worked with Dave Campo and Tony Wise at Syracuse.

The year ended with Jimmy Johnson being named NFL Coach of the Year by the Associated Press.

Coach Tom Landry was inducted into the Pro Football Hall of Fame his first year of eligibility, joining Bob Lilly and Roger Staubach.

1991—UP FROM THE ASHES

On July 27 Tex Schramm was enshrined in the Football Hall of Fame in Canton, Ohio, joining Staubach, Lilly, and Landry, and Coach Jimmy Johnson's third season witnessed a banner draft and a major solidification of the Cowboys' lagging defense.

Assistant Head Coach and Offensive Coordinator/Quarterbacks Coach Norv Turner (1991–1993) became a Cowboys coach after working as an assistant coach at Los Angeles (1985–1990).

At the Rams, Turner oversaw wide receivers Willie Anderson, the NFL leader in yards per catch (1989 and 1990), Henry Ellard, the league's leading receiver in 1989, and tight end Pete Holohan, who caught forty-nine or more passes each season from 1988 to 1990.

Coach Turner took over for Dave Shula (1989–1990) as first offensive coordinator in 1989. In that job, Turner was responsible for developing Troy Aikman into an amazing quarterback. His performance with the Cowboys' offense captured the attention of Coach Johnson, who promoted Turner to assistant head coach after the Super Bowl–winning season of 1992.

Under Turner's tutelage, the Dallas offense exploded with big plays and dogged precision throughout 1992, and by year's end, the Cowboys had assembled what many believed to be the NFL's most balanced attack.

Coach Turner's rookie year at Dallas saw the Cowboys win the 1991 Wild Card Game against the Chicago Bears in Soldier Field, 17–13, but lose the Divisional Playoffs to the Lions in Detroit, 6–38. During his short tenure at Dallas, Turner celebrated the Cowboys' Super Bowl XXVII and XXVIII wins in 1992 and 1993.

Today, Norv Turner is the head coach of the Oakland Raiders.

We drafted cornerback Larry Brown (1991–1995) from Texas Christian, linebacker Dixon Edwards (1991–1995) from Michigan

Coach Norv Turner (second from left) flanked by Beurlein, Staubach, and Aikman

State, wide receiver Alvin "Harp" Harper (1991–1994) from the University of Tennessee, and defensive lineman Leon "Big Cat" Lett (1991–2000) from Emporia State.

Alvin was a complement to All-Star Cowboys receiver Michael Irvin. He left the Cowboys in '94 and went to Tampa Bay. I was told that when a Buccaneers trainer was removing tape from Alvin's fingers, he accidentally severed the tip of Harp's index finger. Harper continued in the NFL, and returned to play for the Cowboys in 1999.

Leon Lett was a great guy and a terrific player, but he was shy.

In the Thanksgiving Day Game at Texas Stadium on November 25, 1993, Big Cat touched a blocked Dolphins' field goal kick late in the game with Dallas ahead, 14–13.

In the mayhem, as players scrambled on the slick, sleet-covered field for the ball, Leon touched it and Miami recovered. The Dolphins went on to convert a field goal and won the game 16–14. After the game, Leon hid from the press in the Cowboys' training room, which was off limits to the media.

The real draft catch that year was defensive tackle, Outland Trophy winner, and No. 1 overall pick Russell Maryland (1991–1995) from Miami of Florida.

Al Walker was my field maintenance man in 1991. A seasoned veteran, Al is with the Cowboys today. Good-natured Al is a smaller spitting image of Russell Maryland.

For his first rookie meeting, Defensive Coordinator/Linebackers Coach Dave Wannstedt (1989–1992) set Maryland up. Wannstedt asked Al to don a No. 67 jersey—Russell Maryland's number. Wannstedt had Al knock on the meeting room door after everyone was seated. Al did so, and Coach invited him in.

Al entered the meeting carrying a helmet, walked up to Russell, and in a booming voice, growled, "Hey, man! You're in my seat."

The startled Maryland bolted out of his chair, and the room erupted in laughter.

A rook's life in the NFL is fraught with uncertainty and mischief. Russell Maryland later confessed to me that he was happy to have taken his rookie licks early.

Wannstedt was a Jimmy Johnson pick from the University of Miami. He was an accomplished motivator and a great defensive coordinator at the Cowboys. Prone to temper tantrums, his idol was Coach Mike Ditka.

As a fitting tribute, Wannstedt replaced Ditka as the Bears' head coach in 1993.

Under Wannstedt, the Dallas defense opened the 1991 season with new starters at six of eleven positions. By year's end, rookies Russell Maryland and Larry Brown were with the first team, leaving only three remaining starters from the previous season.

Offensive Line Coach Tony Wise (1989–1992) was another University of Miami, Jimmy Johnson assistant coach pick and a good friend of Coach Wannstedt's.

In the early 1990s, Coach Wise developed a unit that provided protection and opened holes for a Dallas offense that produced four Pro Bowlers. In 1990, the Cowboys went from twenty-eighth in the league in total yards to ninth place in 1991.

The Cowboys' front wall sprang Emmitt Smith to league-leading yardage, and Troy Aikman completed a team-record 65.3 percent of his passes. In 1991, Michael Irvin led the NFC in catches and the NFL in receiving yards.

Wise oversaw Kevin Gogan's transition from tackle to left guard.

He was instrumental in developing rookie tackle Erik Williams (1991–2000) from Central Ohio State. Erik started three games, including the Cowboys' 24–21 win over the Redskins at RFK on November 24 before a home crowd of fifty-five thousand and change.

Erik Williams was a four-time Pro Bowler (1993, 1996, 1997, and 1999) who was considered one of the best pass protection blockers in the league. Shortly before his retirement from the Cowboys, Erik was involved in an automobile accident in Dallas, severely injuring his ankle. After rehab, he played one more season before retiring.

As big and tough as he was, Erik was a gentle spirit in the Cowboys dressing room, walking about, singing softly to himself. But when he donned his helmet, the big guy became a fearsome and aggressive competitor.

Erik was another low-maintenance player.

Down the stretch, five other rookies contributed to a Dallas defense that held opponents to 82.4 yards rushing per game over the last five games, all Cowboy victories.

No touchdowns were scored on the ground against us in our final three games that season, propelling America's Team to our first playoff appearance in six seasons.

To add to the mix, the Cowboys drafted linebacker Godfrey Myles (1991–1996) from the University of Florida.

Dallas defensive lineman Tony Casillas (1991–1993, 1996–1997) from the University of Oklahoma may have been low maintenance, but he was especially picky when it came to shoes.

Adidas had several types of shoes with varying grip configurations for different turf conditions. Tony generally ran through at least three pairs of shoes prior to pregame warm-up. His first year at Dallas, the former Sooner insisted on taping his jersey to his shoulder pads, a process most players relied on us to do.

Double-sided carpet tape is used throughout the NFL to ensure a tight-fitting jersey that is less likely to be grabbed by opposing players. The process of taping the jersey to the pads is not a one-man job, but Tony insisted on doing the taping himself.

I watched Casillas exit our dressing room, his jersey bunched up so badly that his name was barely discernible. Had Schramm been around, he would surely have had an issue with Tony or me—or both of us—for Tony's unkempt uniform appearance.

After several outings, Casillas saw the light and allowed me to do the taping.

To add to the influx of new players, the Cowboys acquired quarterback Steve Beurlein (1991–1992) from the University of Notre Dame in a trade with the Raiders.

Troy got hurt at the end of the season, and Beurlein stepped in as quarterback.

Beurlein won three of our last five games and helped pull us through that season.

Emmitt Smith and Michael Irvin became the first two players from the same team to lead the NFL in rushing and receiving yardage the very same season. Emmitt had 1,563 yards rushing, and Michael set single-season club records for receptions (93) and receiving yardage (1,523).

Both were named to the NFC Pro Bowl with Jay Novacek and Troy Aikman.

Dallas had not fielded four offensive players at a Pro Bowl in over thirteen years.

That year, Michael was named Pro Bowl MVP.

For a coach and a team to climb out of a 1–15 hole to a 7–9 season record in one year is phenomenal. To go from a 1–15 to an 11–5 season in two short years is miraculous.

After winning the last five games of the season, the Cowboys finished with an 11–5 record—our team best since 1983. To add to the fun, we defeated the Redskins 24–21 at RFK on November 24 after Washington had registered its eleventh straight victory.

The Cowboys went from last place to the No. 2 spot in the NFC East in three seasons. We beat the Bears 17–13 in Chicago to win the 1991 First-Round Playoffs, which put us in the Divisional Playoffs against the Lions in Detroit.

We lost 6–38.

An injured Aikman started the game at Detroit, and Beurlein finished.

Despite the lopsided score, Steve steered the Cowboys through several tight spots.

In the final analysis, Dallas survived a team rebuilding and better days were on the horizon. Once again, the Cowboys were a team to be reckoned with.

1992—SUPER BOWL DREAMS

Tired and ready to hang it up, that preseason I tended my resignation to Bruce Mays. Bruce alerted Coach Johnson and Jimmy stopped by the equipment room.

"What's this all about, Buck?"

"My resignation," I said. "I'm tired, Coach. It's time I spent quality time with the family."

Coach Johnson said that he understood, but asked if I would stay on an additional two years and train a successor. I agreed that I would, and I'm thrilled that I did.

The year began with a 2–3 preseason record and a trip to Tokyo, Japan, where we played the Houston Oilers before fifty-one thousand fans in an exhibition game Dallas lost 23–34.

1992 witnessed the arrival of several outstanding new rookies.

Dallas drafted cornerback Kevin "Pup" Smith (1992–1999) from Texas A&M, safety Darren Woodson (1992–2003) from Arizona State, free agent center Frank Cornish (1992–1994) from UCLA, free agent defensive end Charles Haley (1992–1996) from James Madison, and defensive tackle Chad Hennings (1992–2000) from the United States Air Force Academy.

Dallas secured Haley from the San Francisco 49ers.

#94 Charles Haley with Jerry and me aboard the Cowboys' chartered jet

Charles was small for a defensive lineman, but he made up for his size by studying game films. He was smart, and he was extremely quick with catlike reflexes.

Always vocal upon entering the locker room, Charles loved to give grief to everyone, including this Cowboys equipment manager, whom he called "Old Man."

My retirement was officially announced to the team by Coach Johnson shortly before the Championship Game in Dallas against San Francisco on January 21, 1994.

After the Cowboys' win over the Bills in Atlanta in Super Bowl XXVIII, Haley approached me and insisted, "You know, Old Man, we won this game for you."

The Cowboys' No. 1 draft choice that year was Pup Smith. Our second No. 1 draft choice was linebacker Robert Jones (1992–1995) from East Carolina. That year's No. 2 draft pick, ahead of Darren Woodson, the Cowboys' second No. 2 draft choice, was Jimmy Smith (1992) from Jackson State.

Jimmy had a medical problem all season that required the constant attention of the Dallas trainers and prevented him from playing in any of our games. In 1993, he was picked up by the Jacksonville Jaguars, got past his injuries, and turned into quite a wide receiver.

The last I heard, Jimmy still plays for the Jaguars.

Darren Woodson holds the Cowboys record for solo career tackles—787—and the Cowboys combined tackles career record—a whopping 1,350. He was selected to five consecutive Pro Bowls. At strong safety, Darren Woodson defined the position.

When Darren hit you, you knew you had been socked.

The Cowboys drafted Chad Hennings in 1988. Dallas took a chance with the strapping defensive tackle, much like it had years before with Roger Staubach, as Chad had a four-year military obligation with the U.S. Air Force.

Chad flew an A-10 "Wart Hog" and saw combat during Desert Storm.

Four years later, I could tell right away that the rookie was a military serviceman because Chad was always organized and prompt. He worked hard and lifted weights as part of his demanding regimen to bulk up. Chad was a very smart defensive lineman.

In our first regular season game at Texas Stadium, we defeated the Washington Redskins, 23–10. We went on to win every game but three—losing big to the Eagles in Philadelphia 7–31, and going down in heartbreakers to the Rams at home 23–27 and to the Redskins 17–20 at RFK.

A week before losing to the Redskins, Dallas played the Broncos in Denver on December 6. It was very cold, as most winter days at Mile High Stadium tend to be. I had just received new fleece sweats with cotton lining from APEX for the coaching staff.

Defensive Line Coach Butch Davis (1989–1994) came up to me in the locker room and said he couldn't get his leg through his sweat pants because the lining had been sown together. I told him there were no more sweat pants available and went about my business getting ready for pregame warm-up.

A half hour later, Running Back Coach Joe Brodsky (1989–1997) complained to me that he could not get his leg through his sweats.

I learned we didn't have two pairs of defective sweat pants after I saw Coach Davis walking around wearing a brand-new pair of sweats. I quickly surmised Coach Davis had made the switch with Coach Brodsky—without the latter's knowledge.

Coach Brodsky, "Bro" to the players, always worked in the press box on Game Day. Coach Davis knew this, and he must have felt he needed the warm pants more on the sideline than his former University of Miami fellow coach did in the heated press box.

Coach Davis was intensely competitive. He played college ball at the University of Arkansas, and was the only member of the Dallas staff who had served as an assistant coach to Jimmy Johnson for all fourteen of Johnson's years as a head coach.

After our win in Super Bowl XXVII, Johnson promoted Coach Davis to the defensive coordinator position vacated by Dave Wannstedt when he joined the Bears.

Coach Brodsky oversaw the development of Emmitt Smith, the National Football League's top rusher, and Daryl Johnston at fullback—a blocking complement to Emmitt.

Under Brodsky's guidance, Emmitt led the league in rushing in only his second season as a pro in 1991 and went to the Pro Bowl his first two years.

Moose Johnston added career-highs for receptions and receiving yards.

Coach Brodsky was instrumental in mentoring Cowboys running back Ricky Blake (1991) from Alabama A&M and fullback Tommie Agee (1990–1994) from Auburn.

True to his style, Coach Brodsky was especially tough on fullback Darryl Johnston. In fact, his first two years with the Cowboys, Coach Brodsky nearly drove Darryl crazy by hollering and critiquing him on the field in front of the other players. But that was just an indicator of how much Coach Brodsky thought of Darryl's talent.

Troy Aikman was the Dallas starting quarterback that year.

He had come aboard in 1989, the year the Cowboys went 1–15.

Troy was hurt his rookie season and wasn't up to par through that season.

Dallas went 7–9 in 1990 with Troy and improved our record in 1991 at 11–5.

I believe Troy Aikman really came into his own in 1992.

In our December 6 game at Denver, Broncos All-Star John Elway moved his team the length of the field to score the go-ahead touchdown. Troy rallied the Cowboys' offense, moving the length of the field and scoring the winning touchdown for Dallas.

That year, the Cowboys won the NFC East.

In my estimation, that game in Denver provided Troy the impetus and confidence to lead the Cowboys to a Super Bowl win that season and another in 1994 (Super Bowl XXVII and XXVIII). In succeeding years, Aikman led the Cowboys to four first-place NFC East titles—1993, 1994, 1995, and 1996.

With Dallas Owner Jerry Jones and Head Coach Jimmy Johnson at the helm, the Cowboys continued their winning season, defeating the Atlanta Falcons 41–17 at the Georgia Dome before a national television audience on ABC's Monday Night Football. For our efforts, the Cowboys claimed the coveted NFC Eastern Division Championship.

That victory marked our first divisional title since 1985.

On December 27 in our last regular season game, Dallas defeated Chicago 17–14 at Texas Stadium. That win was the thirteenth of the year for the Cowboys, establishing a new club record for victories during one season.

In the Bears game, Emmitt Smith finished the season with 1,713 rushing yards, making him the first player to win back-to-back NFL rushing titles since Eric Dickerson (1983–1984). That's pretty good company, Emmitt.

On January 10, 1993, we defeated the Philadelphia Eagles in Dallas to secure the 1992 Divisional Playoffs and an opportunity

Emmitt Smith after our Super Bowl XXVII win

to meet the 49ers in San Francisco to determine the 1992 NFC Championship Title.

The Cowboys defeated the San Francisco 49ers on January 17, 1993, at Candlestick Park by a score of 30–20. The victory sent Dallas to Super Bowl XXVII in Pasadena, marking our first NFC title and Super Bowl trip since 1978.

While making an NFL-record sixth Super Bowl appearance, the Cowboys defeated Buffalo 52–17 in Super Bowl XXVII at the Rose Bowl in Pasadena on January 31, 1993.

With that victory, the Dallas Cowboys became the only franchise in NFL history to win more than one Super Bowl under two owners.

That Super Bowl win ranks up there with quarterback Troy Aikman's best memories as a Dallas Cowboy. "Winning Super Bowl XXVII and celebrating in the locker room with so many of the same players that were on the '89 team that went 1–15 was one of my happiest moments with the Cowboys. We went from the worst team in the NFL to the World Champions in four years, and it felt awfully good."

The Pasadena, California, Super Bowl crowd of 98,374 was the largest to ever see a Cowboys game. It was the most-watched event in TV history, viewed by more than 133 million fans. Entertainer Michael Jackson was on stage at halftime and for me, that day stands out clearly—I was nearly crushed by one of the band's heavy metal boxes.

Six Dallas offensive players were selected to play in that season's Pro Bowl: running back Emmitt Smith, tight end Jay

Jay Novacek makes another big gainer

A SPECIAL TRIBUTE TO JERRY JONES

Few NFL owners truly know the game of football like Jerry Jones. Few indeed have actually played the game. As cocaptain of the 1964 National Championship Arkansas Razorbacks, Mr. Jones earned a significant level of success as a football player.

In 1989, when Mr. Jones purchased the Dallas Cowboys, he made his intentions crystal clear: *There would be no substitute for winning*.

In the sixteen years since he has served as the owner, president, and general manager of the Dallas Cowboys, Mr. Jones has made good on that sixteen-year-old promise.

Cowboys Owner, President, and General Manager Jerry Jones

In a few short years, Dallas struggled back into national contention winning three Super Bowls: XXVII, XXVIII, and XXX. Within ten years of purchasing the team, Mr. Jones had led the Cowboys to the three world championships, eight playoffs, six division titles, and four conference championship appearances.

I had the honor of knowing Mr. Jones and working for him (1989 to 1993). When I retired as equipment manager, he agreed to let me stay on in a part-time capacity (1994–1998) to help the team and lend my expertise to the guys in the equipment room.

During my tenure with the Cowboys, I was privileged to earn three Super Bowl Rings—for the season of 1977 (SBXII) and the 1992 (SBXXVII) and 1993 (SBXXVIII) seasons with Mr. Jones. I'm proud to say, the fourth Super Bowl Ring in the Buchanan family belongs to my son, Bucky, the Cowboys' assistant equipment manager who received his Super Bowl Ring with Mr. Jones in Super Bowl XXX on January 15, 1995.

Jerry Jones is a former athlete, a successful businessman, and a philanthropist.

He is a man of vision and unbridled determination.

Mr. Jones, it was a pleasure working with you all those years.

Novacek, quarterback Troy Aikman, wide receiver Michael Irvin, guard Nate Newton (1986–1996) from Florida A&M, and center Mark Stepnoski (1989–1994, 1999–2001).

The six Dallas players set a record for the most offensive players ever selected to the Pro Bowl. The Cowboys set a new team record for road attendance by averaging 72,523 fans per road game in 1992. We also played before a sold-out stadium in all sixteen regular season games for the first time since the

Jay and Jerry after Super Bowl XXVII

1981 season. Jones and Johnson were on a roll, and the Dallas Cowboys—America's Team—were once again riding high.

1993—THE END OF THE ROAD

During preseason, the Cowboys enjoyed an exhibition game against the Detroit Lions in London, England, that resulted in a 13–13 tie. The Brits seemed to enjoy the contest and apparently didn't seem to mind the tied score—unlike the Dallas faithful.

Sports announcer Terry Bradshaw, former quarterback for the Pittsburgh Steelers, the guys America's Team loved to beat up on, had a heyday on air in the announcer's booth, teasing Mike McCord and veteran equipment manager Buck Buchanan.

The score was tied.

On the sideline, I had the kicker's net set up for Dallas field goal kicker Lynn Elliott (1992–1993) from Texas Tech University. I was still the full-time equipment manager for the Cowboys, training my protégé, Mike McCord.

We had the ball in field goal range, and Lynn was warming up on the sideline.

The Cowboys fumbled and Detroit recovered.

With less than two minutes to go, Mike and I took the kicking net down.

Detroit fumbled and Dallas recovered.

Mike and I set the kicking net back up again and Lynn continued to warm up.

Dallas fumbled once more and Detroit recovered the ball.

Mike and I took the net down.

Detroit fumbled and Dallas recovered.

Mike and I put the net back up.

Bobbies, English police stationed on the sideline, were bent over laughing.

In the booth, Terry Bradshaw laughed uncontrollably.

"Coach Johnson is going to jump Buck for this," Bradshaw said, on air.

The game ended and we took the net down and put it in its shipping bag.

Mike and I got off the field as fast as we could.

Dallas Offensive Line Coach Hudson "Hud" Houck (1993–2001) molded our offensive line into one of the premier units in league history. His first year at Dallas, our offensive line allowed twenty-nine sacks, the fewest that year in the NFC and the third fewest in the NFL. At the same time, Emmitt Smith grabbed his third straight NFL rushing title, only the fourth player in league history to do so, while averaging 5.3 yards per carry.

The Pro Bowl selection of Nate Newton, Mark Stepnoski, and Erik Williams at the conclusion of the 1993 season marked the first time in club history that three offensive linemen represented the Cowboys in Hawaii.

Coach Houck coached the Seattle Seahawks and the Los Angeles Rams for a total of eleven years prior to joining the Cowboys. In 1992, he fashioned a Seattle offensive line that opened gaping holes for Chris Warren and helped the Seahawks running back rush for an average of 4.6 yards per carry and a season total of 1,017.

At Los Angeles (1983–1992), Coach Houck helped send more Rams offensive linemen to the Pro Bowl than any other NFL team.

Linebacker Coach Jim Eddy (1993–1995) came to the Cowboys by way of Houston where he served as the Oilers' defensive coordinator. Coach Eddy's timing could not have been better. The Cowboys won Super Bowl XXVIII on January 30, 1994, and Super Bowl XXX on January 28, 1996.

Coach Eddy's second year at Dallas, we defeated Green Bay 35–9 to take the Divisional Playoff Game at Texas Stadium, but went on to lose to the San Francisco 49ers on January 15, 1995, thwarting our hopes to go to Super Bowl XXIX.

A native of Checotah, Oklahoma, Coach Eddy had a great sense of humor.

He coached football at his alma mater, New Mexico State, where he played at defensive back and running back. At Texas El Paso, he served as defensive coordinator.

In Houston, Eddy guided the Oilers' defense, which led the American Football Conference and finished third in the NFL in total defense in 1992. During his three seasons with the Oilers, Houston earned three playoff berths, including the franchise's first AFC Central Division crown in 1991.

During a preseason game at the Alamo Dome in San Antonio, Texas, rookie running back Lincoln Coleman (1993–1994) from Baylor University began his NFL career in embarrassing fashion. He nearly lost his pants before sixty-three thousand fans.

Lincoln had his right game pant leg ripped by a defender, the thigh pad falling to the Astro Turf playing surface. He made it to the sideline and asked Dallas Head Coach Johnson what he should do. Coach Johnson said, "Hell, find Buck!"

Lincoln did, and I taped his pants with heavy elastic tape.

We enjoyed our third winning season with Owner Jerry Jones, culminating in a 12–4 record and a second Super Bowl win (XXVIII) over the Buffalo Bills.

On a postseason celebratory tour of Washington, DC, and the White House, I saw President Bill Clinton, and by season's end, I had discussed retirement with my wife.

Jerry and I decided it was time to call it quits.

After back-to-back Super Bowl wins and my second and third Super Bowl Rings, I was at the end of a long and rewarding athletic career. Coach Johnson officially announced my retirement to the Cowboys prior to our NFC Championship Game with San Francisco although my actual separation date was May 31, 1994.

The club set another benchmark with an NFC-record eleven Dallas players selected to that season's Pro Bowl—five more than the record-setting year before. We sent a club-record eight offensive players to the Hawaii Pro Bowl—Troy Aikman, Michael Irvin, Darryl Johnston, Nate Newton, Jay Novacek, Emmitt Smith, Mark Stepnoski, and Eric Williams.

The three Cowboys defensive players who went to the Pro Bowl Game that year were safety Thomas Everett (1992–1993) from Baylor University, Russell Maryland, and linebacker Ken Norton, Jr. Ken is the son of heavyweight boxing champion Ken Norton, Sr. whom I had the occasion to meet at Valley Ranch.

In the final game of the season, the Cowboys beat the New York Giants 16–13 in overtime at Giants Stadium to claim our fifteenth division crown and our second NFC East title in as many years.

In that January 2, 1994, game with the Giants, running back Emmitt Smith severely bruised his shoulder before halftime. Assistant trainer Jim Maurer (1990–2005) approached me in the dressing room and asked for my help getting Emmitt ready for the second half.

In 1973, I had been faced with a similar dilemma and had outfitted Cowboys running back legend Walt Garrison with a redundant pad. I did much the same with Emmitt in the short time we had before returning to the game. Emmitt, Jim, and I returned to the sideline minutes after the second half began.

The donut-shaped pad was circular with a hole cut in the middle. It fit directly beneath the shoulder pad, with the hole surrounding Emmitt's injury. Showing as much grit as any Cowboy I have known Emmitt toughed it out and finished the game.

The Cowboys pulled it out in overtime and sports announcer, and former NFL great, Coach John Madden left the press booth

Jim Maurer tends to a fallen player

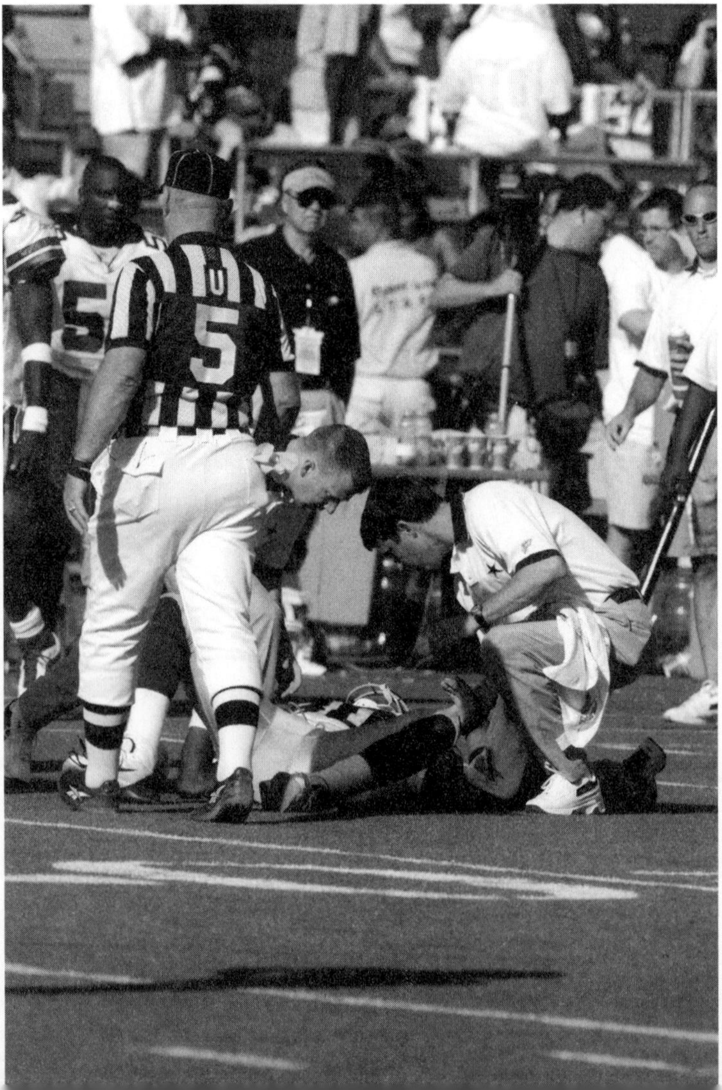

and strode to our locker room to congratulate Emmitt and his teammates.

Madden shook EM's hand and told the Dallas running back how tough he was.

When we returned to Dallas, the press wanted to see the special pad I had used.

Emmitt walked into the room as the members of the media were examining the donut pad, and I pointed to him and said, "The pad didn't do it, the guy right there did."

Emmitt finished the season with 1,486 yards to earn his third straight NFL rushing crown. He became the fourth man in NFL history to win three consecutive rushing titles.

The Cowboys beat Green Bay 27–17 in Dallas on January 16, 1994, to win the 1993 Divisional Playoff. A week later, we played the 49ers at Texas Stadium, winning that contest with San Francisco 38–21 to secure the 1993 NFC Championship title. The 1993 NFC victory over the 49ers gave the Cowboys an NFL-record seventh conference championship title.

With the January 23 defeat of the 49ers, the Cowboys were guaranteed a shot at Super Bowl XXVIII in Atlanta against the Buffalo Bills. We won that game 30–13 before an audience of nearly seventy-three thousand fans.

That Super Bowl victory in Atlanta's Georgia Dome broke another record, making the Dallas Cowboys one of only three NFL teams to win four Super Bowls.

Jerry Jones and Jimmy Johnson had a falling-out after Super Bowl XXVIII and Jimmy would not return the following year as the Dallas Cowboys' head coach.

1994—PART-TIME GIG

Before training camp started, Coach Jimmy Johnson, who had led the Cowboys to back-to-back Super Bowl wins, was replaced with the University of Oklahoma's premier head football coach, Barry Switzer (1994–1997).

In 1994, Coach Switzer became the third man to lead his team to the NFC Championship Game as a rookie NFL head coach. Within twenty-two months, he delivered a pair of NFC East Championships, an NFC title, and a Vince Lombardi Trophy after the Cowboys' 27–17 defeat of the Steelers in Super Bowl XXX at the end of the 1995 season.

Switzer's record as head coach of the University of Oklahoma Sooners is legendary, with a phenomenal 157–29–4 collegiate career record. For all of his accomplishments—collegiate and professional—I remember Coach Switzer as an affable guy and a terrific recruiter universally loved by his players and those he worked with.

Switzer's first year at Dallas, we played the 49ers in the NFC Championship Game for the right to advance to Super Bowl XXIX. San Francisco was ahead in that game, but Troy Aikman brought the Cowboys back. When wide receiver Michael Irvin was bumped by San Francisco defender Deion Sanders, and the officials failed to call the 49ers for a penalty, Coach Switzer flew into action. More accurately, the Dallas head coach flew onto the field, and in the process, bumped an official—resulting in a 15-yard penalty assessed against the Cowboys.

The next year, the Cowboys got Deion Sanders and we won Super Bowl XXX.

Barbara Goodman, executive secretary to four Cowboys head coaches—Landry, Johnson, Switzer, and Gailey, spoke of her former boss, Coach Switzer, in glowing terms: "He seemed to know everyone, and he was so nice. When first introduced to a player, Coach Switzer knew all about that player's life—his team, his former coach and his school and hometown. He is just so wonderful and had a wonderful way about him."

As successful as Switzer was at Dallas, his passion is collegiate coaching.

1994 Team Photo

Coach Switzer

After more than forty years as a coach, Barry still prefers the college ranks:

"College coaches work with young men seventeen to nineteen years old. They develop young men for the next thirty to forty to fifty years of their lives; they know their players' families, their passions, and what they want in life.

"College coaches are more concerned about the young man's development. In pro coaching, these things are irrelevant. Money and performance levels are all-important. It is tragic, but that is the way it has to be.

"I prefer college coaching. I love helping people, developing young men, the atmosphere, the pride in your school and team, and promoting your university and state.

"However, I am glad I could experience both collegiate and professional coaching."

#21 "Prime Time" Deion Sanders

Coach Mike Zimmer (1994–2005) spent his first season at the Cowboys as defensive assistant. He spent the next six years as defensive backs coach. Coach Campo promoted Zimmer to defensive coordinator in 2000, where he has established himself as one of the league's top assistant coaches.

Six times in his eleven seasons at Dallas, the Cowboys defense finished the year ranked in the top ten in total defense. Seven times, Dallas ranked in the top ten in pass defense. During his tenure, Zimmer has contributed to Cowboys teams that have made it to ten playoff games, including three divisional playoffs, two NFC championships, one Super Bowl victory (Super Bowl XXX), and four NFC wild card wins.

For the first time in twenty-one years, I was no longer the SOB in charge of the Cowboys' equipment room—and it felt great. The details of my part-time deal with the team were somewhat vague as my wife Jerry and I left for a two-week vacation to North Carolina.

As far as *this* retired equipment manager was concerned, I was a man of leisure, no longer a slave to the arduous hours and the beck and call of America's Team.

That season, I was exempt from any preseason games, and I didn't miss the frantic pace of packing and moving cross-country. After returning from our Carolina getaway, however, Mike McCord called and I returned to Valley Ranch to lend a hand.

Still not completely up to speed, Mike and Bucky needed my help, so I stuck around two weeks to get training camp set up in Austin. After a déjà vu glimpse of the same old backbreaking grind, I returned home to Jerry and the grandkids to enjoy the fruits of my second retirement. I remained in Plano during the preseason, and I'm glad I did.

On August 15, the Cowboys played the Houston Oilers in an exhibition game in Mexico City, and the trip, from what Mike and Bucky related, was a bucket of worms.

They ran into heavy rain before the game, and the field was muddy and slippery.

The guys had to change out each player's cleats, the Cowboys uniforms were in disarray, and the equipment truck was involved in a fender-bender returning to the airport.

The more the guys shared their south-of-the-border ordeal the more tickled I was that I had retired. I confess I was less than sympathetic to the complaints of my only son and my successor as I listened to their doleful liturgy in the Valley Ranch equipment room after their return.

We had several scintillating draft choices that year. Defensive end Shante Carver (1994–1997) from Arizona State was the Cowboys' No. 1 draft choice. Guard Larry "LA" Allen (1994–2005) from Sonoma State was our No. 2 draft choice. And offensive tackle George Hegamin (1994–1997) from North Carolina State was the Cowboys' No. 3 draft choice. Hegamin and Carver ended their professional careers at Dallas in 1997, never realizing the Cowboys' predraft expectations for them.

Allen exceeded everyone's hopes, rising to the ranks of All-Pro seven times.

As a member of the NFL's All-Decade Team for the 1990s, Larry Allen has long been widely recognized as one of the NFL's premier offensive linemen, and he has established himself as the most decorated offensive player in Dallas Cowboys history.

In eleven NFL seasons since being drafted, Larry has been named to nine Pro Bowls, more than any offensive lineman in Cowboys history. For a big man tipping the scales at 325 pounds, Larry is amazingly fast.

He is also strong, with a career-best bench press of 700 pounds and a squat lift of 900 pounds. Allen is considered the strongest man to ever play professional football.

Larry, who cares about that dirty locker?

After losing the third regular season game to the Detroit Lions in overtime, 17–20 at Texas Stadium, the Cowboys used their September 25 bye week to prepare for the Redskins at RFK. We trounced Washington 34–7 before fifty-five thousand rowdy fans and headed home for another lopsided win over the Cardinals, 38–3.

The Cowboys concluded the season with a respectable 12–4 record.

We defeated Green Bay in the Divisional Playoffs 35–9 at home and fell 28–38 to the 49ers in San Francisco, losing the NFC Championship bid on January 15, 1995.

As I was leaving the Cowboys' dressing room, I bumped into San Francisco linebacker Kenny Norton, Jr., as he was leaving the 49ers' dressing room.

Kenny left the Cowboys after the 1993 season.

Our chance encounter gave Kenny and I an opportunity to catch up on old times. Kenny was in good spirits as he was headed to his third consecutive Super Bowl, and I was somewhat less enthusiastic, about to fly back to Dallas to wrap up another season.

As consolation prize, our staff made another trip to the Pro Bowl in Hawaii, one that I enjoyed for the first time in years from the comfort of my recliner in Plano, Texas.

During that laid-back game, Coach Switzer caught serious flack from NFL Commissioner Paul Tagliabue for eating a hot dog on the bench during the fourth quarter.

I guess Tagliabue, the former NFL attorney elected as the league's fourth commissioner in 1989, the same man who ushered in the salary cap that year, thought Barry should have shown greater interest and decorum in that Pro Bowl contest.

1995—COMMAND PERFORMANCE

The 1994 season worked out so well for everyone—the Cowboys and this old equipment manager—that Mike and Bucky asked to have me back another season.

Our preseason record was as lackluster as the year before—2–3—but it was highlighted by one of my more enjoyable exhibition games. Tex Schramm would have killed me for calling a preseason game an exhibition game: "People don't pay good money to see an exhibition game," Tex would say. "They want to see a real contest!"

On August 12, I helped the guys pack for the trip to Toronto, Canada, for our preseason game with the Buffalo Bills—the team we had defeated in 1993 and 1994 to capture Super Bowls XXVII and XXVIII. Toronto—what a city, and what a nice trip!

Much of my satisfaction from that trip stemmed from the fact, no doubt, that I no longer shouldered the sole responsibility for the Dallas Cowboys' equipment needs.

Rather, I was relegated to a hired hand, willing to lend my expertise to Mike and Bucky—as *they* carried the burdens of the job on *their* shoulders. Despite the Cowboys' 7–9 loss to the Bills, that football game stands out as one of my most memorable.

Our No. 1 draft pick that year was running back Sherman Williams (1995–1999) from the University of Alabama. Sherman had a tough rookie year as he was overshadowed by brilliance—Cowboys running back Emmitt Smith.

It has to be tough for a star running back right out of school to play behind one of the game's brightest NFL stars. But that was the downside to Sherman's season—and his career. That, and the fact that the other Cowboys players razzed Sherman about his name and its similarity to the paint manufacturer.

Too bad for him, the talented Sherman did not get much playing time that year.

The Cowboys' best free agent in 1995 was wide receiver Oronde Gadsden (1995) from Winston-Salem. Oronde has the largest hands of any NFL receiver I have ever known, and that is saying a lot.

Oronde proved to be a huge target for Cowboys quarterback Troy Aikman.

Troy threw the ball so hard that he split the fleshy area between Oronde's thumb and index finger twice that year. The Miami Dolphins picked up Oronde at the end of his rookie year. The last I heard, Mr. Gadsden is still playing football in the Sunshine State.

Cornerback and punt return man Deion "Prime Time" Sanders (1995–1999) from Florida State University came to the Cowboys on a trade from the San Francisco 49ers.

Most players have a pregame ritual they go through preparing for a contest.

His was the most unique.

When Deion entered the locker room, wearing one of his flashy, expensive suits, he went directly to his locker. Before undressing, he laid every piece of his uniform and equipment on the floor as it would be worn in the game.

Deion placed his helmet at the base of his locker.

He placed his game jersey, No. 21, beneath his helmet, with the shoulder pads inside. He positioned his game pants beneath the jersey, and Deion layered the thigh and knee pads in their appropriate position atop the pants. To conclude the process, Deion placed his game socks under the pants and the shoes beneath his socks.

Deion undressed, went to the training room to get taped, and proceeded to get suited up for the game. Prime Time's nickname for me was "Pops."

When Deion came to the Cowboys in 1995, Russell Maryland, one of Deion's former friends and soon-to-be teammate, devised a clever welcoming for Prime Time.

"Deion had cut a record a year before," Maryland reported. "*Must be the Money*" was the name of that rap song, and it never made the top ten, perhaps 199 out of 200. But then, how many of us have actually produced a record?

"To make him feel at home," Maryland said, "Tony Tolbert brought a copy of Deion's recording to the locker room, and I asked Bucky to loan us the Boom Box. The plan," Maryland continued, "was to play that tune as Deion hit the locker room curtains.

"We blasted that song as Deion entered the room, and I think that must have been his most embarrassing moment at the Cowboys. Deion had not met most of the players yet, and I wanted to help them break the ice. We had met at the '94 Pro Bowl, and I knew Deion was a low-key guy, but the Cowboys were wondering what he was really like."

Deion Sanders may have been low-key in the locker room, but he was 180 degrees different when the cameras were rolling. The flamboyant Cowboy was the NFL Player of the Week on September 21, 1998, in a game against the Giants in New York.

Deion led the Cowboys on punt returns from 1997 to 1999.

He is the third all-time Cowboy in yards gained from punt returns with a total of 1,184. Prime Time was selected for the Pro Bowl each year from 1996 to 1999. He leads the Cowboys in average punt return yardage (minimum of seventy-five returns) with 13.3 yards and 89 returns. Deion leads the Cowboys for touchdowns scored on punt returns, with four.

The Cowboys enjoyed a 12–4 season and made it once more to the playoffs.

Our first playoff opponent was Philadelphia on January 7, 1996, in Dallas. We beat the Eagles 30–11, advancing to the NFC Championship Game at Texas Stadium against Green Bay.

Late in the Packers game, with less than a minute remaining, Coach Switzer authorized a Cowboys field goal attempt, ostensibly to set a new league record.

Dallas kicker Chris Boniol (1994–1996) from Louisiana Tech made that field goal and set a NFL-record five field goals in one championship game.

Green Bay's Reggie White took exception to Boniol's last field goal, and a fight erupted on the field, resulting in offsetting penalties. We beat the Packers 38–27 and ensured a Super Bowl berth in Phoenix, Arizona, against the Pittsburgh Steelers.

After the game, Cowboys Strength and Conditioning Coach Mike Woicik voiced his objections over the decision to allow Boniol to kick that last field goal.

At the end of the season, Woicik left the Cowboys and landed a coaching job with the New Orleans Saints. After several years in New Orleans, he secured a job coaching for the New England Patriots and earned himself another three Super Bowl Rings to add to the three he received at the Cowboys. Woicik fared very well after leaving Dallas.

We flew to Phoenix and practiced a week at the Cardinals' plush training facility before meeting Pittsburgh. That Super Bowl trip was highlighted by a walk-down-memory-lane encounter with old friend and Steelers Equipment Manager Tony Parisi.

On January 28, 1996, the Cowboys exacted their revenge over the Steelers 27–17 before seventy-six thousand fans to claim victory in Super Bowl XXX. Bucky asked me to return to our locker room at the end of the third quarter to prepare for the game's conclusion.

It was a good thing there was a TV in the locker room; I was able to watch Dallas cornerback Larry Brown (1991–1995, 1998) from Texas Christian intercept a pass to end the Steelers' final threat.

The first person through the door at the game's conclusion was my son, Bucky.

Bucky yelled, "Now I have my own Super Bowl Ring, Dad!"

"You sure do, son," I beamed, "And I'm really proud of you!"

Bucky and I stood inside the door hugging as jubilant Cowboys poured in.

On Christmas Eve, we won our fourth straight NFC Eastern Division title; Emmitt Smith ended the season with 1,173 rushing yards and a whopping twenty-five touchdowns, and ten Cowboys were selected to go to the Pro Bowl.

1996—HIGH HOPES

Coming off Super Bowl XXX, the Cowboys were brimming with confidence.

Preseason was punctuated by an exhibition game in Monterrey, Mexico, on August 5 with the Kansas City Chiefs. Although the trip wasn't as much fun as the Toronto trip, it was vastly superior to Mexico City, 1994—from what the guys told me.

I didn't make the trip to Mexico City; I was relaxing in my recliner back in Plano.

The horror stories Mike and Bucky shared with me after their south-of-the-border excursion made me feel great that I had indeed retired. When I first made arrangements with the Cowboys to help out in a part-time capacity, I had no plans of going to away games. This old vet was past tired of the commutes. But the experience in Mexico City had been so horrendous for Mike and Bucky that they liked the idea of having me tag along when they ventured to Monterrey.

We lost the game to the Chiefs 6–32, which proved to be an omen.

We played New England in Texas Stadium on August 12 and fell to the Patriots 7–31. It didn't get any better when the Cowboys lost to the Denver Broncos 3–20 at home.

We ended the preseason with a 24–19 win over the Oilers in Orlando, Florida.

Dallas secured the No. 1 draft pick that year with defensive end Kavika Pittman (1996–1999) from McNeese State. Kavika is a military brat who was born in Frankfurt, Germany, so we

Mike McCord, Bucky, and I at Valley Ranch

immediately hit it off. His dad was a retired Army NCO, and Kavika warmed up to the Cowboys' ex–equipment manager, "Old Sarge," right off the bat.

That year's No. 2 draft pick was linebacker Randall Godfrey (1996–1999) from the University of Georgia. Randall was one hard-working, hard-hitting dude who suits up today for the San Diego Chargers.

Safety George Teague (1996, 1998–2001) joined the Cowboys that year. George was a competitive player with a whole lot of Cowboys pride. In a game at Texas Stadium on September 24, 2000, after I had retired, he took offense when a 49ers receiver scored and ran to the 50-yard line. The 49er spiked the ball on the Cowboys star, and fans and players were incensed. George exacted his revenge by leveling the offending player.

George Teague was penalized and the Cowboys lost the game 24–41.

That season's record was 10–6, not that good, but sufficient for us to make it into the playoffs. The Cowboys met and defeated the Vikings in the 1996 NFC Wild Card Game 40–15 at Texas

Stadium. The win pitted us against the expansion team Carolina Panthers in Charlotte, North Carolina, to determine the 1996 Divisional Playoff champ.

That day, the fledgling Panthers bested America's Team.

Early in the third quarter, Michael Irvin was injured—diagnosed with a separated shoulder—and did not return to the game. The Panthers defeated the Cowboys 26–17 to advance to the NFC Championship Game with the Packers in Green Bay.

1997—REVERSAL OF FORTUNES

The Cowboys began the year by splitting the preseason 2–2, losing close games to the Oakland Raiders at home, 27–34, and to the Patriots at New England, 10–16.

You would have thought the tide had turned our last two preseason games when the Cowboys upset the St. Louis Cardinals in Texas Stadium, 34–31, and downed the Tennessee Titans 34–10 at home, but it had not.

In a year's time, Dallas had gone from a 10–6 to a 6–10 record and from first place to fourth place in the NFC East. Needless to say, we didn't make it to the playoffs. The handwriting was on the wall, and by year's end, Coach Switzer would be history.

The Cowboys' No. 1 draft pick that year was tight end David LaFleur (1997–2000) out of Louisiana State. Our No. 2 draft pick was linebacker Dexter Coakley (1997–2004) from Appalachian State. LaFleur proved to be a pretty fair receiver but he was injury-prone. And as far as linebackers go, Coakley was small. But Dexter was solid as steel, making the Pro Bowl in 1999, 2001, and again in 2003. Dexter was traded at the end of 2004.

My last game at Dallas was the Cowboys' 7–20 loss to the New York Giants on December 21, 1997. Late in the fourth quarter, I was in the dressing room, straightening up. One of the guys came in and asked if I would return to the sideline, so I dropped what I was doing and jogged outside.

Any speed I might have once had was all but gone, and the old knees weren't as sound as they once were, but I made it to where Bucky was standing and asked what he needed.

That day, my eleven-year-old grandson, William Thomas Buchanan II, was helping his dad on the sideline while granddad straightened up the Cowboys' locker room.

Bucky pointed to a camera, and the camera operator manning it not far away.

My son proudly beamed, "Fox Sports wants to honor you here today, Dad."

That was the first time I noticed the camera.

After twenty-five years in the trenches, unlike my former assistant, I seldom paid attention to the army of camera crews that were there to televise the games. They were like the rest of the personnel on the sidelines—backdrops in an NFL portrait.

That day on FOX Sports, sportscasters John Madden and Pat Summerall turned their focus from the Cowboys' losing effort and panned to the Buchanan clan—three generations of loyal Dallas equipment managers—Buck, Bucky, and Thomas.

Madden gave the TV audience an overview of the Buck Buchanan Story and introduced my son and grandson. The three of us could not have been prouder.

SIDEBAR: TO THE COWBOY FALLEN

"No man is an Island, entire of it self; every man is a piece of the Continent, a part of the main; if a clod be washed away by the sea, Europe is the less, as well as if a promontory were, as well as if a manor of thy friends or of thine own were; any man's death diminishes me, because I am involved in Mankind; And therefore never send to know for whom the bell tolls; it tolls for thee."

—John Donne, *Devotions upon Emergent Occasions* (1624), "Meditation XVII"

Every hour of every day, my thoughts hearken back to the summer of 1973, my rookie year with the Cowboys, when I was surrounded by such extraordinary talent.

It seems like only yesterday.

Prior to completing *Glory Days*, I attended a Cowboys party celebrating the induction of three of my all-time favorite Dallas players into the Ring of Honor: Troy Aikman, Emmitt Smith, and Michael Irvin.

Coach Tom Landry

No finer players have ever donned an NFL uniform.

As the decades speed by, I am compelled to pay tribute to the fallen Dallas Cowboys who have preceded us in death.

Nearing the completion of this story, I was disheartened to learn that pal Toni Fritsch, our Austrian kicker, had died at the tender age of sixty. As we go to press, the deaths of two Dallas stalwarts have come to our attention. Our deepest condolences go to the families of former defensive coach Ernie Stautner and former quarterback Jack Concannon. Through the years, too many players have preceded us in death. They include:

Ermal Allen—Offensive Backfield Coach; Special Assistant; Research & Development
Larry Bethea—Defensive Lineman
Nate Borden—Defensive End
Lee Roy Caffey—Linebacker
Mike Clark—Kicker
Tom Dahms—Defensive Line Coach
Jim Doran—Wide Receiver
Mike Dowdle—Running Back/Linebacker
Tom Franckhauser—Cornerback
Toni Fritsch—Kicker
Sid Gillman—Special Assistant Coach
Bob Hayes—Wide Receiver
Don Heinrich—Quarterback
Lynn Hoyem—Center/Guard
Buddy Humphrey—Quarterback
Otis Jackson—Field Maintenance
Dr. Marvin P. Knight—Chief Orthopedic Surgeon
Tom Landry—Head Coach
Billy Lothridge—Punter/Quarterback
Amos Marsh—Running Back
Harvey Martin—Defensive End
Jimmy Parker—Business Manager
Ray Renfro—Passing Offense Coach

Colin Ridgway—Punter/Kicker
Bill Roe—Linebacker
Alvin Roy—Strength & Conditioning Coach
Texas E. Schramm—President & General Manager
Derrick Shepard—Wide Receiver
Dave Simmons—Linebacker
Tody Smith—Defensive Lineman
Jim Stiger—Running Back
Andy Stynchula—Defensive End
Mark Tuinei—Offensive Tackle/Defensive Lineman

1998—CAREER'S END

That spring marked the first point in forty-eight years, since graduating from Ballinger High School in 1950, that I was unemployed. Chan Gailey (1998–1999) became the fourth Dallas head coach in the team's history—behind Tom Landry (1960–1988), Jimmy Johnson (1989–1993), and Barry Switzer (1994–1997).

In all, Coach Landry had been responsible for 250 Cowboy wins during his twenty-nine seasons. The combined wins of his successors, to that point, Johnson, Switzer, and Gailey, were 102, by comparison.

I never really got to know or work much with Coach Gailey.

I offered my support to Mike and Bucky in the equipment room early in the season due to their heavy workload. But my days as an NFL part-timer were numbered.

The period immediately after April's draft was particularly busy, so I lent a helping hand with the rooks and the team's first minicamp. Toward that end, I helped fit helmets, shoulder pads, and accessory pads, but when that phase of preseason was completed, I said "Adios, fellas!" and returned to my wife, Jerry, and our Plano home.

1998 Team Photo

The transition to "civilian" life has been gradual.

I kept up with the Cowboys by watching TV and staying in touch with Bucky.

The Cowboys' No. 1 draft pick that year was defensive end Greg Ellis (1998–2004) from North Carolina. Their No. 2 pick was offensive lineman Flozell Adams (1998–2005) from Michigan State.

The 'boys had a new batch of rooks that promised hope for the team's future.

There was defensive lineman Michael Myers (1998–2003) from the University of Alabama, linebacker Darren Hambrick (1998–2001) by way of Savannah State, offensive lineman Oliver Ross (1998) from Iowa State, safety Izell Reese (1998–2001) from Alabama-Birmingham, and running back Tarik Smith (1998–1999) from the University of California.

Mom had plenty of "honey-do's" for me at home. The lawn and the swimming pool required my never-ending attention, and the grandkids had plenty of athletic contests for their proud grandpa to attend.

With time, I weaned myself off the Cowboys.

Other than the rare funeral or get-together, I was out of the mainstream.

I didn't return to Valley Ranch for four years.

In 2002, I returned to my old stomping grounds to chew the fat with the guys.

During the compilation of this book, I visited Valley Ranch and met with new and old Cowboys friends. But I am no longer a young man, and the game of football is, after all, a young man's sport.

Every year, I gaze at the photos and Cowboys mementos in our den and reminisce about the most thrilling twenty-five years of my life—my Glory Days with America's Team, when I walked in the footsteps of truly Great Men—the Dallas Cowboys.

EPILOGUE

In the year it has taken to write this book, I have met with many former Cowboys colleagues and communicated with yet more by telephone or mail. Ours is a loose-knit band of brothers, a fraternity of warriors held together by an uncommon thread. Get-togethers are rare, yet reports of poor health or death are passed by word of mouth.

Some of the guys still work for the Cowboys.

Many have become successful businessmen.

Others retired altogether, shunning the limelight.

Several are regulars on TV, sportscasters and guest hosts.

Lean and handsome, Roger Staubach is a successful real estate entrepreneur.

Restaurateur Randy White is one of the healthiest fifty-something men I know.

Conditioning Coach Ward has excelled in the health industry.

Coach Jim Myers is as tough and brilliant as he has ever been.

But not everyone can still fit into his old uniform.

After a pair of knee surgeries, my feet grew three shoe sizes. Figure that.

Some have gained weight and grayed, if they still have hair.

The ever-youthful Charlie Waters and Cliff Harris wrote a book.

Long-time pal Russ Russell is still going strong at the Cowboys.

Bruce Hardy still manages Texas Stadium—talk about some great stories.

And time marches on for us all, America's Team, with intermittent news of divorce, remarriage, children, grandchildren, surgeries, illnesses . . . and yes, death.